Media Consumption and [

DATE DUE

Consumption and Public Life

Series Editors: **Frank Trentmann** and **Richard Wilk**

Titles include:

Consumption and Public Life
Series Standing Order ISBN 978–1–4039–9983–2 Hardback 978–1–4039–9984–9
Paperback (*outside North America only*)

You can receive future titles in this series as they are published by placing a standing order. Please contact your bookseller or, in case of difficulty, write to us at the address below with your name and address, the title of the series and the ISBN quoted above.

Customer Services Department, Macmillan Distribution Ltd, Houndmills, Basingstoke, Hampshire RG21 6XS, England

---

Media Consumption and Public Engagement

Beyond the Presumption of Attention

Revised and Updated Edition

Nick Couldry
Goldsmiths, University of London, UK

Sonia Livingstone
London School of Economics and Political Science, UK

Tim Markham
Birkbeck, University of London, UK

First published in hardback 2007
This paperback edition published 2010 by
PALGRAVE MACMILLAN

Palgrave Macmillan in the UK is an imprint of Macmillan Publishers Limited, registered in England, company number 785998, of Houndmills, Basingstoke, Hampshire RG21 6XS.

Palgrave Macmillan in the US is a division of St Martin's Press LLC, 175 Fifth Avenue, New York, NY 10010.

Palgrave Macmillan is the global academic imprint of the above companies and has companies and representatives throughout the world.

Palgrave® and Macmillan® are registered trademarks in the United States, the United Kingdom, Europe and other countries.

ISBN 978–1–4039–8534–7 hardback
ISBN 978–0–230–24738–3 paperback

This book is printed on paper suitable for recycling and made from fully managed and sustained forest sources. Logging, pulping and manufacturing processes are expected to conform to the environmental regulations of the country of origin.

A catalogue record for this book is available from the British Library.

Library of Congress Cataloging-in-Publication Data
Couldry, Nick.
    Media consumption and public engagement: beyond the presumption of attention / Nick Couldry, Sonia Livingstone, Tim Markham.
        p.   cm.— (Consumption and public life)
    Includes bibliographical references and index.
    Contents: Theoretical foundations—The public connection project—Conclusion.
    ISBN-13: 978–1–4039–8534–7 (cloth) 978–0–230–24738–3 (pbk)
    ISBN-10: 1–4039–8534–0 (cloth) 0–230–24738–5 (pbk)
    1. Mass media—Political aspects—Great Britain.   2. Great Britain—Politics and government.   3. Communication in politics—Great Britain.   4. Mass media—Social aspects.   I. Livingstone, Sonia M.   II. Markham, Tim, 1974–   III. Title.
    P95.82.G7C68 2007
    302.230941—dc22   2006048786

10   9   8   7   6   5   4   3   2   1
19   18   17   16   15   14   13   12   11   10

Printed and bound in Great Britain by
CPI Antony Rowe, Chippenham and Eastbourne

In memory of Roger Silverstone
(1945–2006)

Contents

Part I   Theoretical Foundations

Part II   The Public Connection Project

List of Tables

List of Figures

Preface

Democracy as a political form assumes some level of participation. While the exact level and nature of such participation is disputed, certain working assumptions underlie democratic practice and theory. This book explores one such set of assumptions about citizens' underlying orientation to the sites where the public business of democracy goes on. Such sites are in contemporary societies always, in part, mediated sites. What does people's media consumption contribute to democracy? As fears in some quarters for the future of democracy grow and as media delivery systems everywhere become more complex and varied, automatic assumptions about the future underpinnings of democratic engagement are no longer adequate. This book reexamines these questions through the lens of citizens' daily practice, including their daily practice as media consumers. While our main research has been based on the United Kingdom, we draw also on new research emerging across Europe and North America.

Our particular focus is the UK study we conducted between October 2003 and March 2006 at the London School of Economics and Political Science. The project was funded by the Economic and Social Research Council and the Arts and Humanities Research Council's Cultures of Consumption Programme ('Media Consumption and the Future of Public Connection', grant number RES-143-25-0011).

We wish here to thank, first, those who in various ways worked on this project: Martin Boon, Ann McIntyre and Chris Menzies of ICM Research for their great efficiency in conducting the Public Connection Survey on our behalf; Zoetanya Sujon, Ellen Helsper and Maria Kyriakidou who provided invaluable research assistance at various stages of the project; and David Brake for useful references on blogging. Particular thanks to those who have supported the project from the outside: Frank Trentmann, an inspiring Director of the Cultures of Consumption programme; Bruce Williams and Andrea Press at the University of Illinois, Urbana-Champaign for their enthusiastic interest in our work and for the stimulation which their parallel US project, funded by the National Science Foundation, has provided us; and other researchers who have showed interest in our project, particularly Ien Ang, Lynn

Schofield Clark, Peter Dahlgren, Joke Hermes, Stewart Hoover, Katherine Montgomery, Dominique Pasquier and Kim Schroder. Thanks also to Jill Lake our editor for believing initially in this book and to her and Melanie Blair for supporting it on its passage to publication.

We owe a special word of thanks to Angela Jones of The Field Department, and her recruiters across the country (Carol Atherton, Anne Bertram, Marilyn Croxford, Anne Drake, Irene Edwards, Lynn Ronayne, Janet Salmon, Margaret Stevens) for their tremendous engagement with our research idea and recruitment needs.

And above all, we want to thank the diarists themselves whose names must remain confidential but without whose generous gift of their time, energy and reflections there would, quite simply, have been no Public Connection project.

We dedicate this book to the memory of our much-loved colleague, Roger Silverstone, who died suddenly as the manuscript was being finalised and whose inspiration and encouragement were crucial to this project from its inception.

Nick Couldry, Sonia Livingstone and Tim Markham
London
July 2006

Preface to the Revised Edition 2010

It is three years since we wrote the preface to the original hardback edition of *Media Consumption and Public Engagement*. That book, and our original study funded by the Economic and Social Research Council, were an attempt to find a methodologically rich way of understanding what we saw as a fundamental question in media research and political science: *are* people in fact oriented to a world of public issues beyond what is of private interest to them, their family, friends and close associates? If so, is it *media* that helps sustain that orientation? If not, or if that orientation is potentially unstable, what are the consequences for the workings of democracy and contemporary societies?

We called the elusive object for which we were searching in that study 'public connection', emphasising two things: first, that it was people's underlying habits of orientation and media consumption in which we were interested, not their actual levels of attention which obviously vary from time to time; and second, that it was people's own understanding of what counted as public issues that we wanted to follow, not any understanding that might be imposed on them from outside. By and large, we found that the UK citizens in our multi-region fieldwork and national survey *did have* public connection, but this took many and varied forms. Much of our attention in the book turned out to be focussed on a further question we had implied at the outset: if people did have public connection, what exactly (and how much) followed from this for the effectiveness of democracy?

From that further question, we became interested in the way people's habits of public connection were linked up with, and supported by, other things they did (for example, their work, their discussion with friends, family and workmates) or – just as important – not linked up with much else at all! We became concerned at the 'missing links' between people's habits of following what was going on in a wider public world, and their possibilities of acting, as citizens, or at least as people with a claim to be treated as citizens. This raised questions both about the consequences of public connection and also about the preconditions in people's everyday lifeworld which serve to sustain (or undermine) it. Put another way, we became interested in what our Swedish colleague Peter Dahlgren had called 'the circuit of civic culture', in the possible breaks in that circuit, and media's role in both circuit and breaks.

Since completion of the Public Connection study, we have been pleased to hear that other researchers found useful the approach we adopted to answering these difficult questions: we have been in public and private discussions about possible extensions or applications of our methodology with colleagues in France (Josiane Jouët, University of Paris II), the USA (Bruce Williams and Andrea Press, University of Virginia), Denmark (Kim Schröder, Roskilde University), Norway (Jostein Gripsrud, University of Bergen), and Australia (Paul Jones, University of New South Wales). Clearly, there is much more work to be done in this area, particularly in developing more closely targeted studies of the young and the socially and economically disadvantaged. Overall however we believe that our mixed diary-based methodology has established its value in researching the experience of living in a complex media-rich democracy such as the UK.

Since 2006 however, the landscape of both media and politics has been moving fast in the UK and internationally. Some basic features remain unchanged, even if their details are new: the tensions, or perhaps symbiosis, within the news landscape between so-called 'serious' news and entertainment-based news, particularly celebrity coverage; the fears about the news engagement and news habits of the young; the uncertainties about the long-term economic models of online media. By contrast, two major developments have occurred which, without question, would be important for a new study started today: the rise, even prominence, of social networking sites such as Facebook especially among the young but also among other age groups; and the start in the US, UK and elsewhere of the first main crack in the traditional media edifice, as public service broadcasting is threatened, multiple local newspapers close and, in the US at least, major national titles are threatened (*Los Angeles Times*, *New York Times*, *Boston Globe*).

Some further key factors have emerged, even if their long-term significance is still unclear: the UK has moved from minority to majority broadband coverage this having been just 24 per cent at the end of our diary fieldwork; online access from mobile devices has increased; and the trend for mainstream media such as the BBC to incorporate 'user-generated content' has grown considerably alongside the increasing prominence of blogs in politics, sport, celebrity coverage and elsewhere.

Particularly in relation to this last set of factors, the difficulty of discerning the *significant* dynamics within today's media and political landscape becomes clear. The range of information, and the forms of 'connection', on offer to today's citizens in many countries is changing, and changing fast in some respects. But how habits of consumption and orientation will change *in response* is a much more difficult question. As the 2009 Digital Britain report acknowledges, over 15 million adults in the UK still do not use the internet; while Ofcom's latest Media Literacy Reports (published in April–May 2009) suggest that only 24 per cent *of internet users* use the internet at least once a week to get news (21 per cent among 16–24 year olds). Indeed, the apparent acceleration of change makes all the more relevant our insistence in this book on some basic questions: are habits of media consumption changing and to what extent, and for whom? Are new complex practices of engagement resulting? How might those new practices link to other changes of practice? Is the result to enhance people's possibilities for action in relation to politics, or to leave them largely unchanged?

These are still the crucial questions. Since 2006, the UK government has vindicated at least two of our concerns: first, by acknowledging that the digital divide remains a serious issue in Britain, and ways need to be found to ensure that a substantial proportion of the UK population is not excluded from the online world (the 2009 *Digital Britain* report); second, by acknowledging that, at present, UK citizens do not generally feel involved in processes of local decision-making (the 2008 *Communities in Control* White Paper). But there is, we believe, a very long way to go before such concerns are adequately addressed. In the meantime, urgent questions remain about how the changing digital media landscape will in practice (not in the abstract) generate resources for more effective engagement with the political process. The fact (reported by Ofcom's *Citizens Digital Participation* report in March 2009) that people can, and do, perform various types of 'citizen action' online (submitting a tax return, registering for voting) does not, in our view, illuminate whether more substantive new habits of engagement are emerging.

We are aware, however, that our 2006 conclusion, which (along with Chapter 8 and some other parts of this book) we have revised and updated for the present edition, may have been too pessimistic for some. We wrote of a 'crisis of recognition' in the UK whereby even those who had 'public connection' and a considerable degree of civic activism still felt disconnected from the process of politics, not because they didn't care about it, but because they didn't sense that *government cared* whether they cared. This bleak view did not necessarily resonate for US readers, for example, during the autumn of 2008, when one of us was living in the US and all of us, along with a large proportion of the world's population, were following the progress of Barack Obama to the White House. We, like countless others, observed with fascination how Obama's campaign energised vast numbers of new voters, young and old. At the very least, this was a process of recognition, in which the participation of citizens in a large democracy was seen publicly and dramatically to matter.

For the UK at least, concerns about voter engagement have certainly not been allayed by turnout at the recent EU elections in June 2009 which at 35% (in some regions close to 30% or lower) was well below the EU average. A basic motivation for the funding bid that led to the Public Connection project was reflection on how long-standing democracies such as the UK would cope if adult voter turnout fell to 50% or below. With a UK general election less than a year away as we write, this remains very much a live issue.

Indeed this book's conclusion was never intended to be pessimistic. As we show, a sizeable minority, sometimes a majority, of people are interested in, concerned about and engaged with diverse civic issues in one form or another. However, our aim was to state as directly and clearly as we could that certain key components of a healthy civic and political culture are missing in the UK, judging by the evidence of our fieldwork. It mattered *then* that only one of our diary respondents ever mentioned a moment when an issue she talked about with others ensued in a shared action, just as it has mattered *since then* that so many US citizens in 2008 would for sure have had a different story to tell. Nothing has happened yet, in the UK at least, to convince us, as authors, either that our original conclusion was too negative or that new contexts for supporting citizens' involvement in the political process have since emerged and stabilised. We wait with interest to see how much of the shared energies of the Obama campaign in the USA will be translated into more lasting shifts in political and civic engagement. In the meantime, we believe that our analysis and its conclusions still offer a salutary account of where one long-established democracy is heading in the digital media age.

We would like to thank Frank Trentmann as co-editor of the *Consumption and Public Life* series and our editor Philippa Grand of Palgrave for their support in making this paperback edition possible.

Nick Couldry, Sonia Livingstone and Tim Markham
London
July 2009

Part I
Theoretical Foundations

1
Democracy and the Presumption of Attention

Introduction

No amount of communication, however stylish and informative, will engage people in politics, unless they are paying attention, at least some of the time. If, with apologies to Plato (and his famous cave metaphor), we can imagine political events as projected onto a wall, then democracy depends on people's backs not already being turned away from that wall.

Two assumptions are involved here which provide, in effect, the bottom line of most political science and political theory, and indeed much media research. The first assumption is that, as citizens, we share an orientation to a public world where matters of shared concern are, or at least should be, addressed: we call this orientation 'public connection'.[1] The second assumption is that public connection is principally sustained by a convergence in the media people consume. Taken together, these two assumptions imply the notion of 'mediated public connection'. The question which this book investigates is whether mediated public connection exists beyond the academic literature and in the practice of everyday life.

'Public connection' is not literally the same as attention – no one believes that more than a small minority give their full and continuous attention to a public world (we discuss our use of the broader term 'public', rather than 'political' shortly). Public connection is rather a basic level of orientation that can reliably, particularly at times such as elections, be translated into attention. Mediated public connection might therefore seem like a very minimal assumption to make, and hardly worth investigating. But there are a number of reasons why this assumption is now worth exploring in some depth.

3

First, there are growing fears of a decline in engagement in the democratic process, especially among younger citizens, as measured by voting in national elections: the impact on the legitimacy of, say, the British political system if voter turnout in national elections regularly falls to around, or even below, 50 per cent should not be underestimated. While both the 2004 US Presidential election and the 2005 UK general election showed a slight improvement in turnouts (to 55 per cent and 61 per cent respectively) over immediately preceding elections, the 50 per cent danger point remains perilously close:[2] remember that since World War II voter turnout at UK general elections *never* dropped below 70 per cent until 2001 when it fell to 59 per cent (the previous lowest being in 1997: 71.4 per cent).[3]

Second, those fears are not allayed, or fully answered, by mainstream political science; indeed it is a puzzle that in the UK political interest remains relatively constant, even as propensity to vote falls (Electoral Commission 2005b: 31). At some level there is a disconnection. If political anthropologist Robin Leblanc is right to suggest political science tells us little about how people 'perceive their citizenship' (1999: 7), then now is a good time for research to address this experiential gap (Lister *et al.* 2003).

Third, 'public connection' may be both particularly complex and particularly threatened in an era of proliferating interpretations of what counts as 'political' and (returning to the second assumption we are investigating) when media outlets and delivery platforms are multiplying. As the complexity of being a citizen of an intensely mediated democracy increases, it is all the more important to listen to citizens' own reflections on these matters.

Concerns about the conditions of effective democracy are not new. They have been debated since Rousseau insisted citizens must be able to meet in general assembly (Rousseau 1973: 240, orig. 1762); concerns about organised communications' contribution to democracy go back almost as far (Garnham 1999). Indeed both sets of concerns have been replayed many times since:[4] it was post-World-War-I fears, particularly in the USA, of the consequences of mass enfranchisement that prompted John Grierson to experiment with film as a new way of engaging the British population (Grant 1994: 17). Indeed, from a historical perspective, the last century has seen a 'persistent fear that media publics are essentially ungovernable' (Barnett 2003: 101). But we need to understand how such concerns are being lived out *now*, not just in the minds of theorists and policymakers but in the experience of citizens.

Some old fears of the 'phantom' nature of the public sphere may rest on false premises. Walter Lippman, for example, assumed that 'the time each day is small when any of us is directly exposed to information from our unseen environment' (1922: 63), hardly plausible today. But this does not mean that analogous problems are not being played out now in different forms. What if the intense mediation of political culture and the visual and interpretative sophistication it instils in citizens are altering the conditions under which a representative political system can retain its legitimacy? What if, after a period during the mid-to-late 20th century when regular attention to a public world through media could be assumed, we are seeing the first signs, adapting Jonathan Crary (1999), of a 'regime of inattention' with regard to politics?[5]

At this point it is worth emphasising that this study does more than register the mediation of contemporary political culture. It goes further by insisting that only by understanding the everyday practices of media *consumption* – and the way those practices fit into the other practices of everyday life – can we begin to understand the problem (if it is one) of public engagement. There is an essential link here from the way democratic systems reproduce themselves as social and cultural forms to the details, often banal details, of 'ordinary consumption' (Gronow and Warde 2001), including ordinary media consumption in all its complexity and variety.

In this chapter we first explain in more detail what we mean by 'public connection', acknowledging the philosophical complexities involved in any use of the term 'public'. Then we review the hinterland of empirical and conceptual work – in political science, political sociology and political theory – that lies behind our notion of 'public connection'. (Chapter 2 will perform the same task for 'media consumption'.) In the last two sections, we review the various academic narratives of whether, and why, democratic engagement is under threat and the immediate context (including the policy context) for investigating this question in early 21st century Britain.

The idea of 'public connection'

The term 'public connection' represents our attempt to capture one key empirical precondition of democratic engagement in a way that does *not* privilege in advance any particular definition of 'politics'. 'Public connection' is at most a heuristic term – an abstraction that isolates a complex component of a working democracy. The term 'public connection' resonates with theories of participatory democracy which conceive of the public sphere as a site where decisions and norms are collectively contested and redeemed,[6] but it is prevalent more widely across political science and political theory, as we show later. Related assumptions are made right across media research (see Chapter 2).[7] Sometimes the word 'connection' has fuzzy normative implications,[8] which is why we emphasise we are using it purely as an analytic concept. For us, it is useful only if it captures an orientation – definitively 'on' or 'off' – that can be established empirically.

We use the word 'public' here – not 'political' – to allow for the complex disputes over the definition of 'politics' in contemporary life. Clearly for some people, perhaps many, 'politics and public life [are] not necessarily the same thing' (LeBlanc 1999: 200). For a start, 'politics' is for many people broader than its traditional definition, electoral politics. This is already clear from one of the more useful definitions of 'politics'[9] ('politics' as the 'authoritative allocation of goods, services and values': Easton 1965, quoted in Delli Carpini and Keater 1996: 12): many forms of political organisation in this sense operate outside electoral politics. But 'public' issues may themselves be broader than recognised in any established form of 'politics'. We write therefore of public connection to capture an orientation to *any* of those issues affecting how we live together that require common resolution (Taylor 2004). Despite broad disagreements over what falls within the definition of 'politics' or 'public' issues, the underlying distinction between the 'public' (any issue that requires common resolution) and the purely 'private' remains important.

In defending this notion of 'public', and building it into the focus of our research, we are taking a normative position about which we want to be explicit. Just as 'citizenship is not just another lifestyle choice' (Delli Carpini and Keater 1996: 285), so too public issues (and potentially therefore politics itself) involve more than just 'social belonging' or expressions of identity.[10] Something crucial remains at stake in the public/ private distinction, notwithstanding postmodernist thinkers[11] who celebrate its breakdown. Democracy requires, we believe, the idea that those affected by decisions can participate in them, which in turn requires some (more or less satisfactory) demarcation of the types of decisions that are, or, just as important, are not public. The term 'public', as just outlined, grounds any notion of democratic engagement; there is nothing radical in dispensing with it or confusing its reference, since 'public' identifies precisely those 'collective action problems' (Pattie *et al.* 2004: 22) that require a common solution. So 'public connection' is not orientation to *any* collectively available space whatsoever. To say this, however, does not mean defending a traditional notion of 'public' as electoral politics – we acknowledge the growing complexity of reference-points in today's public cultures and the new 'multiaxiality' of political communications[12] – but it is to reject claims that group identity, let alone individual consumption,[13] sufficiently demarcate the issues in which citizens are expected, broadly, to engage. 'Public connection' is an orientation to a space where, in principle, problems about shared resources are or should be resolved, a space linked, at least indirectly, to some common frame of collective action about common resources.

We must note, however, the philosophical minefield we have just walked round: that is, the disputed status of the term 'public' itself. The notion of 'public connection' relies on us demarcating the idea of a 'public world': the open-ended set of things that are, or should be, the subject of 'public', not purely private, attention. Some notion of a 'public world' is familiar, for example, from John Dewey's (1946: 15) account of democracy, Jurgen Habermas's concept of the 'public sphere' (1989) and Hannah Arendt's account of a 'public realm' (1958: 52). But the apparently consensual nature of the public/private boundary was famously challenged by the feminist insistence that 'the personal *is* political', a challenge continued in recent research on 'intimate citizenship' (Berlant 1997; Warner 2002; Plummer 2003) and the political significance of an ethics of care (Gilligan 1993).

Some theoretical clarification is helpful here, drawing on the discussion of Jeff Weintraub (1997) and Raymond Geuss (2001). They point out that the term 'public' is confusing precisely because it condenses *more than one* type of public/private boundary. The first distinguishes issues that are broadly 'political' – matters of common *concern*, or 'common decision' (Taylor 2004: 104; cf Barber, 1984: 120–1) – from issues that are 'non-political' (of purely individual concern). The second distinguishes the private *space* of individuals/families from public (or 'accessible') space. In this book we are concerned primarily with the first distinction, not the second; in principle, matters for common decision could come from any space, whether normally accessible to public entry or not. But the problems with the term 'public' arise, as Weintraub notes, because the two types of distinction are confused, inevitably, because their uses are intertwined; if separate, everything political must in principle be made visible, even if not everything visible need be political. Indeed, the two reference-points of 'public' are fused in much liberal thought, that unhelpfully reifies 'private experience' as immune from public intervention and beyond politics (Geuss 2001:1–3). We can however retain the public/private distinction (in the first sense) as a reference-point, while relaxing the absoluteness of liberalism's interpretation.[14]

Returning then to the challenge of feminist and other argu-ments about intimate politics, they can be interpreted in two ways: either as rejecting any distinction between 'public' and 'private' matters or as contesting specific versions of where the public/private boundary should be drawn. Only the first challenges the notion of public connec-tion itself, and it is a position few directly hold.[15] The second argument implies the contestability and historicity, not pregiven naturalness, of how the public/private distinction is mapped onto daily life (Zaretsky 1976). We would not only acknowledge this, but emphasise that media institutions have been involved in constructing and reconstructing such boundaries (Flichy 1995); indeed some aspects of everyday life currently sit ambiguously between private and public status (Livingstone 2005a). We assume *only* the distinction between public and private issues is meaningful in everyday life; this is quite consistent with acknowledging that the distinction is *inherently contestable* (and often rightly contested, as feminism has shown).[16] Perhaps, following Charles Taylor (2004), we can go further and say that the distinction between public and private issues is part of the 'social imaginary' of modernity. Indeed the public/private boundary may be an even more important reference-point when some political forces on the right (in the USA at least) are intent on collapsing the public into the merely private.[17]

Public connection: the conceptual and empirical background

We have introduced 'public connection' to capture a key assumption amongst writers who understand democracy as a structure of participa-tion, not a façade for elite control. It is time now to look at that wider literature.

The background in political theory

Something like 'public connection' is necessary in most democratic theory, since it is implied by the notion of political participation itself. Some form of citizen participation has been intrinsic to democracy since the dawn of political theory (Aristotle 1981: Book III). Of course, there have been debates for almost as long as to the limits of actual popular participation. This is the basis for substantive disagreements between, crudely, 'representative' and 'participative' theories of democracy, and between both of those and 'elite' models, which are more pessimistic about the feasibility of extensive popular participation. These disputes do not concern us here, since we are interested in an assumption – public connection – which is common to all such theories.

In liberal theories of democracy an assumption of 'public connection' is at least implicit. Robert Dahl argues that effective participation and enlightened understanding are necessary preconditions of a working democracy (1989: 108–14), implying a basic orientation to public affairs. Public connection receives great emphasis in social/ liberal approaches to democracy, for example T. H. Marshall (1992, orig. 1950) who incorporates within his account of citizenship a 'common culture' which citizens share. Cosmopolitan extensions of broadly liberal models make the same assumption, if only in telegraphic form.[18]

The notion of participation (and implicitly public connection) works very differently within republican political philosophy, where it is a core concept. Republicanism is distinguished by its emphasis on active citizen participation as the basis of democratic life.[19] Republican theories vary of course on the degree of that necessary participation (similarly for communitarian models of democracy), but some notion of 'public connection' is universally implied. 'Public connection' is also assumed in models of deliberative democracy linked to Jürgen Habermas. Clearly some orientation to a world of public issues is a precondition for people to become involved from time to time in public deliberation, even in Habermas's (1996) more recent model of a 'networked' public sphere. A notion of 'public connection' is equally presumed in Iris Marion Young's difference-based model of participatory democracy (2000) and in civil society models of democracy.[20] In such writings, the emphasis is less on public connection itself (its presence is assumed) than on the institutional structures necessary to channel particular forms of democratic participation in complex societies. Finally, public connection is at least implicit (even if not explicitly developed) in 'radical' models of democracy as permanent contestation.[21]

However, there is one version of political theory where public connection is, on the face of it, absent: 'elite' models of democracy. Such models are characterised not necessarily by a disdain for participation, but by a pessimism about its contemporary feasibility; one type of liberalism (Page and Shapiro 1992)[22] comes close to elite models in this respect. Classic here is Walter Lippman's discussion of the myth of democracy where, he argues, the citizen is at best a 'back-row spectator': 'men make no attempt to consider society as a whole'.[23] Along similar lines, Joseph Schumpeter (1943) argued for the 'unreality' of the modern ideal of citizenship compared with actual practice, and Seymour Lipset (1963) argued that lower classes are inevitably disconnected from the sphere of political/civic action, while Samuel Huntington (1975: 114) notoriously claimed the *necessity* of apathy, if governments are to do their job. Lupia and McCubbins (1998: 36) put it even more starkly: 'we assume people *choose* to have little information about politics' (added emphasis).

It can, however, be argued[24] that even elite models of democracy rely upon something like public connection (an orientation that yields the potential for some, however intermittent, attention to politics), if democracy is to have any legitimacy. Similarly for quasi-elitist liberal approaches that downplay the necessity of active political participation, for example Michael Schudson's notion (1998) of 'monitorial citizenship': how can we understand 'monitoring' without a shared orientation towards the space being monitored? Indeed this is the weakness of this last model, that by normalising general inattention to politics it risks making it permanent. What stands in the way is precisely the notion of an *orientation* to a public world that sometimes (but regularly enough) issues in actual attention.

The background in political science/sociology

In political science, 'public connection' intersects with strands in the important literature on 'civic culture'. Here we must acknowledge Gabriel Almond and Sidney Verba's key concept of 'participant political culture' viz 'orientation to political structure and process' (1963: 29). There is, however, some ambiguity about the explanatory weight Almond and Verba put on this orientation, for they also argue that political 'culture' is based on a 'necessary *myth*' of citizen involvement (1963: 481),[25] but the idea that there is a dimension to political engagement which is orientational rather than based in specific knowledge originates here (1963: 15, 34).

In cultural citizenship models, the notion of political culture is given maximum emphasis, and so notions of 'public connection' are close to being explicit. We have in mind not only left models of 'common culture' (Williams 1961) as the basis of re-energised democracy and more recent work on cultural citizenship,[26] but also T. H. Marshall's classic model of citizenship (which is at the roots of both). Marshall's celebrated account is distinctive not just for its emphasis on complex historical dynamics, but for its insistence on multiple dimensions – civil, political and social. Citizenship, Marshall argues, acquired a cultural dimension through 'the great extension of the area of common culture and common experience' in the early 20th century (1992: 42). This notion of an overarching public space is in fact surprisingly resilient in accounts of politics that emphasise 'difference'.[27]

We are sympathetic to such versions of 'public connection' in political science and sociology as normative ideals, but sceptical about their empirical applicability. There is a great danger of exaggerating the degree of value consensus in complex societies (Mann 1970; Abercrombie *et al.* 1980). For that reason, we sharply distinguish 'public connection' from any value consensus, while remaining open to the possibility that public connection might under certain conditions lead to important shared values emerging. Here Peter Dahlgren's work, while still seeing a 'shared public culture' as the 'centre of gravity of politics' (2001: 85), usefully rethinks 'civic culture' in terms of a six-moment circuit of civic engagement: values, affinity, knowledge, practices, identities and discussion (Dahlgren 2003). This challenges not only Almond and Verba's model but also the implication of the Habermasian public sphere that formal public deliberation *in itself* is enough to ground effective democracy (Dahlgren 2005, 2009). Public connection is not explicit in Dahlgren's model but it is clearly implied, and we return to it in Chapter 3.

There remain accounts of politics and political engagement where 'public connection' receives apparently no emphasis. Leaving aside Foucauldian political sociology (Rose 1999; Isin 2002), where attention is on how the *possibility* of political discourse is produced, potentially more problematic are accounts of civic and political engagement that bypass the cognitive and emotive dimensions of individuals' public orientation, and concentrate on citizens' material incentives to act. Here Pattie *et al.* (2004) summarise five different models of the factors that support active citizenship. They distinguish broadly between 'choice-based' and 'structural-based' models: the former split into 'cognitive engagement' or 'general incentives to act' whereas structural theories of citizenship can be divided into the 'civic voluntarism' model, the 'equity-fairness' model and the 'social capital' model. It is striking – and apparently undermines the salience of both 'public connection' and media consumption – that mediated attention only features explicitly at two points in their survey: positively in the 'cognitive engagement' model, and negatively in the 'social capital' model. But the incompatibility with our approach is only apparent, since Pattie's discussion highlights the causal factors *isolated* by particular models of citizenship; they are not concerned (as we are) with background, often latent, assumptions. From the latter perspective, it is difficult to see how citizens can assess the material benefits of becoming civically involved without an orientation to a public world by reference to which they make their choices.

'Public connection', then, (whether explicitly emphasised or not) is a key assumption in accounts of how democracy does, or should, work. What makes investigating public connection urgent, however, is the sense of writers and policymakers in many countries that democracy is no longer working effectively.

Accounts of the crisis of democracy

These concerns have come in overlapping waves over many decades, and each is relevant to the UK's current situation.

The *first* wave of concern regarding the preconditions for effective democracy related to the skills of citizens. An influential early argument was that these could only develop through regular civic involvement; Mill and Rousseau saw crucial links between voluntary association or local community action and wider interest in politics (Pateman 1970), a point developed further in the 20th century by John Dewey (1946) among others. A version emerged in Almond and Verba's (1963: 144) 'capillary action' model of democratic activism spreading from local to national. Here what matters most for democratic engagement is the learned practice of acting with others in public. On this account, the threat to democracy comes from the decline of such practices, although national differences in social norms of voluntary action are important (Skocpol and Fiorina 1999). A variation of this argument emphasises civic education. Many writers have identified 'cultural', particularly educational, factors as essential preconditions for an engaged citizenry, whether in republican and liberal accounts of 'civic education'[28] and 'civic literacy',[29] or in T. H. Marshall's historical model of citizenship (1992: 34). The UK government's recent introduction of citizenship education into the national school curriculum is a practical application of this argument.

Account must, however, be taken of a major counter-argument which emphasises the *social* stratification of political culture. That education is marked by social stratification is well established, and the consequences for civic engagement have long been noted.[30] Concern about social segmentation of course goes much wider than debates about the work-ings of politics,[31] but the argument is that political culture at all levels is stratified. Particularly powerful was Carole Pateman's critique of Almond and Verba's civic culture research (1989: 76, 77): in the UK and the USA the working class was, she argued, socially prepared for its 'not very civic place' in the democratic polity. Similarly, but in greater sociological detail, David Croteau (1995: 103, 172) has analysed the lack of 'cultural context' for working class people to be engaged in politics.[32] The same broad argument can be extended to other dimensions: age and gender,[33] ethnicity,[34] and occupational status.[35] A parallel argument can be made for more specific areas, such as involvement in voluntary organisations (Skocpol and Fiorina 1999: 499–504). Such arguments lead Michael delli Carpini and Scott Keater (1996: 60) to ask, how democratic is US or indeed any democratic society, *and for whom?* We hope to cast some light on this question.

The concern with systematic exclusion from politics has generated responses both theoretical and practical. Theoretically, communitarianism (Sandel 1982; Walzer 1983; Taylor 1989) rejects the Rawlsian theory of justice in which the basic units of society are discrete, atomised individuals and argues that preceding individual deliberative positions are the natural communities of which each of us is a member. In policy-making, communitarianism has been associated in the UK most strongly with the social inclusion agenda. We are, however, cautious about any assumptions that there are natural 'communities' in contemporary Britain.

A *second* wave of concern at democratic decline that grows out of such responses to the first centres on the question of 'social capital', brought to prominence particularly by Robert Putnam's work (Putnam 2000). While there are many reference-points for 'social capital' (from family and friends to membership of social groups to networks of acquaintances), 'the idea' it has been claimed 'at the core of the theory of social capital is extremely simple: social networks matter' (Putnam 2002: 6). Starting out from the general fabric of social interaction, as the foundation of civic activity, Putnam is concerned with both the overall decline in social trust and the uneven distribution of the resources (social 'capital') that build on social trust, and the long-term implications of each for effective democracy. Putnam is specifically concerned with the decline of formal associations, captured in his famous image of 'bowling alone'. In the late 1990s such arguments had considerable resonance in USA, UK and other countries' policy circles, and that influence has recently developed into a broader concern with measures that will restore 'respect' within communities.[36]

There have, however, been many fundamental critiques of Putnam's thesis. Ignoring disagreements as to whether social capital and civic involvement *have* declined in particular countries such as the USA and UK (Hall 2002; Wuthnow 2002), the most important criticisms for our purposes are: exaggerating the importance of formal associations in social life generally (compared with other forms of organisation, not least online networks),[37] ignoring the disjunctures between voluntary activities and the actual space of politics,[38] and exaggerating the importance of horizontal trust for political engagement.[39] In addition, Putnam's well-known isolation of high levels of television consumption as negatively correlated with social capital and civic participation has been heavily criticised (Norris 2000) for ignoring the *positive* correlation between television consumption and public engagement for many people (see Chapter 8).

Our own position, given this intense debate, is to look for the social preconditions of declining engagement not just in the formal associations whose reduction Putnam laments but more widely in the organisation of everyday practice. Not only is the evidence for a tight relationship between social trust, civic involvement and political engagement increasingly ambiguous,[40] but the contribution of *mediated* networks and practices (including those online) needs to be investigated. It is striking, for example, that the UK Electoral Commission's *Audit of Political Engagement* (2004a) suggests a split between 'good causes [i.e. non-political] activism' and propensity to vote: even if social trust/ capital contributes to the former, it need not contribute to the latter. A more helpful concept than 'social capital' for unlocking the social preconditions of democratic engagement may be Etienne Wenger's (1998) 'communities of practice'. For, as Wenger argues, it is 'communities of practice' that provide the 'social configurations in which our enterprises are defined *as worth pursuing* and our participation is recognisable *as competence*' (1998: 5, added emphases). Whatever our levels of interpersonal trust and social capital, we need access to communities of practice which specifically *make sense* of citizenship as something individuals can and should do. Whether UK citizens have such access is an open question.

A *third* wave of concern about democracy's future focuses not on individuals' skill or resources, but on the features of public discourse that undermine it as a shared space of debate. This is the other side of the 'common culture' argument. A recent argument is that the internet is leading to the fragmentation of publics (Gitlin 1998; Sunstein 2001). This is not a new debate, since John Dewey (1946) had feared the consequences of 'too much public' leading to the impossibility of any 'public' identifying itself as such, but it is intensified by the increasing specialisation of political discourse itself (Mayhew 1997; Blumler and Kavanagh 1999; Bennett and Manheim 2006). The argument is as much about the separation of each of us from each other, as about the separation of political elites from ordinary citizens. What if the world of online consumption means that increasingly 'individuals... [will] actually feel better about knowing less and less about the world around them' (Gandy 2002: 452)? The only answer, we propose, is to investigate how and to what extent people remain oriented to a public world through media both traditional and new.

Any such study must, however, take account of broader sociological analyses of democratic decline. One foregrounds overlapping factors within the nation-state which have undermined any coherent model for citizenship (Walzer 1974: 605–6). Sociologists and historians have long acknowledged that citizenship is multi-causal and geographically specific (Tilly 1997); T. H. Marshall's model of the development of citizenship in Britain was similarly complex. The relevance of Marshall's model is however threatened by the fears of a growing gulf between public and private spheres, between civic commitment and consumerism, indeed a collapse of 'the social' itself (Bauman 1999; Touraine 2000). Two detailed accounts, one by a political scientist and one by a sociologist, of the complex intersections between work and leisure, public and private practices, are important here. Lance Bennett (Bennett 1998: 755) in an essay on the 'uncivic culture' suggests that people's psychological investments and values have over time been reorientated away from central political and economic institutions to local and personal projects, for a variety of reasons including increased economic and labour market instability.[41] The sociologist Bryan Turner, by contrast, traces 'the erosion of citizenship' to the marginalization of workers from decision-making through changes in education, rationalisation of the voluntary sector and many other factors; as a result, Marshall's model of citizenship has become a 'thin' model instead of a 'thick' one (Turner 2001: 203). Leaving aside Turner's simplistic blaming of a 'passive world of television' (2001: 203), his suggestion that the matrix of linked practices which make citizenship meaningful has unravelled is powerful. Thomas Janoski expresses a similar point: 'citizenship presumes some determinate community or civil society with some connections and networks between people and groups, and some norms and values that provide meaning to their lives' (1998: 24). So where is that 'determinate community' now?

At this point, a final wave of concern intervenes, arguing that globalisation has seen the supersession by transnational flows of the 'mythic compact' of nation-state-focussed politics (Miller 2002). Some argue that the very concept of 'citizenship' (implying a bounded national territory) should be replaced by a transnational notion of 'denizen-ship' (Soysal 1994),[42] or that globalization has outmoded the national arena for citizenship (Roche 2002). More plausibly and less drastically, Saskia Sassen insists upon the 'partial embedding of global in national' (Sassen 2002); this transforms our practical understanding of 'citizenship' and replaces an older 'bounded' notion of politics with an 'infinite' model of politics operating across and without regard to national boundaries (Dahlgren 2005: 154).[43] The local, however, remains important (Cammaerts and Van Audenhove 2005), creating a new risk that a global civil society will increasingly move out of reach of people's lifeworlds.[44] The point, as ever, is that we should not assume theory is the best vantage-point from which to predict how these contradictions are experienced in practice: we need detailed evidence from people' reflections on their daily lives.

Finally, against these concerns at the decline of democracy, we must register an important counter-argument. What if, instead of declining, political orientation is simply taking new, more dispersed forms? Russell Dalton (Dalton 2000; Dalton and Wattenberg 2003) has sought to test empirically current diagnoses of disengagement, rejecting both the traditional idealised view of the democratic citizen and the 'realist' conception of the 'deferential' voter in traditional political science of the 1950s. Against this, Dalton argues that changes to social structures encourage political participation – albeit not in the form of traditional electoral politics.[45] He argues for an *increase* in community activism and participation in referenda, concluding that contemporary western societies are characterised not by disengagement but transformations in the reference-points of public practice, towards life-style-oriented issues.[46] Is it here that a new 'determinate community' is emerging?

The current UK and international context

The debate remains unresolved. As Pharr, Putnam and Dalton put it in a review of the international evidence, while there is 'no evidence of declining commitment to the principle of democratic government . . . by almost any measure political alienation [from electoral systems] soared over the last three decades' (2000: 7, 9). An international Gallup/World Service survey (BBC Press Office 2005) is equally bleak, suggesting that only in Scandinavia and South Africa do a majority of citizens believe their country is run by the will of the people.

In the UK concerns have until recently been targeted on the young, and with good reason. After a significant decline in young people voting in the 2001 general election (Hansard Society 2001), various researchers have confirmed that young people's interest in the political process is low.[47] In the 2005 UK general election only 37 per cent of 18–24 year olds and 48 per cent of 25–34 year olds voted (Electoral Commission 2005b). While below-50 per cent turnout among the under 24s is not unique to the UK,[48] the 'generation gap' in voting propensity appears particularly wide in the UK (and also Japan).[49] More recently, concerns have been registered about other groups: less than 50 per cent of Class C2D consider themselves certain to vote (Electoral Commission 2006: 15), confirming earlier concerns that political disengagement is crucially linked to deprivation,[50] while less than 47 per cent of ethnic minorities voted in the 2005 election.[51]

There is however a broader problem here, not limited to one population sector. The BBC (2002: 22) has voiced concern about 'political disconnection' amongst the whole UK population, while one online survey reported that 72 per cent of UK citizens felt 'disconnected' from their political representatives (Coleman 2005). Not surprisingly the problem of 'disconnection' is now regularly noted in the literature,[52] and concern about voter disengagement was registered by both journalist commentators and leading politicians during the 2005 election,[53] although disengagement has not further increased since then (Electoral Commission 2008). But the issue of disconnection is complex, as the example of young people shows: disinclination to vote may be distinct from unwillingness to follow politics through media or disinterest in political issues,[54] while some researchers point to considerable civic activism among the young alongside their disenchantment from the formal political system.[55] Nor do such disconnections occur in a vacuum: the national press, it appears, *reduced* the priority it gave to election news in 2005, while media's established practice rarely represents 'ordinary' citizens as active agents in political deliberation.[56]

The problem of democratic engagement rightly therefore exercises governments and policymakers, but ways forward are anything but clear. One possibility is restoring the electorate's trust in politicians and the political process, and here hopes are sometimes invested in new technological possibilities (blogging, social networking and the mobile phone, or more broadly online interactivity).[57] UK e-government initiatives play back the language of 'connection' (for example the 'Government connect project' or the direct.gov.uk site), but it is unclear whether they make any difference: according to one recent survey, only 13 per cent of internet *users* (not the general population) look online for information about an MP, local councillor or politician.[58] Even at its boldest, the New

Labour government's vision of an e-democracy acknowledged that 'the notion of a formal space on the web where any one can initiate policy ideas, contribute evidence or debate with others is a long way off'.[59] While the BBC's Action Network tried to facilitate online engagement in civic and political activism, its success was limited. Nor have experiments in e-voting clearly solved disengagement problems, and they are beset with their own difficulties.

Indeed there is an increasing momentum behind the view that the problem of democratic engagement is not amenable to a 'quick fix'. Some critics have suggested that it is government trust in voters as much as voters' trust in government that needs to be boosted,[60] while The Power Report (Power 2006) moves away from the Putnamesque idea that the problem is a decline in voluntary association membership, towards a more disturbing conclusion: that civic engagement remains healthy in Britain, but those who are civically engaged remain nonetheless disengaged from, indeed despairing of, Britain's *political* process. We return to these concerns later.

There are important comparative issues here. In our conclusion we note parallels between our research and research from Europe and the USA. But the problem of disengagement affects each country from very different historical starting-points. What are the distinctive features of the British situation?

First, Britain is broadly an elitist, not a participative, democracy:

in which citizens have traditionally thought of themselves as 'subjects'. In such a context, it may seem natural [for citizens] to place a strong emphasis on civility and the preservation of community norms while downplaying the importance of those political duties which involve considerable political participation. (Conover *et al.* 1991: 814)

In Britain the link between citizen engagement and government action has *usually*, not exceptionally, been problematic, and the agenda of 'community norms' cannot, automatically, be assumed to encourage 'naturally' an agenda of political participation or engagement. Trust in political institutions in Britain has been low for a long time,[61] which makes less surprising our finding (Chapter 8) that levels of political trust contribute little to the explanation of political engagement or public connection. This also helps us understand how the increase in centralising pressures on UK local government over the past three decades (Mulgan 2006) has generated relatively little protest, even as it has reduced opportunities for local civic activism. Over the longer-term still, the character of Britain as an 'elitist' democracy must be linked to the relative weakness in Britain (compared, say, with the USA) of religious or other civil society institutions as independent political actors. This, we must remember, is the historical context that shapes whether experiments in encouraging citizen involvement, online political innovations (Moveon.org)[62] or global civil society movements (Indymedia) will become integrated into political and civic culture in Britain. Certainly people's political engagements may go beyond the national framework with all its limitations,[63] but the national setting may still be a major constraining force.

It is in any case vital to contextualise our study of mediated public connection in the space of *action-opportunities* available to citizens; this is the material context in which (mediated) public connection has meaning, if at all. For people's orientation to a world beyond the private to matter, it must have some link with practice:[64] a democracy of citizens must be based on more than 'myth' (Eder 2001). But, as with the notion of 'the public', we need to be as open as possible on where, and in what specific forms, those action-opportunities may occur. In this context, we will think of civil society both as including the space of media (Cohen 1999) and allowing for a broader range of 'communities of practice' than the formal associations with which Putnam was principally concerned. It is crucial also to consider to what extent this space of action is acknowledged as legitimate (or not) by government. Since citizenship is oriented ultimately towards what governments do, citizens' commitments must be recognised by governments or in a struggle with governments (Young 2000: 189–90): otherwise citizenship is indeed based on 'myth'.

Finally, in thinking about Britain's distinctive context, we need to remember the complexity of the UK's media audience. Britain, of course, has a distinctive media history: long established public broadcasting, an even longer established newspaper market, with the relatively slow introduction of high-speed, unlimited-access domestic online use (no free local dial-up as in the USA or heavy investment in broadband installation as in South Korea). These distinctive conditions are shaping Britain's entry to the digital media age. Perhaps broadband is changing everything as a connected majority[65] starts to link together in unexpected ways! But even here we need to note evidence from the USA that broadband internet users differ by being *less*, not more, concerned about solidarity with other users (Pew 2002).

In any case, technological change is not the only factor, since history, in the sedimented form of *habits* of news consumption, remains vital in shaping how change occurs: so the older habit, for example, of watching

TV news bulletins at a fixed time and having a newspaper delivered to one's door is not trivial, even if it is destined to decline, even disappear, in the long-term. It is worth remembering that the third term in Albert Hirschman's famous dialectic of 'exit' and 'voice' was '*loyalty*': loyalty which 'holds exit at bay and activates voice . . . [so serving] the socially useful purpose of preventing deterioration from becoming cumulative, as it so often does when there is no barrier to exit' (1969: 78–9). Loyalty, or 'habit' – and its social stratifications – will be a major factor in later chapters.

Conclusion

We have established so far that the notion of public connection under-lies most political science and political theory, but a complex set of social changes require that we no longer take it as a given. In Chapter 2 we examine what media consumption contributes both to the assumption of public connection and its reality.

Notes

1. For earlier papers developing the notion of 'public connection', see Couldry and Langer (2003; 2005).
2. The US figure is a percentage of voting-age population (2000 figure: 51%), based on US Census Bureau (2004). We choose this figure because of the uncertainties over figures for registered voters in the USA: 64% of US voters registered to vote turned out in 2004 (http://www.census.gov/Press-Release/www/releases/archives/voting/004986.html).
3. UK Election Statistics 1945–2003 (2003).
4. Lippman (1925), Schumpeter (1943), Kierkegaard (1962).
5. Cf Dimaggio *et al.* (2001) on the link between attention scarcity and inform-ation abundance.
6. Benhabib (1996b: 68); Cohen (1999: 59).
7. See for example Blumler and Gurevitch's (1995: 24) insistence on the need for 'mutual orientations to communication content' in a democracy.
8. Coleman (2003).
9. Contrast looser definitions of 'politics' as 'public-spiritedness' (Eliasoph 1998: 16), or power relations (Bhavnani 1991: 52).
10. But contrast Garcia Canclini (2001: 20), Costera Meijer (1998), Hermes (1998), van Zoonen (2003).
11. Ankersmit (1996), Pels (2003).
12. Delli Carpini and Williams (2001).
13. Cf Barber (1999), Elster (1999:10–11).
14. Indeed many non-liberal versions of democratic theory do so: Unger's (1998: 248) progressive democracy theory where the distinction makes room for the notion of social property, Charles Taylor's communitarian rethinking

of the public sphere as 'the locus of a discussion . . . in which [a] society can come to a common mind about important matters' (2004: 87), and Van Gunsteren's 'neorepublican' framework that draws on post-structuralist theory (1998: 136–8).

15. See for a recent example Gerson (2004), but also note Elshtain's (1997) critique of those who reject the public/private boundary explicitly while holding onto it implicitly. We acknowledge however the broader issue of secularism. Within Islamic thought or Christian evangelism we might expect a very different view of the public/private divide, since the division between secular (public?) everyday life and individual (private?) religious practice is not recognised. But such questions are not of primary importance in the overwhelmingly secular context of UK public life.

16. Fraser (1992); Phillips (1996); Young (2000).

17. Berlant (1997: 3); Giroux (2001).

18. Held (1995) on 'cultural rights' and Beck (2000b) on the cultural basis of mediated global politics.

19. Barber (1984: 132) on 'political community'; Dewey (1993: 110) on democracy as a 'mode of conjoint communicated experience'.

20. See Cohen and Arato (1992: 456) on 'communicative coordination'; and Walzer (1998: 308) on 'connection' as basis of mutual responsibility; and see generally Keane (1998).

21. See Rasmussen and Brown (2002: 179) on representation and Mouffe (2000: 13) on the 'common symbolic space' of politics.

22. Drawing on the liberal idea of the 'naturally inactive citizen' (Pateman 1989).

23. Lippman (1925: 13–14, 45), cf Lippman (1922).

24. Zolo (1992: 130); Bucy and Gregson (2001).

25. Pateman (1989) critiques Almond and Verba for a purely nominal notion of political participation, that masks deep forms of gender/ class stratification in political engagement.

26. Stevenson (1997); Murdock (1999).

27. Cf Narayan (1997: 65) who retains a notion of 'shared national life' in her feminist account of citizenship.

28. Dewey (1946); Almond and Verba (1963: 34); Barber (1984); Delli Carpini and Keater (1996).

29. Miller (2002).

30. Almond and Verba (1963: 379), Verba *et al.* (1995), Nie *et al.* (1996).

31. Young (1999) on 'the exclusive society'; Graham and Marvin (2001) on 'splintered urbanisms'.

32. See Conover and Shearing (2004) on how civic discourse does not treat various groups equally as actors.

33. Bhavnani (1991); Delli Carpini and Keater (1996); Pattie *et al.* (2004: 75, 85, 103).

34. Bhavnani (1991).

35. On work status as the basis of social connection see Croteau (1995) and, Wilson (1996).

36. An example of Putnam's influence on UK policy is a 'social capital' survey within the London Borough of Camden (Khan and Muir 2006). On the new 'respect' initiative, see extensive reports in the UK press on 11 January 2006 of a Tony Blair speech on 10 January.

37. See theoretically Cohen (1999), Meyer and Tarrow (1998), Fine and Harrington (2004), and for empirical support Hill and Matsubayashi (2005), Thiess-Morse and Hibbing (2005). For online community, see Wellman and Hampton (1999).
38. Eliasoph (1998: 236).
39. Milner (2002: 23, 37) cf Barbalet (2000).
40. A recent collection (Putnam 2002) confirms these doubts.
41. Cf Croteau (1995: 190); Boggs (1997); Putnam (2000: chapter 5).
42. For counter-views, see Dahrendorf (1974); Preuss (1995); Miller (2000).
43. Cf Held (1995); Hermes (1998); Beck (2000a).
44. Stevenson (1997: 44–6); Miller (2000); Schlesinger and Kevin (2000).
45. Beck (1997); Tarrow (2000).
46. Compare on the shift towards 'postmaterialist values' Inglehart (1997: 305).
47. Livingstone *et al.* (2005); Haste (2005); Electoral Commission (2004c). A recent increase in engagement among younger voters is reported by the Electoral Commission (2008).
48. See Keater *el al.* (2002) for the US where voting in this age group has been below 50% since 1992.
49. Electoral Commission (2004c: 8–9).
50. Electoral Commission (2005a: 9).
51. Electoral Commission (2005b: 25).
52. Electoral Commission (2004c); MORI (2004: 6).
53. Cook (2005); Moore (2005).
54. Electoral Commission (2004c: 12); Haste (2005: 7–9).
55. Morris *et al.* (2003); MORI (2004: 5, 14).
56. See respectively Loughborough University (2005) and Lewis *et al.* (2005: 49).
57. Coleman (2005); for pessimism, see Sunstein (2000), Dahlgren (2001).
58. Dutton *et al.* (2009: 27).
59. Office of the E-Envoy (2002: 37).
60. Toynbee (2005).
61. Kavanagh (1989), Topf (1989).
62. For online civic engagement by young people in the USA, see Center for Social Media (2004).
63. For interesting discussions of scales within and beyond the nation, see Schlesinger (2003) and, Held (2004: 114).
64. Cf in republican democracy theory Pateman (1970), Barber (1984) and Bader (1995).
65. Broadband connection had reached 66% of households by February 2009, a rapid rise over recent years Dutton *et al.* (2009: 13).

2
Media Consumption and Public Connection

Why media consumption?

In Chapter 1, we reviewed the debates regarding the basis of the public's engagement with democratic politics. We observed that, while there are many explanations of the so-called crisis in democracy, these generally focus on changes in political institutions and social structures; much less often is serious attention paid to the media. Yet at the heart of many of these explanations lies a set of assumptions about people's 'public connection' – their lived relationship with public culture – which make little sense unless grounded in the material realities of people's daily lives. Firmly embedded in these material realities are the symbolic realities of the media (Couldry 2005a; Silverstone 2005).[1]

We also began to map out some key processes now shaping public connection, particularly the putative shift away from 'traditional' politics towards single-issue or life-style politics, the decline in public trust in democratic institutions, and the increasingly contested boundary between public and private. Media are highly relevant to each since so much that is 'political' or 'public' is presented through media. Indeed as Putnam (2000: 218) notes, 'newspaper reading and good citizenship go together', while according to the *British Social Attitudes* survey, alongside a 'gradual erosion' of trust in government through the 1990s, people's willingness to contact the media is the only form of political action that has increased (Bromley *et al.* 2004).[2]

Attracting and sustaining citizens' attention is a central challenge in modern democracies and a prerequisite for most political or civic action, from opinion formation or public discussion to voting or direct participation in democratic institutions. But how such attention is managed raises important questions, particularly since this attention is likely to be uneven, and perhaps also unequally distributed. This complexity is compounded by the contestability of the public/private boundary itself. We thus join with a growing number of scholars who are interested in how the transitions across boundaries (from personal to political, from opinion to action, from individual to collective) are mediated, in either direction.

This chapter will first argue against the position that simply blames the media for today's supposedly high levels of political apathy. We then examine the claim that media can, and in some ways do, sustain collective attention. We do not advocate the naïve view that media consistently act as a force for the public good. Instead, if, as Craig Calhoun (1992: 13) put it in relation to the public sphere, 'the public define[s] its discourse as focusing on all matters of common concern [and] the emerging public establishe[s] itself as inclusive in principle', we wish to ask: what are these matters of common concern, how are they engaged by the public, how does public engagement relate to political participation, if at all, and how important are media in facilitating, shaping or impeding such participation?

The plurality of media

Any such analysis must start, however, from a recognition that media are plural in their cultural forms, modes of address, technological features and, hence, in their effects. We must disaggregate the generic term, 'the media', too easily reified in public, sociological and political debate.

One aim is to acknowledge the range of opportunities for people to use media to engage actively with civic concerns. Beyond 'the news' (the main, widely valued, means by which public connection is mediated) are various other, less obvious means by which particular media genres may open up new routes to public participation.

Another is to clarify what aspect of media is under discussion. Two frames are frequently confused in both popular and academic discussion. Roger Silverstone (1994) used the concept of double articulation to contrast the media *qua* material objects such as the television or walkman (i.e. technological objects consumed in particular spatio-temporal settings), with the media *qua* texts such as the news or the soap opera (i.e. symbolic messages located within particular sociocultural discourses and interpreted by audiences). So when, for example, research critiques 'the media' for undermining public participation, we need to be clear: is the target of this critique the media *qua* material objects – keeping people at home on the sofa, filling their ears so they can't hear conversation around them, distancing them from each other in time and space – or the media *qua* texts – infusing the news with commercial values, reinforcing normative perspectives through the soap opera, or replacing genuine debate with the managed show of the phone-in? Similarly, when the claim is made that 'the media' bring the nation together, is the claim that they do this because people simultaneously consume the same programme, and so can share experience over the water cooler the next day, or is the claim that people receive the same communicative content and so come to share a particular perspective on the world and a language for discussing it? The answer is probably 'both', but the analysis depends greatly on which aspect of media we emphasise.

Research must also disaggregate 'the audience'.[3] Murdock *et al.* (1995) identify three categories of resources – the material (income, space, etc), social (support networks and local expertise) and symbolic (educational and cultural competences) – which contextualise media consumption and which are differentially available. In charting the multiplication of media goods in the family home over recent decades, Sonia Livingstone (2002: 41–2) distinguishes between 'media rich' (online, digital television, multiple media options), 'media average' (computer, multichannel television), and 'media poor' (no computer, terrestrial television). While the precise combination of technologies continues to change, the principle of differentiation persists, since with each new market innovation, social stratification works to maintain class distinctions. Other kinds of differentiation – by gender, ethnicity, generation – are perhaps less predictable; in relation to media goods at home, the picture for gender is changing as early technophobia among women evaporates, largely because of the ubiquity of technology in the workplace (Wajcman 2002) though attitudes to other media may remain gendered (Gray 1987). The picture for ethnicity, at least in the United Kingdom, is complex, with some minority groups being among the early adopters while others are disproportionately represented among the digitally excluded (Ofcom 2008).

Similarly research on how people interpret media texts has generated a thoroughly differentiated conception of audiences. Social class, gender, age and so forth all shape audiences' interpretative activities, and their ability to construct a meaningful world view that may accept but also re-interpret or resist media's often-normative encoding.[4] Research is now turning to the rather different tasks – increasingly framed as media literacy – implicated in making sense of new media, especially the internet.[5]

In addition, disaggregating audiences, and adjusting the broader narrative of mass consumption to take account of people's everyday responses to media, has tended to move audience research away from an overly media-centric approach. Being part of an audience is just one of many activities in daily life, and media just one of many sources of meaning and influence. The charge of media-centrism criticises at audience research for reifying its objects of analysis ('the movie-goer', the 'soap fan', 'the audience') and so blinds us to the diverse social and cultural contexts within which media reception is embedded. Various concepts have been proposed to counter this media-centrism: the 'embedded audience' (Abercrombie and Longhurst 1998), the 'dispersed audience' (Radway 1988), the 'extended audience' (Couldry 2005), and the call for 'ethnographic' research (Drotner 1994; Ang 1996). These debates have opened the way to a more contextualised approach to people's everyday relations with media.

By opening up the black boxes of 'the media' and 'the audience', the empirical analysis of later chapters will explore how people's diverse, often contradictory participation in democracy is thoroughly mediated.

'The media' – legitimate object of blame?

Since the advent of broadcasting, opinion has been sharply divided between those excited by its potential to stimulate, engage and integrate, and those fearful of its potential to distract, disengage and fragment. Each new medium has attracted surprisingly similar public hopes and anxieties (Drotner 1992).

A commonplace, pessimistic discourse about media use is that the media, especially television, transform the public into a passivised, individualistic, mindless mass audience, sapping their motivation to get off the sofa and engage. This discourse – familiar through such well-worn tropes such as the couch potato or telly addict – reinforces a highly critical view of the media. The view that the media are irrelevant or even harmful to democracy, and political engagement in particular, goes back to elite models of democracy (Lippman 1922: 63; 1925). More recently, Jürgen Habermas (1989) argued that the media have played a key role in undermining the public sphere through the 'refeudalisation' of public discussion into the mere 'publicity' of a pseudo-public sphere. By contrast with face-to-face communication, where one can check whether communication is trustworthy, authentic and reliable, the increasing mediation of the public seems to open the door to the inauthentic, the motivated and the untrustworthy.

In the lively debate following Habermas' original thesis, many have judged the media to have 'undercut the kind of public culture needed for a healthy democracy' (Dahlgren 2003: 151) by various means, including (1) keeping people at home and away from civic and community spaces, (2) distracting people by easy entertainment away from more demanding news and current affairs, (3) commodifying news into branded infotainment and dumbing down journalistic values, to the point where fact and fiction are indistinguishable within politics itself,[6] and (4) focusing attention on the activities of the traditional (privileged) establishment and silencing difference and dissent.[7]

A recent and influential version of those arguments is Robert Putnam's *Bowling Alone* thesis (Putnam 2000). Noting time-use data that shows most of Americans' increase in free time in the past decades has been taken up by television viewing, Putnam argues that high television consumption (television as entertainment, that is) is a major cause of declining levels of social capital and civic engagement. As he puts it, 'a major commitment to television viewing – such as most of us have come to have – is incompatible with a major commitment to community life'; consequently, 'just as television privatises our leisure time, it also privatises our civic activity, dampening our interactions with one another even more than it dampens individual political activities' (2000: 229).

Both Putnam's argument and his evidence have since been widely criticised (see Chapter 1). Nonetheless, blaming television remains a popular explanation for the apparent loss of civic engagement and Putnam's argument has been reworked theoretically in Henry Milner's argument that low civic engagement is associated with the high knowledge dependency associated with high TV viewers (Milner 2002). Yet arguments such as Putnam's based on how we use our time, while they cannot easily be dismissed,[8] are far from straightforward. American research based on time-budget data (Robinson and Godbey 1997) has concluded that subjectively the US is a 'time-famine society', even though the average American actually had *more* free time in the 1980s and 1990s than previously. Gershuny (2000) argues that recent years have seen increasing *convergence* in time use by gender and class in the UK, like many Western countries, with time 'pressures' increasing not because of overall hours spent in employment, but because a growing range of activities impinge upon leisure time.[9] The relation of time to socio-demographics is therefore complex.

Reasons for blaming media are, then, multiple. The risk is that blaming 'the media' without disaggregating these different claims obfuscates the broader, complex and co-dependent relations between media and society. The critique too easily loses its force especially as, when expressed in its simplest form, it can be sidelined as a mere scapegoating of the media as a convenient target, motivated either by the covert desire to distract attention from other likely causes of political apathy (for example, failing political institutions) or by an elitist disparaging of 'ordinary' interests (a consistent pitfall of arguments around the Habermasian public sphere).[10] A more subtle and nuanced account of media's consequences for public life is needed.

Mediating a shared frame of attention

If, as in much liberal thought (see Chapter 1), the public world is taken to mean that which is *both* collective *and* accessible (or visible), then private experience can offer little scope for public connection, which obscures the potential fluidity of the public/private boundary. While not arguing necessarily that everything private has a public or political significance, we do argue against the idea that everything private (i.e. inaccessible to others) is without public or political significance. Why? For our present purposes, the main reason is the crucial positioning of the media, *linking* the private and inaccessible realm of the home (where most media are consumed) to the public (visible, accessible) world beyond. That, many argue, is the point of the media; engaging with media at home, as part of a collective audience, has long been regarded by media and communication scholars as potentially a public activity.

So mediation may facilitate shared attention and, as Daniel Dayan (2005: 44) puts it, we need to 'pay attention to attention'. Dayan argues that collective attention takes many forms: the public, but also the spectator, the activist, the witness, the community and the crowd. If shared attention can be constitutive of the collective, media may also serve to divide, fragment, silence or exclude members of collectivities – a question that can only be resolved through empirical exploration.

It is widely assumed, however, that media constitute the public's sense of its collective identity and community. In Europe particularly, the classic public service vision of electronic media as connecting community, even building the nation, has long been influential. The BBC's manifesto for public service broadcasting in the twenty-first century proclaims that, to build 'public value', it must enable citizenship, strengthen social capital and connect communities (Grade 2004). Indeed, throughout the history of mass media,[11] nations have relied upon the assumption that media can and do play a key constitutive role, an assumption held in fascist as well as democratic states and long before the advent of broadcasting.[12] Paddy Scannell (1989: 155) has argued media play a role in the 'resocialization of private life', while Bird sees media as providing the 'cultural frame' for everyday life (Bird 2003: 3), notwithstanding questions about whether media really did play such an integrative role in nation-building as so often now taken-for-granted (Schlesinger 2000).

Many have agreed with this analysis but offered a much more critical reading of its consequences. George Gerbner's claim that 'television tells most of the stories to most of the people most of the time' (Gerbner *et al.* 1986: 18) pointed to media's ideological power to draw people into a normative mainstream, masking diversity and undermining dissent, whereas a more recent critique of (American) public service television challenges its distinctly middle-class vision of what it means to be a 'good citizen' (Ouellette 2002: 138).

As we move into a new media and information environment, characterised by convergent, ubiquitous and interactive communication, this now-familiar agenda has focussed on the internet (Lievrouw and Livingstone, 2006; Livingstone 2005a).The internet seems to some uniquely equipped to 'build' community, whether a social cosmopolitanism (Hannerz 2002) or an enhanced deliberative democracy (Bentivegna 2002). As one of Maria Bakardjieva's interviewees said, the internet offers 'a link to everywhere' (Bakardjieva and Smith 2001: 76), a statement reminiscent of Robert Park's comment, many years ago (Park 1984: 81, 85), that the newspaper provided a 'window on [the] world' for US immigrants seeking community in the modern metropolis.

A significant shift is suggested if we contrast these last two quotes: in both, the media are crucial to public connection, but in relation to the newspaper, the media do the connecting; by contrast, with the internet, citizens are the agents, for without their activity, the link exists only as a potential (Burbules 1998). However, if there are expectations that the internet will simply 'take over' television's role in connecting community, history suggests otherwise, for rarely do new media replace old media (Marvin 1988); rather, the new 'remediates' the old (Bolter and Grusin 2001). We do not know as yet whether television's audience will further fragment (Webster 2005) or, perhaps, continue to provide the centre-stage for national culture, albeit an often mainstreamed and normative stage, leaving the internet to afford opportunities for the expression of diversity and difference.[13] Once again we will leave the implications of this point open until we examine our fieldwork.

From the collective to the public

Television seems 'to project its images, character types, catch-phrases and latest creations to the widest edges of the culture, permeating if not dominating the conduct of other cultural affairs' and yet it also has 'the powerful capacity... to draw towards itself and incorporate (in the process, transforming) broader aspects of the culture' (Corner 1995: 5). But, even if one accepts media's importance in attracting the public gaze and so setting the agenda of our shared attention, what are the implications of this beyond a collective experience? When is mediated connection also *public* connection? Is media consumption necessarily significant for democracy and the public sphere? Even if true in the past, can the media retain such a role, now the mass media that dominated the twentieth century are diversifying into the manifold interactive media of the 21st century?

One way forward is to argue that conceptually 'the collective' and 'the public' are one and the same. But this fails to capture the normative expectations held of the public, especially by theories of democracy (Taylor 2004: see Chapter 1 above). In seeking to distinguish the two, Daniel Dayan (2005) argues for a conception of the 'public' that goes beyond mere common experience. 'A public' must engage in actions that constitute a visible performance – it must take action, and it must be seen to do so. Further, it must be seen by itself to act, for a public (unlike, say, a crowd or a community) is reflexive: 'a public not only offers attention, it calls for attention'. Forming or joining a public takes commitment; it is not entered into lightly, for once joined, the public is imagined by its participants in the first person, as 'we'.

The publics in which ordinary people, in their daily lives, might participate – the 'we' that is open to them to join – include 'the general public' or 'the nation', but also various counter-publics, local publics or subcultural publics. These may not always meet Dayan's normative standards but they do, nonetheless, represent a range of ways in which people experience and enact a connection to the public. To allow for this range, our phrase, 'public connection', repositions 'public' as an adjective rather than a reified (or idealised) noun. Degrees and types of publicness may, thus, vary; indeed, the nature of public connection is, for us, an open question, inviting empirical exploration.

Developing Dayan's analysis also helps to reveal media's potential role. The media provide a means, perhaps the key means in late modern society, not only for offering but also calling for attention. Media are frequently reflexive and are engaged with reflexively by their audiences.

Media choices reflect a certain degree of commitment, as a form of identity display, not least to oneself, although as a corollary we must realise that media exclude as well as include. As Mirca Madianou (2005) observes, in Greece the 'national' news presumes the public to be Greek, thus discursively excluding the Turkish-speaking minority in a manner strongly felt by that subsection of the audience who, in their turn, 'switch off', simultaneously switching on to an alternative form of news and, so, to a potentially subcultural public. Research indicates that levels of mistrust in media are much higher in UK certain ethnic minorities than the general UK population (Ofcom 2006a). More generally, as critical scholarship has long made plain, it is endemic to news discourse that it divides the world variously into 'us' and 'them'.[14]

   That qualification aside, what grounding in democratic theory can be found for these claims that media sustain the public's attention? First, John Dewey's argument (Dewey 1946: 114–15) that traditionally, citizens' duties have been threefold – to vote, participate in the social life of the community and communicate, expressing opinion and discussing issues of the day, and so communications ('shared experience') provide the basis of democratic revival. Barnhurst (2000) however suggests that for young people in the early 21st century, these duties are perceived and enacted differently and now encompass various types of expressive and resistant identity, in which media are variously involved. T. H. Marshall's (1992: 44) argument, that citizenship relies on the 'extension of common culture and common experience', like Dewey's, makes no specific mention of media institutions, though Raymond Williams (1961) draws out Marshall's implicit assumption that media play a central role in sustaining a 'common culture', providing 'representations of what living is now like' (Williams 1976). Scannell (1989) emphasises the role of 20th century national broadcasting in generating a new 'communicative entitlement' for whole populations. However, with the notable exception of Habermas' (1989, 1996) initially negative and later more positive reading of media's contribution to democratic engagement, most political theory has given media limited explicit attention until recently.

   It is much easier to find examples of the assumption of mediated political connection in political science,[15] even if the nature of media's role remains little explicated.[16] But if it has only become common recently within mainstream political science to be explicit about media's contribution to public connection, the sub-discipline of 'political communication' research, is premised precisely on the salience of mediated political connection;[17] we draw on insights from this field in what follows.

The traditional centrality of the news

For most people, the media are the main source of news about political matters (Electoral Commission 2008) and, notwithstanding the media environment's diversification, television remains 'the main source'[18] of news, cited as such by 2 in 3 British adults (Ofcom 2006). The same survey finds that nearly 4 in 5 trust television to provide fair and unbiased news, though interestingly those of higher socio-economic status are less likely to prioritise television news (preferring newspapers or radio).

In part, such high trust reflects people's acknowledged dependency on television news at times of conflict or crisis, especially international crisis.[19] At such times, people may have complex and ambivalent responses to media images of global suffering over which audiences have little control (Hoijer 2004), while also being critical of the coverage (Michalski *et al.* 2002).

Under more everyday circumstances, however, and notwithstanding generally high levels of public trust in the objectivity of television news, there are many uncertainties whether people accept, or even understand, the news. Research consistently shows that few can recall many of the news items watched just a few minutes before, and that many confuse, or misunderstand key aspects of the message content.[20] Key barriers to understanding include the use of technical terms, lack of context or explanation for events, the rapidly shifting news agenda, and mismatches between visual and verbal information. These are increasingly being raised in policy contexts as 'media literacy' questions, though this shifts responsibility from producer to receiver,[21] a problem when news is institutionally organised according to priorities that often do not match those of the citizen.[22]

Understanding presumably influences decisions over trustworthiness. The 2004 British Social Attitudes survey found that while 65 per cent of broadband users trust the internet as a source of news (the same proportion that trust newspapers), the balance is different among potential internet users and non-users who trust both the internet and newspapers *less* overall; in particular the internet is a much less trusted medium among non users (59 per cent trusting newspapers versus 19 per cent internet news) (Bromley *et al.* 2004). Pew (2004: 33) also reports considerable scepticism towards news sources among the American public, with 53 per cent agreeing that they 'often don't trust what news organisations are saying'. However, all this begs the question, does greater trust indicate *higher or lower* levels of media literacy? Is there a 'right answer' to the question: 'how much of the time can you trust newspapers'? One

American study (Tsfati 2003: 65) found that: 'when people did not trust the media, they tended to reject the mediated climate of opinion. On the other hand, when people had faith in the media, they tended to consistently converge with the media's election predictions'.

Understanding and trust is not simply a matter of the public's 'media literacy'. In a survey for the BBC among 16–44 year olds, it was argued that not only does the public 'find it difficult to relate politics and its presentation to their everyday lives' but also 'more media, in all forms, can mean more coverage but less clarity', especially as 'many people do not have a grasp of the basics of on-going political and news issues . . . or even democracy's structure and workings' (BBC 2002: 4; see also Hargreaves and Thomas (2002: 4)). These reports suggest a failure of news media as much, or more than, a failure of the public. Further, when people distrust media representations, they may either seek out a wider range of information sources or 'dismiss coverage' altogether (Reilly 1999). The latter rejection is more characteristic of lower socio-economic status, ethnic minority and marginalised populations.[23]

In short, people's interest in news is shaped by whether or not they understand it, and understanding depends on the form of the news, and the ways in which it addresses people. Research shows that if audiences do not understand, they lose interest and become disengaged (Graber 2001). Hargreaves and Thomas' (2002) study identified 'a strong demand for clear direct explanations from journalists which cut through 'waffle' and 'spin' and which explained why these events were happening' (Philo and Berry 2004: 257). Greg Philo and Michael Berry also found that people were more engaged (and understood news reports better) if they could empathise with the people depicted, or there were common values in the news to which they could relate. But, recalling Putnam's argument, Ron Lembo (2000) has suggested the 'sociality' of TV for many adults is comparatively 'disengaged', requiring the news to overcome such disengagement if it is to sustain public connection.

Yet far from media seeking to overcome disengagement, some research points to media institutions ever more motivated to communicate with themselves, and with society's elites (Raboy 1992: 142). Nick Couldry's work (2003a) sees the idea of media as socially integrative as a myth whose relationship to social reality cannot be assumed. Taking a different tack, Nina Eliasoph (1998) seeks to understand the role of apathy in everyday life, through the patterning of everyday talk and action, where people may want 'to create a sense of community, but [do] not want to talk politics' – precisely the problem in moving from the collective or civic to the political that we saw in another context at the end of Chapter 1.

For young people particularly, the internet is becoming an increasingly important source of news, raising new questions about people's skills in locating, comparing and critically evaluating an expanding range of news sources, many of which lack traditional gatekeepers or editorial quality checks. The 'UK Children Go Online' survey found that 24 per cent of UK teenagers read the news online (Livingstone and Bober 2004), while the Electoral Commission (2008) found that 25 per cent of 25–30 year olds turn to the internet as a major source of political and current affairs news, compared to just 4 per cent of those are 55 years. However, Pew internet surveys (2000, 2002a, 2004) suggest that young people's interest in the internet is insufficient to counter their generally lower levels of news consumption overall, though online news does now comprise a larger proportion of their news consumption than for older people. Reliance on the internet as news source may rise among the whole population during times of emergency such as the September 2001 attacks (Hamilton and Jenner 2003: 136). Other American research also suggests that the public is increasingly using the internet as a news source (Eveland *et al.* 2004), and this is a growing trend also in the UK (Ofcom 2004b). Online news appears to supplement more than displace traditional news sources (Althaus and Tewksbury 2000), and since many rely on the main news 'brands', the content thus obtained does not differ greatly from broadcast news (Tewksbury 2003). Research on the internet, however, is still in its early phases, and our research will make no *a priori* assumptions about the internet's importance for ordinary people in their daily lives.

Moving beyond claims that the public is irrational, news media simply irresponsible, or that the internet will solve the problems in the media-citizen relation, we need a complex account that relates media consumption to public connection in multiple ways.

Engaging with media in late modernity

The very factors that threaten the taken-for-granted centrality of traditional routes to mediated public connection may point, simultaneously, to new routes. Crucial here is the increasing individualisation in society, including the individualisation of media use, especially among young people. 'Individualisation' refers to a continuing process not a radical break, proposing that traditional social distinctions (social class, but also gender, ethnicity, region) are declining in importance, resulting in a fragmentation or undermining of the norms and values which have, hitherto, defined how people live their lives.[24] Regarded critically, this arouses popular fears of the selfish, 'me-generation'. More positively, it suggests new freedoms through self-actualisation and intensified reflexivity.

In terms of media consumption, one may point to the gradual fragmentation of audiences for the main terrestrial channels in a multichannel environment (Webster 2005), to the multiplication of media goods and increasing independence of time-schedules within the household (Livingstone 2002), and to the gradual displacement of mass media (television especially) by the internet, mobile and digital media (UCLA 2003). Observers of recent media history predict that the long-term consequences of media will be further to stratify (Dahlgren 2001: 83), fragment (Lievrouw 2001; Sunstein 2001) or polarise (Jones 2002) lifeworlds, not integrate them. Alternatively more diverse media content, together with the rise in creative or user-generated content, may facilitate the project of the self.

However we resolve this, media's mode of address is clearly changing as we move from a mass mediated to an increasingly multi-mediated culture. Media have never addressed all parts of the population equally: the press never tried, television tried but failed for many decades though public service retains such an ambition (Grade 2004); while the internet is built on the assumption of diversity and heterogeneity. Audience research strongly suggests that audiences are, in practice, just as disaggregated as we already know media organisations, texts and technologies to be (Livingstone 1998). Even the exceptional case of a national or global 'media event' (Dayan and Katz 1992) – a coronation or royal funeral, a major football game, even the finale of Big Brother – may have audiences that are more heterogeneous, diverse, stratified than we first suppose (Turnock 2000; Couldry 2003a). Indeed, it is a standard finding that audiences – or media consumers – acquire, make choices about, and interpret media texts and technologies in a manner strongly shaped by their sociodemographic background (social class, gender, age, ethnicity) and individual life history. In this regard, media consumption is part of the broader analysis of mass consumption that seeks to understand the complex ways in which people choose, interpret and appropriate goods within their daily lives (Csikszentmihalyi and Rochberg-Halton 1990: 139).

In any case we are concerned in this book with more than convergent national habits of media consumption, even if to some extent they persist. For such convergent consumption may not be focussed on media that link to the world of public issues. What if media connection is mainly used by most people for entertainment genres, not news, so that the presumption of 'public connection' is unfounded (Morley 1999: 139, 152)?

When addressing such concerns, the research literature often finds itself challenging the boundaries of the political. A case has been made, across a wide range of entertainment genres – the soap opera, the talk show, music and, most recently, sports – that these too may provide a basis for what we are here calling public connection. The argument is not, generally, made in terms of a shared knowledge of political facts, but rests on claims regarding identity and life-politics (gender, ethnicity, age), on mobilising shared emotional connection, and making visible the lived reality of ordinary people (especially the poor, the marginalised and those usually denied a voice in traditional political formats).[25] We take such arguments seriously: now that the public agenda is preoccupied by contentious issues once considered private, 'such as affirmative action, abortion, and the rights of sexual minorities... issues about which large publics are either disinterested or unalterably divided' (Bennett 1998), who is to say that the treatment of such issues in a soap opera is any less influential than its treatment by the news? But the empirical question remains: how effectively are such genres linked to 'the political' in the broadest sense (that is, the world of public *deliberation* and public *action*)? For public connection is more than a matter of expressing belonging to a specific community (see Chapter 1).

One area of entertainment where, in principle, we might expect such links to a broader public agenda is celebrity culture. Celebrities, we are often told, are role models for millions, especially younger citizens; the detailed narratives of celebrity lives – their struggles over identity, sexuality, giving birth, performing in public – certainly fascinate many of us. And celebrities are increasingly involved in, and used by politicians to further, political narratives, as part of a general blurring of the boundary between news and entertainment (Delli Carpini and Williams 2001). From here, some have made a stronger case, that celebrity culture is an essential component of public debate about the issues which require public resolution, whether as part of an increasing personalization of politics (Corner 2003), or as part of a broader narrativisation of democracy that includes a wider section of the public (Hartley 1999; Lumby 1997). This contradicts a longer negative tradition which sees celebrities and the mediated events constructed around them, as pseudo-personalities and pseudo-events (Boorstin 1961). But such is the proliferation of celebrity culture (Rojek 2001; Turner 2004) that it can no longer simply be dismissed as external to the world of public issues. We have taken an open view on this question: we asked our diarists to talk, as they thought relevant, about celebrity and other aspects of popular media culture, and then looked for any connections *they* made with issues of public contention.

In contemporary large-scale democracies, it would be absurd to ignore media's potential contribution to democracy as both information sources and foci of public attention and orientation. But the key question is: how are such possibilities enacted and embedded within the broader structuring of daily life, and how are such possibilities perhaps now being transformed?

New and emerging sites of mediated public connection

In the face of voter apathy and the supposed decline of civil society, we are witnessing a range of initiatives to engage audiences in public fora, often aided by new technological forms of interactive and participatory media. The familiar, mass communication model – with its centralised organisation, elite gatekeepers and established relations with institutions of power – no longer has a monopoly, with new opportunities emerging for the public to communicate, connect and deliberate online (Delli Carpini and Williams 2001; Lievrouw and Livingstone 2006). Following Habermas' later work, Sara Bentivegna (2002) argues that the internet is 'democratic' in that, while each of its features (interactivity, facilitated horizontal communication, disintermediation, reduced entry costs for small groups/individuals, and increased speed and flexibility of transmission and circulation) are not intrinsically new, when combined they enable the internet to introduce a qualitative shift in the potential for democratic communication.

Governments appear optimistic that civic or political participation can be thus revitalised, supporting a variety of mediated initiatives in relation to cultural citizenship, political socialisation, participatory deliberation, e-democracy, the digital divide, citizen engagement, and so forth (Bentivegna 2002; Coleman 2005; Livingstone 2005b). At present, however, evaluations of these initiatives are less than optimistic (Liff and Stewart 2001; Phipps 2000). An American survey of 15–25 year olds found that the internet to be even less effective than traditional means of engaging disaffected young people though very effective at mobilising the already-interested (Levine and Lopez 2004) while a survey of UK teenagers (Livingstone *et al.* 2005) found that those from more privileged homes, and with higher quality internet access, were better positioned to take up civic information available online (see also Ofcom 2009).

It is important here to avoid polarising the (passive, mass) audience and the (active, collectivist) public. After all, they may be the same people, and such a binary opposition blinds us to the complexity of people's relations with media and, so, to ways in which media consumption may sometimes work for the democratic cause. The growth of borderline public/private phenomena across both traditional and new media are important complications here, whether talk shows (private issues aired in the public television studio), internet chatrooms (publicly visible discussion accessed from private bedrooms), or voting in media contests or commenting on the news via text message (participation at a distance);[26] the BBC's Action Network[27] was another interesting development. Without overstating their consequences, these new genres at least 'create a space for us to understand each other. Such understanding stops short of real political efficacy. But it does contribute to democratising the discourse of news' (Lewis *et al.* 2005: 89).

There is evidence also that citizens are challenging more established media for the right to interpret public discourse, particularly through citizen-created online magazines or the much-vaunted 'blogs' (Boczkowski 2004). In the US particularly, bloggers have been influential in, for example, securing the resignation of Republican Senate majority leader Trent Lott (Cornfeld 2005; Drezner and Farrell 2004a; Regan 2004). Some have suggested that they constitute a new kind of governing institution, a 'fifth estate' that 'keeps watch over the mainstream media' (Drezner and Farrell 2004b), while the argument that computer-mediated communication provides intrinsically new possibilities for the general public and specialised groups to connect and debate is at least a decade old (Rheingold 1995). Yet there are good reasons to be cautious in the face of such optimism. One American survey found that only 17 per cent said online news led to them being exposed to a wider range of political opinion (Pew 2003). The 'blogosphere' may in large part be an elite phenomenon: in the US there is evidence that media elites including leading editors, publishers, political reporters and influential columnists all read blogs, and when 140 editors, reporters, columnists and publishers responded to a survey about which blogs they read, the top 10 blogs were responsible for 54 per cent of the citations, and the skew was even more marked among 'elite' publications (Drezner and Farrell 2004a). The authors caution that:

> To the extent that blogs become more politically influential, we may expect them to become more directly integrated into 'politics as usual,' losing some of their flavor of novelty and immediacy in the process. The most recent evidence of co-option was the decision by

both major parties to credential some bloggers as journalists for their nominating conventions. (Drezner and Farrell 2004a).

Commentators on the many experiments in e-democracy (Tsagarousianou *et al.* 1998) similarly observe that it appears easier to attract the already-interested or politically active than draw in new initiates to democratic deliberation: consequently, initiatives directed at the marginalised risk instead further advantaging the privileged.

One must ask not only about whether online information will improve the quality of public connection but also, more broadly, about the prospects for civil society online (and, indeed, offline). Steve Jones (1997: 25) suggested some time ago that the internet contributes to the fracturing of social realities, while Pippa Norris (2000: 277; Norris 2001) argues that the internet is likely to intensify the 'democratic divide' between 'those who do and do not use the multiple political resources available on the internet for civic engagement'. Thus Michael Bimber (quoted in Lievrouw and Livingstone 2002: 54) fears that the internet is producing the 'democratisation of elites'. Meanwhile James Katz and Ronald Rice (2002: 150)[28] conclude in their survey of the internet's social consequences that:

> even with higher bandwidth and richer format, [the internet] does not fit well with the way people get politically socialized. Rather it is our view that the Internet is a form of syntopia – an extension of, but still heavily integrated with other face-to-face and media channels and processes.

All this is without taking into account the online strategies of existing power groups: Robert McChesney (2000) charts the growing power over the internet of dominant commercial players, reducing the diversity of voices that get heard online, while Anthony Wilhelm (2000) complains that online politics takes the form of monologues, not dialogue. This is echoed by young people when they complain that online they are invited to 'have their say' yet rarely are listened to (Livingstone and Bober 2004; Livingstone 2009). Interestingly, following the successful use of the internet in the 2008 US election, Pew internet reports that online citizens also expect to be active in the Obama administration (Smith 2008).

We return here to the suggestion at the end of Chapter 1: that even enhanced civic engagement and mediated public connection will mean little unless on a larger scale it contributes to people's possibilities of effective action, which means government responding to the conversation as well.

Conclusion

As throughout this chapter, the best response to such complexities and ambiguities about digital inclusion/ exclusion is further empirical research. We have tried to show that, notwithstanding many uncertainties and doubts, the *idea* of 'mediated connection' – that media consumption sustains, in crucial respects, the shared attention of whole populations within, and perhaps now, beyond, national borders – remains pervasive and important. But what empirical support is there for this idea? How is it enacted in people's lives?

In Chapter 3, we ask specifically: how can such broad questions be translated into an empirical programme of research?

Notes

1. On most measures, media's role in our lives goes on increasing. For UK data on the acquisition of media goods over decades, see MacKay (1997), for US data on television viewing over recent decades, see Robinson and Godbey (1997). There are some exceptions, of course, notably signs that in the US time spent on the internet may be displacing time spent viewing television (USC 2004).
2. Although it remains at a low level (3.9% of population) (National Centre for Social Research 2006).
3. Alasuutari (1999; Livingstone (2005a).
4. Morley (1986); Press (1991).
5. Snyder (1998); Kress (2003); Livingstone (2004); Jensen (2005).
6. Delli Carpini and Williams (2001).
7. McChesney (2000).
8. See Hirschman (1982) on political scientists' underestimation of the time necessary for political involvement, Verba *et al.* (1995) on time as a key determinant of higher voluntary participation, and Croteau (1995) on the lack of time left over from work for working-class families.
9. Cf van Frissen (2000) on dual income families' sense of living in the 'rush hour of life'.
10. Calhoun (1992), Fraser (1990).
11. Reith (1924: 219), Arnheim (1943), Rath (1989), Lacey (1996).
12. Anderson and Levin (1976), Gellner (1983). Compare early 20th century accounts of sociality in the modern city (Park 1984).
13. Contrast Bentivegna (2002) and Luke (2006).
14. van Dijk (1988), Liebes (1992), Gamson (1998).
15. See Norris' 'virtuous circle' argument (Norris 2000) and earlier research on 'the knowledge gap', namely, the more you already know, the more the media inform you, and vice versa (Ettema *et al.* 1983).

16. Street (1994).
17. Delli Carpini and Keater (1996), Cappella and Hall Jamieson (1997), Graber (2001).
18. Robinson and Levy (1986).
19. Ball-Rokeach (1985), Cohen *et al.* (1990), Sancho (2003).
20. Graber (2001), Robinson and Levy (1986).
21. Berg and Wenner (2004), Livingstone *et al.* (2008).
22. Lewis *et al.* (2005).
23. Croteau (1995), Hargreaves and Thomas (2002), Michalski *et al.* (2002), Morley (1992), Towler (2001).
24. See, for example, the writings of Beck (1992), Reimer (1995) and Ziehe (1994). More critical positions regarding the individualisation of youth culture are developed in Lieberg (1995) and Pollock (1997).
25. Livingstone and Lunt (1994), Hermes and Stello (2000), Costera Meijer (1997), van Zoonen (2001), Coleman (2003).
26. Coleman (2005), Gamson (1992), Livingstone and Lunt (1994), Shattuc (1997). Cf. Drotner (2005) on the potential of mobile telephony generally.
27. Previously called iCAN, this provided an online public forum and resource site for civic activism: www.bbc.co.uk/dna/actionnetwork.
28. Castells (2001: 118) and Gandy (2002) on the instrumental nature of online use.

3
Tracking Public Connection: Methodological Issues

So far we have reviewed a range of arguments (both empirical and theoretical) about the uncertain future of democratic participation (Chapter 1) and media's role in democratic systems (Chapter 2). We use the term '(mediated) public connection' heuristically to *cut beneath* that complexity and suggest an underlying precondition for democratic legitimacy. Our wider aim is to trace this precondition in everyday practice in contemporary Britain. In this chapter we detail our multi-method strategy, explaining in particular our diary methodology.

Overall design

Public connection is part of how people reflexively inhabit their role as citizens. In so far as 'public connection' involves uncertainties, these are uncertainties for all citizens, ourselves included. This overlap between the reflexivity of researcher and 'researched' generates a 'complicity' that George Marcus (1999) suggests is the condition of all contemporary qualitative research.[1] However that may be, we knew in advance that the reflexive process of public connection could not be adequately understood 'at a distance': it was essential for us to generate individuals' accounts of that process.

This is why we chose the diary form (both written and spoken) as a major tool of research. We asked a range of people across England to produce a diary for up to three months during 2004 on the following issues: what did the 'public world' constitute for them? How was their sense of a public world linked to the media they consumed? How was it linked to their occasions for talk with others[2] and their wider reflections on the workings of media and democracy? Our aim was to stimulate reflection, not constrain it, leaving room for a variety of responses on these complex, open-ended, questions. It was important also to contextualise the diaries using a range of evidence: interviews with individual diarists conducted before and after diary production, and, if possible, their talk in focus groups with other diarists.

Because of the intensity of this research process, the number of diary participants was necessarily small: 37 men and women from six regions across England (see Appendix IA for summary details of the diarists). That was why we wanted to place the diary research within a broader context of a nationwide survey (see Appendix II). The overall result we believe is a rich and complex picture of whether and how citizens orientate themselves to a world beyond the private, and what role media plays in this 'public connection'.

Research precedents

As Chapter 1 explained, the term 'public connection' is deliberately much broader than electoral 'politics', and so we did not aim directly to explore people's views about specific 'political' issues. Indeed, given the problems researchers have found with that term's negative connotations (Barnhurst 1998; Lister *et al.* 2003; Livingstone 2009), it is arguably an advantage to approach people's political engagement *indirectly*.

At the same time, little political science has been expressly interested in media-related activity/ consumption when assessing habits of public/ political participation.[3] This is a symptom, perhaps, of a wider problem. Recall Carole Pateman's argument nearly four decades ago (1970: 104) that political theorists were insufficiently curious about the 'ordinary man's everyday experience of political participation of the: many have noted a similar absence in political science,[4] an absence that naturally covers the 'ordinary' experience of using media too (so we risk missing that the complexity of media culture's role in politics entirely: Street 1994). Further afield, in the study of consumption generally, too little attention has been paid to the 'narratives mobilised by consumers' when they give a detailed account of what they do (Longhurst *et al.* 2001: 125–6).

At this point two approaches are possible. One – pursued in political communication research – aims for large-scale generalisations entirely based on surveys. Our approach by contrast responds to the current uncertainties over the nature of democratic engagement through a detailed attention also to engagement's embedding within the textures of everyday life. This requires a qualitative, broadly phenomenological, approach with precedents not so much in political science, as in political sociology. Following Neuman's 'constructionist' approach to political knowledge, we are interested in discovering the 'meaningful structures' through which people relate politics to 'their immediate life-space' (Neuman *et al.* 1992: 18, xiii). We want to treat the subjects of our research as 'thinking individuals' (Gamson 1992: xii), and take seriously the complex ways in which individuals, or whole classes of people, may be alienated from politics and public life (Croteau 1995), or from possibilities for public discourse (Eliasoph 1998). How are the abstract categories of political science tracked, or not, in everyday experience (LeBlanc 1999: 7)?[5] We need here to be sensitive to the detailed spatio-temporal organisation of daily life.[6]

There have been, until recently, very few studies that link the experience of civic or political engagement to people's practice of media consumption. Two earlier studies were David Buckingham's interview-based research (2000: 17) into how television news enables young viewers to 'construct and define their relationship with the public sphere'; and Kevin Barnhurst's (1998) interview-based study of how young citizens act out broad understandings of politics through their relations to media. Other more recent work has focussed on the place of internet use specifically in the daily practice of political activism by young members of specific alternative political movements (Olsson 2005). Perhaps the closest precedent for our research, in aiming to research the general population, not a specific group, is recent Danish research on how citizens use news media to acquire the resources for citizenship in everyday life (Schrøder and Phillips 2005; cf also Lister *et al.* 2003): while differing from us in its choice of focus groups as primary method, the Danish project was similar in its concern not to privilege traditional politics as its emphasis and to listen to citizens' own accounts of their participation (2005: 181).

As important, however, as direct methodological precedents has been the theoretical inspiration provided by Peter Dahlgren's model of civic culture (Dahlgren 2003, 2009: cf. Chapter 1), which opens up civic culture to a multi-dimensional analysis: not as a single attitude, or even set of attitudes or cultural conditions, but rather as a six-point process or circuit (values, affinity, knowledge, practices, identities, and discussion), in which causal influences may flow in more than one direction. The very complexity of this model encourages detailed attention to individual citizens' reflections. Of course, like any model, it raises unanswered questions: what is the relative importance of its components? Are some components necessary starting-points for becoming engaged? What *types* of knowledge, practice and discussion actually contribute to the circuit of civic culture, and what types do not? Where are media consumption habits (rather than knowledge derived from media) in this circuit? And, most importantly, to what extent does this circuit's efficacy depend on a *broader* public action-context, something implied but not developed in Dahlgren's mention of 'practice'? The disaffection of young people provides an important reminder here: their sense that, whatever they do, they will make no difference is surely crucial to whether they enter the 'circuit' of civic culture. As one 17-year-old respondent in the UK Children Go Online study put it: 'yeah, you can email him [her MP]. But is he going to listen?' (quoted in Livingstone 2004: 7).

Let us now turn to the diary method in detail.

Diary methodology

The diary literature

The use of diary methodology in social science research goes back to the 1920s.[7] Time-use diaries became established as the most prominent form from the 1960s, and time-use research achieved broader prominence in the 1980s.[8] However, by the 1970s, the limitations of time-use diaries were already acknowledged (De Grazia 1962; Robinson and Converse 1972). Criticisms of time-use diaries focussed on low response rates, their reliance on clock-oriented time, so overriding the subjective experience of time (Gershuny and Sullivan 1988), respondents' difficulty in reliably estimating time actually spent on habitual activities, and those diaries' crudeness as analytic tools – especially the inability to generate accounts of simultaneous events, and the arbitrariness of the relative importance assigned to the various tasks involved. Nonetheless, the countervailing benefits of diaries were also clear. First, data were collected closer to the time of the event reported; second, diaries produced detailed inform-ation (allowing the sociologist to refine ever more detailed questions during the course of the diary process); third, diaries could produce evidence of seasonal variations in time-use such that diary-based studies could 'control' for the season in which research took place (Fleeson *et al.* 2002). Most important for our research, self-produced time-diaries generated evidence about the context (social or otherwise) of everyday action that would not otherwise be available. Lively debate continues on the classic time-use diary's usefulness (Thiele *et al.* 2002).

Time use, however, was only one area where diaries became an established research tool. In medical research, a substantial literature developed (Elliott 1997; Stensland and Malterud 1999; Thiele *et al.* 2002) for example to monitor individual response to drug use. This literature did not always make links with the sociological literature on time-use, but nonetheless contains useful insights. Elliott (1997), for example, provides an interesting justification for the *combined diary-interview* (that is, a diary process contextualised by a linked interview) in observing phenomena (such as patients' coping strategies) that the presence of a researcher would distort (1997: para 2.8). Elliott notes the complex interrelations between interview and diary data, with some interviewees being more predisposed than others to talk about their diary-writing (1997: para 4.3), and with the diary evidence providing a way round some patients' embarrassment at talking directly about their illness (1997: para 4.21). The relevance of these points to our own combined diary-interview will become clear later. In addition, time-diaries are used in a variety of fields including economics, social policy, criminology, anthropology and psychology.[9]

Underlying this range is a basic distinction between 'subjective' and 'objective' approaches. By contrast with the 'objective' approach so far described, researchers using a 'subjective' approach have avoided constraining the *objects* of reflection (for example Meth 2003, Jones 2000). The emphasis here is on 'the twin principles of giving voice and empowerment' (Meth 2003), which generates the 'narrative' diary style more common in ethnographic approaches where the researcher must be as unobtrusive as possible in collecting data. (More rarely, researchers augment objective time-diaries with subjective measures (Ujimoto 1990), though most research tends to emphasise one pole or the other.) If we take, for example, the case of pain diaries (from nursing and psychology), they may in principle be either subjective or objective, since they are designed to track subjective responses to objective conditions. 'Objectivists' might argue that specific and regular prompting of responses generates more differentiated data, but Gershuny and Sullivan (2004) argue that overly prescriptive instructions or too frequent observations 'produce' the regularity they claim to measure; more subjective pain-diaries can also address broader topics (for example Keefe *et al.* 2001 on pain and religion).[10]

While the details of the medical literature do not concern us here, the underlying polarisation (between instructing diarists to report the facts without reflection, and inviting them to reflect on anything in whatever form appeals) is highly relevant to the methodological choices we faced, because we wanted through diaries to combine 'subjective' reflection with some 'objective' structure for reflection. There was little direct precedent for this particular hybrid approach, but this does not pose a problem. Indeed the possibility of such a hybrid is discussed in the diary literature: Gates (1991) and Smith (1994) Bell (1998) all discuss the interpretative structure which a researcher should impose on otherwise unstructured data. In any case, *only* such a hybrid approach (combining *some* openness with *some* structure) can track reflexive practice of a particular, rather than completely general, nature.

Diary form

If participants' reflexivity about their practices of 'public connection' (or lack of them) was a key part of what we were trying to under-stand, it seemed important to allow participants to reflect so far as possible *without us, as researchers, being there.* While one-on-one inter-views are very useful and, through the rapport between interviewer and interviewee, may allow some things to be articulated that might not emerge in a group setting (Lindlof and Grodin 1987), the interview still has limitations. The apparent spontaneity of interviewee responses is inevitably structured, not least by the power imbalances (in both direc-tions) inherent in setting up the interview situation in the first place. 'Researcher-absent' data (Bird 2003), while not removing those power relations, offers the possibility of something different from what could be produced in an interview alone, and a *sustained* process of researcher-absent data generation may allow more complex processes of 'internal' reflexivity to emerge.

Diaries allow for the regular tracking of participants' reflections over time. A diarist's opinions may not explicitly change over time, but the subtle, sometimes conflicted ways in which information is processed, ideas mulled over and responses contemplated can be registered by asking participants to reflect over an extended period. The 'Public Connection' diaries were kept for up to three months, and with interviews before and after this period and later focus groups we often had contact with diarists for four months, at least and sometimes up to a year. In many cases this led diarists to articulate significant insights into their own practices. One diarist (Kathleen) realised later that in her first interview she had exaggerated her news watching, while another (Stuart) became aware, more negatively, of the regularity of his issue selection: 'it was interesting at first but as I said [in a letter] towards the end, I felt I was getting a little bit repetitive because the things that interest you, you know you tend to harp on . . . about them'. Still other diarists achieved a regular second-order reflexivity about *why* they pursued certain stories, gathered certain information and formed certain opinions over time. We tried to encourage the full range of reflections through a double strategy: first, we introduced the project's themes of in a general way (in writing and in the first interview); second, we tried to avoid giving any structuring signals in the diary form itself. Diarists were given pages in hard copy or electronic format which were largely blank as shown in Figure 3.1:

Diarists were not directed as to length, style or structure, but told it was up to them to choose what suited them. This led to a wide range of approaches, from literary to conversational, and from journalistic

MEDIA CONSUMPTION AND THE FUTURE OF
PUBLIC CONNECTION

Diarist No: _____
Week No: _____
Date: / / 2004

*Please turn over if you want to add more
– and feel free to attach extra pages*

Figure 3.1   Weekly diary format

to polemical. Such variations in style inevitably raise questions about artificiality and performance, but they also enable us to understand the diarist's style, contextualise it within their overall 'voice' (across all the data) and, where necessary, discount certain elements that then appear artificial.

Since our aim was to encourage (in people with whom we had no preceding relationship from across England)[11] a reflexive process lasting up to three months with later follow-ups, we decided that *weekly*, not daily, diaries were essential (cf Havens and Schervish (2001) for a precedent). Daily diaries are more common in social scientific research, but boredom and frustration are inevitable factors with most precedents lasting for one or two months only. The extended period also allowed us to track the consequences for diarists' public connection of any changes in their personal circumstances (several diarists were in the middle of life-changing events: relationship break-ups, moving from school to university, family illness).

There is always the risk, however, that diarists will acquire a stable, abstracted narrative voice. Hirschauer (2001) terms this over-contextualisation, and suggests it is a practically inevitable consequence of both structured reflection and a context which seems to require narrative consistency. One response to such a trend is feedback: not prompts, but a gentle prod away from patterns that are becoming entrenched, while avoiding directing the diary like 'homework'. Of course, some degree of feedback is necessary to avoid the opposite problem of insufficient context (or isolation). In general minimal, though regular, supportive feedback proved sufficient to sustain diarists' commitment, if not always for the entire three months, then for a substantial period. In giving (and recording) our feedback, we were careful to avoid reinforcing any idea that the project was limited to traditionally public or political topics.

Contextualising interviews and focus groups

The interviews were designed to address the problems of under- or over-contextualisation and artificiality in the diaries. The first interview stressed the openness of the project's themes, and emphasised that it was the diarist's voice, not our own preformed assumptions, in which we were interested. The first interview also allowed for the construction of a personal background against which the diaries can be compared. Notes were taken on diarists' living arrangements – neighbourhood, house set-up, domestic situation.

We also stressed to diarists that the project gave no priority to any one form of media, (indeed we acknowledged that media might *not* be of particular importance to diarists). This led, interestingly, to some diary entries where media were hardly mentioned at all, and in some cases there were reflections on the comparative attention given to mediated and non-mediated sources. We also asked diarists to tell us when they talked to others about the issues mentioned in the diary, not only because talk can be important in sustaining engagement but also because this gave us a clearer sense of how issues and media were woven into everyday practice and reflection.

The second interview served several purposes. First, it allowed the diarist to reflect on how typical the diary period had been; it also provided an opportunity for feedback to us on the project. Most importantly, perhaps, it gave diarists the chance to recount the experience of writing the diary – whether for example they became bored, or resentful, or more inspired as time went on. The logistics of diary production – when, in what context, and how issues were chosen (spontaneously or as the result of accumulating material during the week?) – were also recorded. The second interview allowed us to analyse more precisely what elements in a particular diary were artificial for particular diarists, including topics that were not intuitive for them, thereby giving us a broader insight into their thought patterns.

The focus groups were planned to bring together diarists, who had so far been isolated in the research process, to see to what extent that social context modified their reflections. The aim was to encourage open discussion around the sorts of issues raised by diarists and by the project: to that extent, our focus groups were very different from the classic use of focus groups in media research, to test out how audiences interpret particular media texts.[12]

Issues of interpretation

Demographic factors

We were aware from the outset that the evidence generated by the diary method would vary according to one or more demographic factors. Elizabeth Bird (2003) has suggested plausibly that women are more likely than men to be comfortable with keeping a diary (of course people vary also in their degrees of comfort with a semi-structured interview!). Our diarists' sample in this project had a slight under-representation of men under fifty (see introduction to Part II), although this may have been as much to do with time constraints as anything else. We considered whether alternative names to 'diary' (report, consultation?) might appeal more broadly, but decided each would have its own conceptual baggage which might also be gendered. The term 'diary' best evoked the personally-styled, self-analytical, informal recording of thoughts and actions we wanted. That said, there were gendered variations in diarists' style, women tending to write with more of a sense of narrative complicity and with more references to social contexts, while male diarists – not exclusively, but as an identifiable trend – tended to present an issue and their opinion on it more formally.

The key point, however, as our broadly balanced sample indicates, is that the diary method proved suitable for a project researching the general population.

Medium

Diarists were offered a range of media through which to record their thoughts, including voice recorder and email.[13] We asked diarists to choose whatever would fit best into their routine. Diarists' choices had stylistic consequences. Email, for instance, was a popular option among younger diarists and those who worked full-time, but it was also more likely to be sent spontaneously when a diarist thought something interesting. For three diarists, emails were often sent from work during lunchbreaks, very different from diaries written by hand on a Sunday night from press clippings accumulated at home throughout the week. The voice recorder option produced its own distinct form of data, with reflections tending to be less structured but having a more detailed focus on one or two issues prominent in diarists' thoughts and feelings. Tape recorders were also useful in broadening the sample, particularly it seems among non-white diarists (all three who used tape exclusively were non-white).

We also took the decision, when diarists expressed a preference, to send their material back to them and before the second interview. This generated a further layer of reflexivity – some were genuinely surprised at what they had written, while others had a clear sense of how their diaries developed over several months – which in turn revealed the varying importance the diary had retrospectively for different diarists.

The drop-out rate was very low for a project of this duration: only five of the forty-two recruited diarists (38 original recruits and 4 replacements) pulled out without making a solid contribution, while an overwhelming majority found a style of diary production that they could maintain.

Evidence for public orientation

How did we set about establishing a diarist's *orientation* (or lack of orient-ation) to a public world, as s/he defined it? Our diary method aimed to avoid imposing preestablished criteria for what counts as 'public' and instead to discover how diarists themselves understood their relation to whatever counted as 'public' to them, and how that relation was embedded in their daily practice. Certain types of engagement with, or disengage-ment from, an assumed public world, may generate little in the way of concrete evidence, precisely because they are seen as unproblematic and taken-for-granted, whereas an orientation that is constrained or blocked, for example by a lack of action context, may be more clearly signposted. One useful criterion for establishing orientation is the absence or presence of a frame through which the diarist interprets media or public events. To this end diarists' descriptive or explanatory language, including their points of reference or sources of authority, were catalogued. We also looked for the links diarists made both between topics and from issues to possib-ilities of action or social interaction.

This approach proved helpful in resolving one of the more complex interpretative challenges we faced: distinguishing evidence of mere regu-larity in media consumption from evidence of the *active* following of an issue, that is, an active orientation. In these cases it was a matter of estab-lishing what links a diarist regularly made, if any, between the issues they mentioned and any other context (another issue or reflection, a social context, or an action of any sort, whether private or public). It seemed significant that some diarists mentioned topics without mentioning or even implying any wider context. We return to this in later chapters.

A common issue in collecting evidence was reflexivity, which also had to be sensitively handled. Explicit self-reflection tended to occur in the context of conflicted orientation: most commonly, self-awareness of a knowledge lack on an issue, or frustration at the lack of an action context. Sometimes however reflexivity is a response to perceived expectations, and may suggest an element of artificiality. Signs of self-discounting were also common in some diarists but could be purely habitual, rather than providing substantive evidence of a diarist's disen-gagement. Equally, a *lack* of reflexivity (about how a diarist understands, interprets and acts on an issue) requires careful interpretation: it was perhaps too tempting to interpret a lack of registered interest in public issues as 'alienation', when, as we discuss in Chapter 7, it may rather be a sign of a distant relationship to the public world which is unproblematic for that diarist.

Performance and discursive context

In addition to the complexities of interpreting reflexivity, we needed to be attuned to a level of performance in each diary. However at ease a diarist might be in making sense of the project's themes, being asked to make these reflections *explicit* was always artificial to some degree and invoked certain expectations about what was 'required'. Keeping an extended, largely unstructured diary was unfamiliar to most, generating a variety of responses: only one diarist (Arvind) had kept anything like a diary before. Some treated the diary as a literary endeavour: one diarist (Harry) wrote about his father's involvement in local council politics when he was young, providing a vivid narrative context for the thoughts about politics which followed. Others appeared to reproduce the reflective processes of specific media outlets: for example one diarist often typed a headline verbatim from a newspaper, and then responded to it in something like the style of a tabloid editorial. Other diaries came to resemble personal correspondences with individual researchers. While some did find the format difficult and told us so, the majority of diaries appeared candid and unfiltered.

There was of course a danger, as in all research, that diarists would try to tell us what they thought we 'wanted to know'. We addressed this by emphasising that we had no expectation in them of news engagement or public orientation; since the overall levels of interest in news and politics (and public actions) registered amongst our diarists and our survey sample are broadly comparable, this suggests our strategy was successful. By contrast, diarists who displayed the opposite tendency – alienation from news and public issues – might also have been performing in a cynical mode in order to meet expectations, perhaps a perceived social expectation. This was where our *multiple* data sources were crucial: we were able to look for consistency across diaries, interviews, focus groups and diarists' accounts of their own practice, and pick up performance elements in one setting not reproduced elsewhere.

We were keen also to establish the broader discursive context for the diaries, particularly because the absence of a regular context for talking about public issues may (Eliasoph 1998) be important in contemporary democracies. As a result we asked all our diarists whether they talked to anyone else about the issues they raised with us in their diary, and asked them to note this talk in the diary itself. Thirty-three of the thirty-seven participants reported talk, including about issues, on a regular basis, although others complained about the lack of 'serious' conversation with their families, friends or colleagues (see Chapter 5). Not that an absence of references to conversation in a diary is straightforward evid-ence of an absence of real life conversation; diary style may have affected what diarists told us. Once again it was a matter of looking across all the data and collating explicit evidence of *links* between accounts of social interaction or isolation and reflections on practices. A clearer picture of discursive context often emerged in the second interview, when parti-cipants were asked if they spoke not only of issues but of the diary process itself to family, friends and colleagues. One diarist in particular (Susan) mentioned that her being involved in the project generated a talk context otherwise absent in her rambling group, which hinted at that diarist's normal lack of opportunities to comment on public issues.

Not only did diarists to varying degrees perform for us but diarists sometimes came to reflect on their own mode of performance. Four diarists for example became aware that their diaries was making them sound more like 'angry old men' than they actually saw themselves. While we might see this as a fairly conventional form of self-discounting, other diaries (see Chapter 7) exhibited more individual processes of reflection and self-correction as the diary developed.

Generalising from the diary phase data: diarist 'types'

While our interpretative strategies had to be sensitive to the dynamics of reflexivity and performance, it was important also to move beyond the 37 individual diarist narratives towards larger patterns. How could we do this systematically and rigorously?

The process began early in the diary phase. Our research team met frequently to discuss the transcripts of the first interviews. In terms of coding the diaries, an analytic framework was developed both through discussion of emerging themes, and through experimentation: two members of the research team coded the diaries and interviews in parallel (and several times) to ensure consistency in applying our coding framework. Further readings of the accumulated material also informed the design of the second interview and focus group proto-cols (Appendix IB). The data's complexity and subtlety, and the varying closeness of team members to individual diarists, required this safeguard.

No diarist could be reduced to a static 'type' of connector; the complexity of their accounts suggested dynamic trajectories depending on changing circumstances and constraints, with both consumption and reflective practices shifting, not always predictably, over time. That said, it was clear there were important trends which could be identified. One way of seeing patterns was to isolate two diarists demonstrably similar in one way or another, and to try to explain the detailed ways in which they varied, not in a definitive way, but simply to open up areas of analysis that otherwise might not have emerged. This close reading of the data generated a set of analytical terms which we then sought to apply more broadly, first by generating individual diagrams of diarists' social contexts and media use, and then by constructing overall diagrams and maps which sought to locate the diarists relative to each other (see Chapter 4).

The Public Connection Survey

Towards the end of our fieldwork in June 2005 we conducted a nation-wide 1000-person survey, whose results are presented in Chapter 8. The original, and principal, aim of this survey was to provide context for the data generated in the diary phase. While diarists' individual accounts were interesting in themselves, a contextualising framework was needed to assess to what extent they mapped onto a national scale.

However, the survey's usefulness went beyond contextualising the diaries. A review of the main UK surveys over the last decade revealed that our principal themes had not been addressed. Attention to media consumption in the British Social Attitudes survey, for example, is erratic: television consumption appears in only some years, newspaper readership is often limited to a yes/no response, though internet usage is increasingly the subject of detailed questioning. Such surveys do not give a full account of amount or type of consumption and, importantly, media questions are treated as discrete from any other questions. What was missing therefore in the survey literature was the hows and whys of media consumption, and its links to public connection: how does media consumption fit into everyday practice? What motivates media consumption? Is there a sense of duty to follow the news? And what is the connection (or lack of connection) between practices of media consumption and opinions on, or actions around, public issues?

We designed our survey questionnaire during the diary phase, and its design reflected the diary phase's emerging themes. For example, it was clear that social expectation often played a role in guiding media consumption, and that people had a clear sense of what sort of media consumer they were; it also became clear that the link between talk about, or interest in, an issue and related public actions was by no means straightforward. The team met frequently throughout this period, revising survey questions in the light of our readings of the qualitative material. In the case of action, it led us, instead of asking respondents about their general history of public action, to prompt them to name an issue *they* saw as particularly relevant to them, and then ask them about what actions they had taken specifically related to that issue.

Comparing the diary and survey data

The distinctive character of the diary data means that comparison with the survey data is necessarily complex. Both interviews and surveys rely more heavily on spontaneous answers to questions, whereas the diary's hybrid (semi-structured, semi-open) format could generate far more complex data as already noted. How then can data about similar topics be compared across diaries, interviews and surveys?

If we start with something as apparently straightforward as levels of media consumption, this is expressed in a complex manner in the diaries and interviews. The diaries also offer space for descriptions of the *quality* of consumption (passive or active, for example), and a far more detailed account of how consumption practices fit into a respondent's daily life – not possible in a survey. That does not prevent, however, the broad patterns emerging from the diary phase being compared to the patterns emerging from the survey data.

In assessing themes of orientation or engagement, the position is also complex. News engagement in the survey was measured (and could only be measured) by adding responses to a series of questions about regularity of news consumption and attitudes to following news (see Chapter 8): we could not have access to the thought processes behind survey responses. In the interviews and diaries there was space to explore gaps between attitudes and practices: a respondent may be interested in news 'in principle' but not follow this interest up with regular consumption, or there may be regular consumption (mere habit) with no link to engagement or action.

The methodological question remains whether one can then directly compare the relationship between phenomena across both samples. The potential difficulties – which cannot be avoided – emerged most clearly around the question of trust. First interviews with diarists tended to elicit low levels of trust in media and politics when the question was put directly, matching the general trends in the survey (see chapter 8). However, the same diarists in reflective rather than spontaneous practice wrote about trust in the media and politics in a less starkly negative fashion. By contrast, the survey data on trust and mistrust were necessarily in the form of unqualified opinion: levels of trust/ mistrust were relatively uniform. In that respect, the two types of data cannot fully be reconciled since they focussed on quite difference time-slices from the process of everyday reflection. This only demonstrates the importance of having more qualitative data to contextualise the survey data which dominates political science.

Conclusion

We hope to show in the next five chapters that having both qualitative and quantitative data is a major advantage and enables us to produce an account of public connection which is both accountable for its reliability and validity, and subtle enough in its details to capture the complexity underlying people's uses of media to sustain, or not, a relation to a world beyond the private.

Notes

1. Cf Couldry (2003b).
2. The issue of 'talk' in particular is complex and has recently generated a large literature that emphasises the importance for political engagement of talk about political issues and news coverage: Huckfeldt and Sprage (1995), Dutwin (2003), Delli Carpini *et al.* (2004), Nisbet and Scheufele (2004), Scheufele *et al.* (2004) and for a general review Kwak *et al.* (2005).
3. For an explicit statement of disinterest, see Burns *et al.* (2001: 5).
4. Kavanagh (1989: 166); Conover *et al.* (1991: 801); Bennett (2001: 9).
5. In addition to LeBlanc's (1999) ethnographic study of Japanese house-wives' conception of public life, see also Bhavnani's (1991) study of young working-class UK attitudes to politics (using interviews and focus groups) and Huggins' (2001) focus-group based study of young people's attitudes to politics in the UK.
6. There is a large literature on time-scarcity, both objectively and as a subjective experience: see for example Robinson and Godbey (1997) and for recent work Southerton and Tomlinson (2004).
7. Federally funded studies of (mainly rural) women in the US were prominent early examples: for discussion, see Vanek (1974); Gershuny (1998).
8. For discussion see Gershuny and Sullivan (1998); Gershuny (2004).
9. Especially significant are the edited collections of Campbell and Converse (1972) and Szalai (1972)
10. See generally Cruise *et al.* (1996); Griffiths and Jordan (1998); Stensland and Malterud (1999), Grant *et al.* (2002), Schwebel *et al.* (2002).
11. Diarists were paid a small incentive fee in return for their commitment, paid half at the outset and half at diary completion.
12. For example Morley (1980); Philo (1990); cf Schrøder and Phillips (2005).
13. In all, 16 diarists submitted only handwritten diaries; 13 emailed their contributions; three used voice recorders exclusively; three used a combination of written and emailed diaries; two used a combination of written and recorded spoken diaries.

Part II
The Public Connection Project

Introduction

Part II discusses the diary and survey phases of the Public Connection project. These introductory remarks provide some initial context for each phase of the project.

Diary phase

Recruitment of diarists

In January 2004 we asked a market research company, The Field Department, to find people in six different regions across England who would be willing to submit a weekly diary for twelve weeks. Recruiters were instructed to avoid respondents with a likely professional or institutional interest in our principal research questions (politicians, current party activists). The first diarists were recruited during February 2004, and began diaries shortly afterwards. Recruitment in the remaining five regions was staggered weekly, with diarists from the sixth region starting in late March. Five diarists dropped out in the first few weeks and the last of their replacements began their diaries in June.

Demographic factors

Thirty-six diarists were initially recruited with two further diarists quickly being recruited to improve the geographical balance of the rural region; of those diarists who subsequently withdrew, all but one (who withdrew in exceptional circumstances) were replaced, leaving a final sample of thirty-seven diarists. The details of each diarist are summarised in Appendix IA.

Our aim was to achieve equal numbers of men and women, but in one region (South London) there was some difficulty in recruiting men of any age. As a result our initial sample was 20 women and 18 men, and our final sample (after replacements) was 20 women and 17 men. Eleven diarists (4 men and 7 women) were under 30, 13 (4 men and 9 women) were aged between 30 and 50, and 13 (9 men and 4 women) were over 50. We were concerned to achieve a gender and age balance so far as possible: however, since, as expected, men aged 30–50 were difficult to recruit, the gender balance within age groups was affected.

As to class, 11 (6 women and 5 men) were AB, 13 (6 women and 7 men) were C1, 8 were C2 (4 women and 4 men), one woman was D[1] and 4 (3 women and 1 man) were E. We had no direct class quota (this would have complicated recruitment too much), but we aimed for a class balance through two indirect means. First, regions were selected to encompass a socioeconomic range: two poor inner-city areas, two middle-range suburban areas, one high-income suburb and one mixed rural area (Appendix IB). Second, recruiters were asked in each region to achieve a spread of media access: from media poor (no computer) to media rich (online at home but no broadband) to media super-rich (broadband at home). A very wide span of class and economic circumstances was achieved, from unemployed single mothers living in council housing in poor urban areas to retired chief executives living in rich suburban or rural areas. As expected however (this problem affects nationwide surveys also), Class 'D' category (manual working class) proved very difficult to recruit and correspondingly our sample over-represented classes ABC1 (65 per cent as opposed to the 2001 national census figure of 52 per cent); representation of Class C2 (21.6 per cent: census figure 15 per cent) and Class E (11 per cent: census figure 16 per cent) was more satisfactory, given that no strict class quota was applied.

While we had no ethnicity quota, recruiters were asked to ensure a range of ethnicities as appropriate for each region. Of the 37 completing diarists, 9 were non-white (5 Afro-Caribbean, 3 South Asian, and 1 mixed ethnicity). This is high compared with census percentages, but we felt it was important to ensure that ethnic minority voices were well represented.

Withdrawals and completion

Our attrition rate was low compared to precedents in the diary liter-ature: just five diarists withdrew before or just after starting their diaries. These were mainly male and all under 50, and reasons ranged from life crises to lack of time. Replacements were always of the same gender and from the same region as the person replaced. Of the 37 people who contributed substantive diaries, 27 completed diaries spanning between ten and twelve weeks; 8 contributed for four to nine weeks, and, while 2 contributed only two diaries, these were both long taped entries, yielding significant material. As expected, keeping a diary proved particularly difficult for 30–50 year olds in 'the rush hour of life' (van Frissen 2000).

Interviews and focus groups

We met all diarists for a semi-structured interview (for 60–90 minutes) shortly after recruitment. 31 out of the completing 37 diarists were re-interviewed in autumn 2004 or early 2005 (for between one and two hours), a very high retention rate. 13 diarists took part in focus groups with other diarists at the end of the fieldwork period (fewer than we had hoped, but understandable given that up to a year had elapsed from initial recruitment): for interview and focus group protocols see Appendix IC.

News context of the diary phase

The news in this period was dominated by events in Iraq, the Madrid bombings and other global security issues, the expansion of the European Union ('EU') to 25 members, the 2004 Budget, local and European elections, the aftermath of the Soham murders and rumours of an extra-marital affair concerning footballer David Beckham. For detailed analysis and comparison with the issues selected by diarists, see Chapter 5 and Appendix ID.

Survey phase

Recruitment

On our behalf, ICM carried out a national quota survey of 1017 people by telephone during the weekend of 3–5 June 2005, asking people about their media consumption, media attitudes, political attitudes and political efficacy; questions were also asked about a specific issue named by respondents as important to them (see Appendix IIA).

The context was one month after the British general election, the same weekend as the French vote on the EU constitution, and with Iraq continuing to feature prominently in the news media. As with the diary phase there was a current celebrity scandal (the Michael Jackson trial).

Demographics

Comparison of the survey sample against the 2001 Census demonstrates that the sample was statistically representative for age and gender. There was a slight socioeconomic bias built into the sample, although no greater than in comparable samples such as the British Social Attitudes Survey, with appropriate weighting being made. All figures quoted from the Public Connection Survey data are weighted figures. (For the sample and weighting procedures see Appendix 2B.)

Note

1. One diarist (Arvind) who was unemployed had previously been employed as Class D.

4
Mediated Public Connection: Broad Dynamics

Introduction

We have introduced the term 'public connection' to capture a dimension of daily life: that is, an orientation towards a public world beyond matters of purely private concern. We talk of 'mediated public connection' where that orientation is sustained principally by our practice of consuming media. We wanted to track evidence of public connection across the huge range of diarists' language (both accounts of daily practice and direct or indirect evidence of that practice). 'Mediated public connection' is a complex practice, involving at least *two* dynamic components: media consumption and public orientation. How in particular cases these components are articulated together must vary: we cannot expect to find a single 'ideal type' of mediated public connection. Tracking the resulting varieties of mediated public connection was a key part of our research.

This complexity and heterogeneity is captured well by the notion of 'dispersed practice', introduced by social theorist Theodor Schatzki (1996: 89). Practices may be ordered, according to Schatzki, in various ways and to different degrees. Schatzki distinguishes between general or 'dispersed' practices such as 'describing' (linked only by shared understandings) and 'integrative practices' (such as cooking or going swimming, which are held together also by 'explicit rules' and 'ends, projects and beliefs'). All practices are made up of many heterogeneous elements (Reckwitz 2002), but dispersed practices are particularly heterogeneous. Given that media – and our media uses and their contexts – are so various (as are forms of public involvement), 'mediated public connection' is clearly more like a 'dispersed practice'[1] than an 'integrative practice': certainly it has no explicit rules, although it may involve 'ends, projects and beliefs', that is, motivating values.

To track mediated public connection rigorously and openly, we developed a 'model' (not a predictive model, simply a thinking tool) to map the key features of different diarists' practice in relation to media and a public world. This visual mapping enabled us to grasp the *complex* of dynamic factors which regularly sustain, or undermine, public connection in a mediated democracy such as Britain. This chapter outlines the understanding of those dynamics that emerged from the model.

Modelling individual diarists' public connection

Diarist diagrams

After we had coded and completed a first analysis of all our fieldwork data, we evolved a diagram on which we could represent, for each diarist, first, their overall sense of public orientation (or 'public connection'), second, the various factors which appeared to contribute to that orientation, and, third, its public outcomes (the public actions, if any, in which that diarist was involved). Each element or link in the diagram drawn by us as researchers for a diarist was based on specific evidence gathered from the interviews and diaries. By way of illustration of how we approached the analysis, two sample diarist diagrams (drawn for Henry and Edward, discussed below) are shown as Figures 4.1 and 4.2. Note that each diagram shows the full template that we used to compare diarists with each other, while highlighted boxes are those that proved relevant (and were backed by specific evidence) for a particular diarist.

Starting at the left-hand side of the top layer in Figures 4.1 and 4.2 and moving across, the top layer records the 'objective' factors, both positive and negative, that may contribute to a diarist's media consumption or public orientation. Some diarists had regular habits of media consumption (a certain balance of media every day, certain fixed patterns for getting the news); however particular constraints – a very busy period at work – may disrupt even the most regular of habits temporarily. By contrast, a family context may help coordinate media consumption on a daily basis and so may reinforce media habits. Occasionally – but less than we might expect – lack of access to media was a constraining factor.

Moving across the diagram, there are certain demographic factors, particularly age and gender, that may reinforce an orientation to a public world, particularly to traditional forms of electoral politics. We found

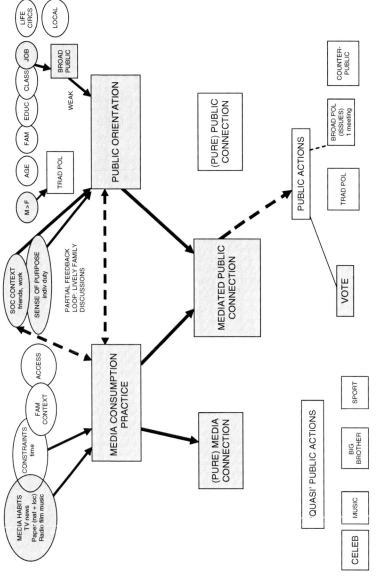

Figure 4.1 Diarist's diagram: Henry

68

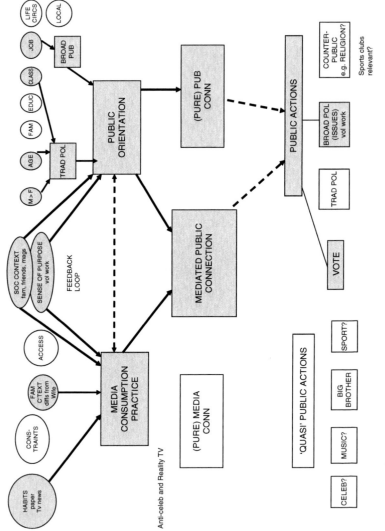

Figure 4.2 Diarist's diagram: Edward

gender to be important right across our diarist sample: the naturalised sense of some women in our diarist sample that politics is not 'for them' ('I'm not the politics girl unfortunately' (Janet)),[2] but also the naturalised sense of some men that their interest in a public world was appropriate to them (and not their wives), for example:

> I watch totally different programmes to what she watches. She watches the soaps, and plays, and I watch documentaries, the news . . . Parliament. (Harry)

Family, education and class may provide specific formative contexts that encourage a stable orientation to a public world. Other factors may supervene later in life to attune a particular diarist to certain sets of public issues, whether job, life circumstances (the responsibility of bringing up young children) or local context, the last set of factors providing incentives to follow issues and contexts where knowledge about them, once acquired, can be displayed.

Since a key factor in the overall practice of mediated public connection is the *linkage* between media consumption and public orientation, we also noted for each diarist factors which regularly and stably linked their media consumption to a public orientation, and vice versa. These 'feedback loops' are shown in the middle of the top layer. In the top right-hand side of each diagram, we allow for 'public orientation' *both* in the sense of following traditional politics *and* in the sense of following a range of specific issues that exclude traditional politics. On the far margins of each diagram's top layer, we note factors which may pull diarists *away* from mediated public connection: either (on the far right-hand side) factors which may undermine their sense of public orientation (disenchantment with how democracy works?) or (on the far left-hand side) an alternative sense of what is public, focused not on matters requiring public resolution but on matters of collective attention (sport, entertainment or celebrity).

The lowest level of each diagram records for each diarist their *degree* of mediated public connection, whether clear, weak, or none at all. By 'clear' mediated public connection, we mean diarists who exhibited a stable pattern of using media to orientate themselves to one or more non-private arenas where issues of public concern – that is, ultimately requiring public resolution – were at stake. By 'weak' mediated public connection, we mean diarists whose diary and interviews indicated a regular use of media in this way, but where that practice was interrupted from time to time or in other ways weakened. By 'none', we mean diarists whose media consumption did not seem overall to be orientated towards a world of public concern, but rather to private or 'collective' (but not contentious 'public') matters.

The bottom level of each diagram records the public actions in which diarists were involved. Note however that on the 'media consumption' side of the diagram, we allow for 'quasi-public actions'(such as visiting the last night of *Big Brother*) that are *not* oriented to matters of public contention (so are not 'public' in the sense we mean when we discuss 'mediated public connection').

Media world connectors versus public world connectors

The diarist diagrams are simply a convenient way of representing the components which either make up the complex practice of mediated public connection or *fail* to be articulated into that practice. The concept of mediated public connection itself implies some basic possibilities. We can imagine people who consume media but have no public orientation, or conversely people who have a public orientation but do not consume media (except purely instrumentally: to find out the weather, to watch a film). We call these possibilities *'pure' media connection* and *'pure' public connection*, to emphasise that such people have some sort of 'connection', but it is not *mediated public* connection. A few diarists got close to these abstract possibilities: Janet enjoyed media in a way that carried very few traces of any orientation to a world of public concerns (pure media connection), whereas Eric was intensely engaged in the public world of a particular Christian church in a way that had no overlap whatsoever with the media he consumed (pure public connection). Their diagrams are shown as Figures 4.3 and 4.4.

Such case were however rare. A more important distinction was between people whose mediated public connection was primarily shaped by a strong pull towards some aspect of media, versus people whose mediated public connection was primarily shaped by a strong pull towards a world of public concern: we call these respectively *media world connectors* and *public world connectors*. (For many people, of course, these two dynamics were broadly in balance, either because both were relatively weak or because both were relatively strong: we call them *multiple connectors*.)

Although both media world connectors and public world connectors have mediated public connection, its quality is quite different. The first group regularly follows public issues through media forms (news, documentary, etc.) but has relatively few other means of engagement with those issues; whereas the second regularly follows public issues through

71

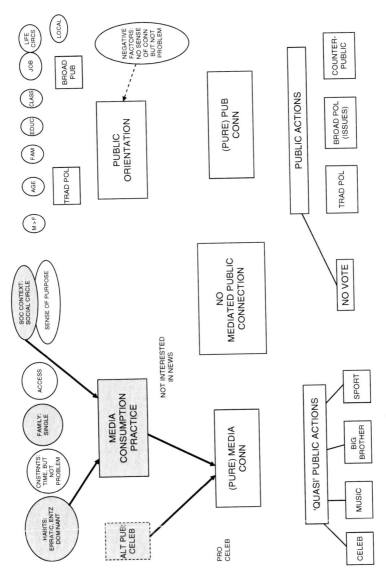

Figure 4.3 Diarist's diagram: Janet

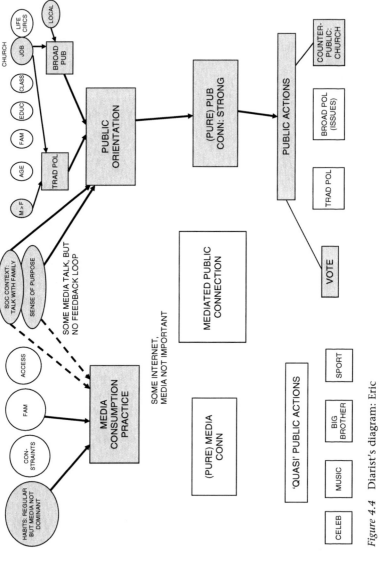

Figure 4.4 Diarist's diagram: Eric

media forms, but has other ways of orientating to a world beyond the private (work as a school governor, religious practice, and so on).

It is worth explaining this crucial distinction through the examples of specific diarists. Henry (Figure 4.1) was a voracious media consumer who took great pleasure from media and the way media connected him to a world beyond his own:

> I start off [the day] with Radio 2 . . . and I'm reading [the papers] by that stage while I'm breakfasting. . . . And then because I catch the [bus] into work and there's a local free paper that you get . . . the Metro . . . and that has just soundbites . . . but again – it sets you up.
>
> *Do you follow up these stories?*
> Some of them yeah . . . well a lot of them you catch them . . . it's mentioned several times throughout the day . . . and it's seeped into your consciousness anyway.

Henry's public connection was focused on the public world of which he was a member as a listener, viewer and reader, rather than other public constituencies to which he belonged independently of his media consumption; mediation was crucial to the substance of his public connection.

This was not the case with Edward (Figure 4.2) although he enjoyed aspects of media too, especially newspapers:

> I read the business section [of *The Times*] everyday and I read all of it, partially because I'm interested and there's people who I still know and so forth. But also I still have money invested and I'm interested in how that's doing. And I'm just interested in what happens to the financial world in general, just to see what's developing. And . . . I'm interested in the country and the politics of the country and so forth. And worldwide events. I like to keep up to date and see what's going on.

Edward's public world, however, was not so much the shared world of a media audience, but the public world to which he had contributed, initially, as a businessman and now as a magistrate. There is an underlying contrast between people for whom the public world emerges principally *out of* their media consumption (media world connectors), and people whose orientation to a public world is something they *bring to* media (public world connectors). Neither type of mediated public connection is 'better', but they have different dynamics and instabilities; as already noted, many people fall somewhere in between.

If we put together degrees of mediated public connection (clear, weak, none) with types (media world connectors, public world connectors, multiple connectors), a more complex space of comparison emerges (Figure 4.5). This brings together degrees of mediated public connection (as a 'vertical' dimension) with types of mediated public connection from the most strongly mediated to the minimally mediated (as a 'horizontal' dimension).

Note a further possibility represented in the bottom left corner of Figure 4.5: diarists whose relation to both media and public worlds was characterised by ambivalence, even indifference. We call these diarists *weakly connected*, because to position them anywhere but marginally in the space of Figure 4.5 would exaggerate the degree to which they were orientated either to media or to a public world. Some felt they could easily live without media (Lisa: 'TV . . . I could quite happily live without really'), yet also lacked an independent sense of a public world to which they were orientated; for these diarists other frames of references (particularly family or social life) might be more important than media or public issues (Kathleen, Lisa, Lesley, Marie: see also below under 'underlying orientations'). Others (Nigel, Paul) had become so alienated from

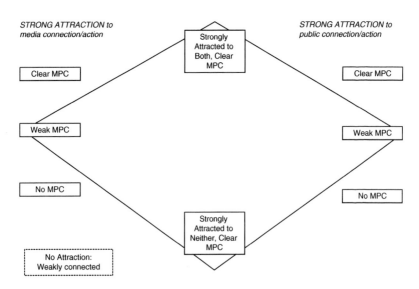

Figure 4.5   Diarists' diagrams: dimensions of comparison

the public world that their media use was no more, or less, than an individual routine without wider significance.

Figure 4.5 also registers the contestability of the 'public'. If a media connection can orient someone *away* from a world of public concern and public decision-making (see discussion of Janet's 'pure media connection' above), another possibility is important: someone with a clear sense of engagement through media in a public world beyond the private, but a public world which bears *no relation* to dominant definitions of 'public concern'. Ross (discussed later in the chapter) was a clear case of this. For him sport was his entire public world: neither politics nor general public issues featured. He had therefore a connection to a public world which was intensely mediated, but it was not the public world, as conventionally understood. Such cases must be registered since they remind us that the normative framework built into Figure 4.5 is only ever provisional: we placed Ross on the left-hand side of the space of Figure 4.5, although arguably Ross might be placed instead on its right-hand side (however as we shall see this would probably misrepresent his distinctive relation to the 'public').

Overall patterns and demographic factors

What happens if we map each of our 37 diarists onto the space of Figure 4.5? The result is Figure 4.6.

It seems that people are fairly evenly divided between those who connect to the public world principally through media and those who principally connect in other ways (for example, work, church, voluntary work); further, most – but crucially not all – media consumption contributes to public connection in one way or another, though for some diarists this is not necessarily the case. In numerical terms out of 37 diarists, there were 12 media world connectors, 12 public world connectors, 7 multiple connectors, and 6 weakly connected. In terms of strength of mediated public connection, 9 lacked mediated public connection (including those weakly connected), 8 had weak mediated public connection, and 20 had clear mediated public connection.

Women diarists were slightly more like to be media world connectors (8 out of the 12 media world connectors) and men were slightly more likely to be public world connectors (7 out of the 12 public world connectors). Diarists' type of public connection was not principally determined by age, except that media world connectors were found disproportionately in the youngest age-group[3] (perhaps they have so far had less time to have built up a range of networks and opportunities for public involvement). Similarly there was no major relationship

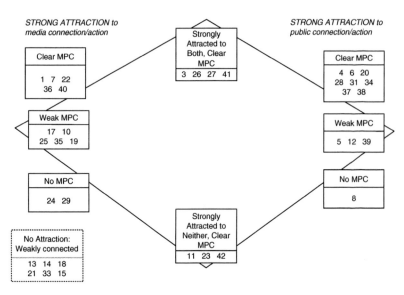

Figure 4.6   Diarists' diagrams: the overall pattern

between type of public connection and ethnicity, although interestingly none of the 9 non-white diarists was weakly connected. Class is more complicated. Among classes ABC1 there was an overall balance of public world connectors and media world connectors,[4] although no unemployed (class E) diarists were public world connectors (perhaps because the unemployed are more cut off than others from public and civic networks).

The dynamics of mediated public connection

What dynamics shape individual diarists' mediated public connection or, just as important, its absence?

Negative factors

It is striking that, in our diarist sample, there were few cases where identifiable negative factors undermined people's *media consumption*. Clearly, without a basic level of regular media consumption, there is no possibility of a stable practice of mediated public connection. But almost all our diarist sample appeared able to access sufficient media if they wanted to, as most did.

The exceptions, however, are interesting. Only one diarist (Mary) regarded a reduction in media access (the loss of personal computer, in-room television and money to buy magazines when she became a university student) as decisive. We might have expected lack of time to constrain people's media consumption, but, contrary to our pilot research (Couldry and Langer 2005), we found only indirect traces of this. Edward recalled that, when he had been a chief executive he had had little time to follow anything but financial news; another (non-completing) diarist whose job involved him intensely in community work explained in his preliminary interview that he had very little time for consuming media. But others, in spite of very busy working lives, absorbed media in fragments or from other people: through the nature of their work (in a newsagents shop or garage where newspapers were sold), or by chatting in office work breaks.

In only one case (Jonathan) did *disillusionment* with media threaten to undermine the practice of following the public world through media. Jonathan was among the clearest in the diarist sample in the explicit value he gave to his mediated public connection ('I'll always watch [the news]. I think the day that I stop watching it, will be the day when I don't know, will be a sad day anyway'). However in writing his diary his increasing frustration became evident:

> There seems to be a domination of negative journalism and sceptical political reporting. Although some (possibly most) of the reporting maybe true, it does make you sceptical and, at times, reluctant to update your knowledge and interest in the media.

Jonathan was not the only diarist to be highly critical of media (Sheila, as we will see in Chapter 7, went through a similar struggle), but other diarists felt on balance that they could find, with effort, the media they needed.

There were by contrast a range of negative factors undermining people's *public* orientation. Some are predicted by the literature on civic culture, for example lack of political efficacy:

> I suppose I'm not an out-there person...everyone has their views and everyone has a right to their views and I don't see why my views should be pushed onto them.... I do get shy.... I can be quite a shy person. (Sherryl)

I have written to newspapers but not on a regular basis or spoken to an MP because again, it's this, this thing at the back of my brain, it doesn't move fast enough. (Nigel)

For some diarists their lack of efficacy was rationalised as a taken-for-granted distance from politics. For others, lack of efficacy was reflected upon with some tension, and developed into a criticism of the mediated public sphere (cf Chapter 7): 'I don't know, we don't seem to be aware of everything we need, I don't think the message is put across' (Samantha). A second negative factor, equally anticipated in political science, was specific political disenchantment: three diarists who were Labour voters were disenchanted with the New Labour government, and in two cases (Jane, Patrick) with the loss of older local working-class politics more generally.[5] Two of our more politically engaged diarists, Jonathan and Josh, ironically, reported isolation from friends *because of* their (unshared!) interest in politics. Finally, time sometimes constrained public orientation: for example, Gundeep had a very busy life running a garage, which, while it didn't prevent him from absorbing media, did reduce his participation in organising community events.

The negative factors identified so far could be 'compensated for' by a strong and regular habit of media consumption, so diarists' orientation to a public world (their mediated public connection) was retained. But other negative factors are unlikely to be 'compensated', for example a strong sense of the priority of the private domain *over* the public. Two diarists both emphasised their concern to protect the boundaries around their private life, and linked this to their avoidance of stating opinions about major public issues:

this is my property, this is my family and if anybody tries to harm it or invade it in any way then yes, I would, yeah, I would pull all stops out to protect, yeah.

. . . have you ever got involved in any public discussion on those issues? . . .

No, no. No, I haven't, no. . . . I suppose it's fear. . . . I don't want anyone else outside of my circle of like friends, people who I can trust, to know because [I might be] penalised for it . . . for what I think. (Lesley)

when I come in here, nobody interferes, not even my family come in and I protect that fiercely. I don't like, I hate to think that I'm being talked about. I don't like being the centre of attention with anybody.... Politics I try to keep away from. (Frank)

This was not just a concern with keeping one's political allegiance private: it emerged elsewhere that each had an alternative valuation of the public domain not linked to politics at all, but to questions of art and creativity: Lesley wanted to return to art college and greatly valued her own artistic creativity, while Frank loved keeping up to date with the latest theatre and musicals, as well as watching arts-related media. Also difficult to compensate were weariness with the world in general (including personal distress for family or other reasons: one diarist) or a general disenchantment or disillusionment with the state of the public world (five diarists).

Positive factors

One pattern positively associated with being a media world connector was a broad interest in media as access-point to a collective world. For some (generally women) this was a world of celebrity, reality TV, fashion or music:

Yeah, that's it you know, everyone, I enjoy reading gossipy stories. Everyone enjoys reading gossipy stories. (Andrea)

I would say that I do keep up to date with what's going on. Maybe mainly the gossipy side of the media, you know like Heat and OK magazine, yes I get those every week. So I tend to keep up with who's doing what with who and where and what have you. What girl isn't into that really? (Janet)

Very unlike me this week. I don't know what is no. 1 in the music charts. Hopefully next week I will have more to write. (Samantha diary)

The male 'version' of this relationship to media appeared[6] different: pleasure in a wide range of light entertainment media (comedy, music, sport) but including also a wide range of factual material with politics watched as a form of entertainment:

My hero of the moment is a guy called Boris Johnson (laughter) I think he's an absolute scream ... he stood up in Parliament a few weeks ago ... and he was doing one of his speeches. And all the guys in the Tory rows behind, they were curling up because he's so funny

but he makes a point, you know, in a humorous way which is what
appeals to me. (Harry)

In both 'versions' diarists prioritised the pleasure that media afforded
them, rather than its public relevance.

Factors positively associated with being a public world connector were
a work context which sustained that interest (including here voluntary work, as well as work that was inherently entangled in public
issues: nurses, teachers, a trainee architect). Some diarists were involved
in a network of community or neighbourhood interactions, whether
based on ethnicity, class, or religion. Three diarists had previously
canvassed for a political party. In addition, diarists could positively
value, indeed enjoy, media's ability to keep them 'up to date' with the
public world: we will discuss examples of this in Chapter 7 (Josh, Bill,
Sheila).

Feedback loops

Feedback loops (that link people's habits of public-related media
consumption to a reinforcing context) may be crucial in stabilising
habits of mediated public connection so they can persist in spite of the
inevitable ups and downs of personal life. We identified such feedback
loops in nearly half (18) of our diarists.

Feedback loops are not always readily isolated; after all, they *reinforce*
preexisting factors and motives, so rarely make a difference on their
own. Two examples, however, illustrate their background importance.
Jane had a long term history of political activism but difficult personal
circumstances now made that world seem distant from her. By the time
of our second interview, even her long-time habits of publicly-oriented
media consumption seemed difficult to maintain. But here a second
feedback loop intervened – the family habit of talking issues through,
often by reference to media:

And politically, my daughter is now far more aware than what I am.
She . . . reads the Independent or the Guardian and she takes . . . a lot
of notice of what's going on in the world. . . . she's been doing that
for quite a while . . . we talk politics.

By contrast, we noted earlier Mary's loss of media access when she moved
from school to university. In other circumstances, this might have been
compensated: she noted that fellow students circulated magazines, she

had collective computer access and there was a common-room tele-vision. The crucial difference, perhaps, was losing the social feedback loop: talking about issues and media with family and schoolmates. Indeed a new context of talk for her (she was a medical student) looked *beyond* media for its sources: 'I mean I'm in a completely different place now. More people here are interested in [science] than they were at school . . . it's just really nice not being the only person that knows something about it'. These explicit examples illustrate well the types of feedback loops: some are *social*, drawing on settings where media and public issues are discussed (family, friends, work); others draw on *individual* values, embedded in daily practice, with values of course some-times being socially reinforced as well. We turn to the specific value of 'keeping up with the news' (Hagen 1994) in Chapter 6.

Underlying orientations

As we have already made clear, 'mediated public connection' is an analytic abstraction designed to capture a complex and dispersed prac-tice. It had a relation nonetheless to diarists' broader sense of who they were and what mattered to them. What was this relation?

To grasp this, we traced which frame of reference occurred promin-ently in each diarist's account of their practice. Figure 4.7 shows the result: where a diarist had more than one important frame, an arrow is shown moving from the more important frame to the other: the gendering of this pattern is also indicated (numbers refer to diarists' identifying number).

Family was an orientating frame for more diarists than any other (14) – all but 8 of our diarists had children, and relations with parents could be an important frame within which non-parent diarists oper-ated (Mary, Samantha) – with work (10 diarists) and social (9 diarists) the next most important frames. Second (shown on the right-hand side of Figure 4.7) are the frames linked to public institutions or practices that may overlap with everyday life but be readily separable from it: religion, politics, sport. Third, on the left-hand side of Figure 4.7, there were many diarists for whom none of those frames figured as important, and for whom individualised orientations were more important: five diarists with a clear sense of media as providing their main interface with a wider world, and six (one overlapping with the first five) for whom the individual routine of keeping up with the news seemed primary.

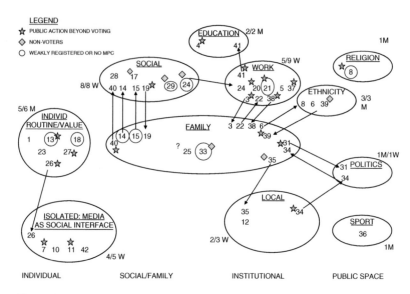

Figure 4.7   Orientating frames

When we relate this pattern to levels of mediated public connection, the results are interesting. Taking diarists with weak or non-existent mediated public connection, the majority (7 out of 11) had social and/or family as their orientating frame. As to the six diarists who were weakly connected in our overall model, only one (Lisa, a teacher) was orientated by frames related to institutions or public space, but this is not because those diarists were all 'individualists' or 'isolated', for, as just hinted, three of the six weakly connected diarists appeared strongly motivated by family. The nexus of social and family (which from most perspectives would be seen as positive) emerges, paradoxic- ally, as important in explaining both *low* mediated public connection and the *distance* from media and public worlds we call 'weak connec- tion'. By contrast, the *absence* of social and family as principal orient- ating frames is associated with a clear tendency *towards* mediated public connection: most of the diarists who were 'individually' motivated had clear mediated public connection. The 'social' frame is the only frame associated with diarists of whom a *minority* had clear mediated public connection.

There are then many positive reasons (family, social networks) asso- ciated with *not* having mediated public connection, whereas absence of social networks may sometimes be associated with high mediated public connection (because media consumption compensates): a trend that surely complicates any social capital model of public engagement. We can also see in Figure 4.7 the importance for many diarists (nine) of *work* as an orientating frame, another theme downplayed in social capital models, but one to which we return in later chapters.

Public/private

As we noted in Chapter 1, the 'public/private' distinction elides two different but related boundaries: the boundary around things that are *issues* of public concern and so require public resolution, and the boundary between privately controlled *space* and publicly accessible space. In so far as our notion of 'public connection' relied on the term public, and particularly the meaningfulness of first type of distinction, it was important to confirm this among our diarists.

Inevitably both public/private distinctions overlapped when we raised the term 'public' with diarists in the first interview:

> Public is anything outside my four walls . . . these walls. In my flat. Are private. Anything that happens out there, that the public can also gain access to, then that's fair enough. Anything that involves . . . the collective. (Abby)

We sensed in some diarists an unease, although it was not expressly articulated, when we introduced the term 'public'. Rather than enter into detailed discussion of the multiple definitions of the term 'public', our approach was to explore with diarists an open-ended series of issues of public concern (or areas of practice that might generate such issues), while emphasising that they were free to define the 'public world' to which they were orientated, and that it was *their* orientation, not our preset definitions, in which we were interested. What was already clear in first interviews however was that there was not always a 'ready-made' specification of 'public' issues, or a 'public world', upon which diarists could draw. No diarist however had overall difficulties because s/he found the 'public/ private' boundary confusing, still less from a desire to contest its usefulness or meaningfulness. Some applied and reflected on that boundary; others gave their accounts without explicit reference to it. Our embedding of the public/private distinction in our framing of the project was therefore justified heuristically.

What about the substance of the distinction? Even though the 'public/private' (issue) distinction and the 'public/private' (space) distinction often overlaid each other, a substantial minority of diarists produced clear and explicit definitions of what counts as a public issue when the term 'public' was introduced into the conversation:

> If it's public, it's not just an individual's issue, it's more a group of individuals with the same issue or varying issues that kind of relate or inter-relate. I guess really it's anything that doesn't just involve one person. (Josh)

This could happen, even if the term produced momentary confusion: 'Not quite sure how to answer that. Do you mean things which I think are, the issues which I think are of consequence to the country which may well affect me indirectly' (Edward)? As expected, the dominant association of 'public' issues with whatever is current news was found among many diarists, for example Samantha: '[public issues are] just the general day to day, what's going [on], anything in the world from . . . the Spanish . . . bombing to celebrities'. But others, while registering that non-reflexive use of the term 'public', could also work with it reflexively, displaying an implicit sense of the boundary demarcating public issues. Sherryl for example distinguished boxing (which you could follow without it mattering either way) from 'things that happen to . . . young children'. Of the latter, she was quite clear: 'I think people should be interested in that.. . . The war I think they should be interested in, things like that. Because those things involve us, even though it's not directly us, it involves us, and it could be directly us.'

There was no diarist who, in the end, did not prove to have a working definition of the public/private distinction. Indeed cases where the boundary between public and private issues was discussed were not particularly common (seven cases). It would seem that it simply wasn't problematic enough: perhaps the notion of 'public issues' is more taken-for-granted than academic discussion acknowledges.

An alternative definition of the 'public' world?

We have noted, however, the contestability of what counts as 'public'. Certainly it is important to emphasise that our diarists ranged well beyond traditional politics in their account of 'the public world': covering health, education and family morality, race and identity, religion, sexuality, music and film, and celebrity culture.

Celebrity culture is often claimed to offer an alternative opening into the world of public issues. How important was this in diarists' accounts of the public world? We did find one topic where celebrity culture raised questions about the public/private boundary and therefore, prima facie, about the public world. This was in discussions of media's intrusion into private life (17 cases): the Beckham 2004 sex scandal in spring/ early summer 2004, the controversial 2004 US television showing of the dying Princess Diana's body. This regularly developed into criticisms of media news values that evidenced a level of media literacy:

> Why do we (the public) need to know what the Beckhams do with their private lives? (Lesley, diary)

> I don't understand why the private life of the England Coach should have anything to do with anyone but him. Private business is just that – between him and his partner – and so what if it's his secretary? (Josh, diary)

Note here however that it was diarists' separation between celebrity culture and topics of public interest – not the connections between them – that was primary. Nor did discussion of celebrity, although frequent among our diarists, emerge elsewhere as a reference-point for broader debates on matters of wider public concern.[7] Nor, perhaps surprisingly, were the 'water-cooler' media formats (soap operas and increasingly reality TV) used in this way by diarists. We are therefore skeptical about suggestions that one key to expanding political engagement might be to shift the attention of those more likely to be *Big Brother* fans (Coleman 2003).

We need however to discuss one diarist whose practice did in effect offer an alternative definition of the public domain from the dominant one. Ross was a graphic design student at a university in the centre of a major southern English town; he lived in a student residence, though his parents lived in a nearby town and he spent much of his time at the home of his girlfriend's parents. In his interview he said he was to an extent active on online sites related to his studies, and demonstrated, if briefly, a knowledge of traditional political issues. However, in his diary, when asked to write about whatever he thought of as public issues, he wrote exclusively about sport.

To an extent this was explicable by biography: his grandfather played football professionally, he himself played in more than one team several times a week, and he watched a great deal of football on television at the weekend. However, the way he wrote about sport suggested more than a practical interest. For him the world of sport – and football in particular – had many traits we would associate with public worlds otherwise conceived. One was a value placed in knowledge as a prerequisite for deliberation: he stressed people should talk from facts, himself included ('I am slightly biased here because I support Arsenal but when you look at the facts I feel that I am being objective in my claims': diary). Another was a distinctly moral or principled framework which Ross brought to bear when discussing sporting events. The World Cup was described as part of a historical narrative characterised by rights and wrongs, justices and injustices:

> the cruel hand of fate steps in and France have a penalty, which he duly converted, and we cruelly lost in a major tournament again. Why does this always happen to us. England usually perform well at major tournaments only to be dealt a cruel blow. . . . Surely this year will see the change of luck that we must deserve. (diary)

He also used a moral evaluative framework when discussing off-the-field events: 'the way they have treated Claudio Ranieri [ex-Chelsea manager] is disgusting but the humour he has shown during all the speculation can only have increased his reputation' (diary). His language suggested he had a sense of what was properly public in a given domain, and what should be excluded: 'this week the footballing world is again concentrating on matters that shouldn't be the main focus of sport' (diary). Alongside these diary comments were frequent criticisms of the media: 'I think the Daily Mail and the British press should think more carefully about the relevance and interest levels of what they are writing'. There is little doubt then that for Ross football, and sport generally, constituted a public world with its own principles of differentiation, values, matters of shared concern, and frames of reference for resolving them.

However, while Ross maintained a clear orientation to this public world, he remained isolated without any social feedback loop to sustain his engagement in it, nor any possibility of acting publicly with others. In one sense, of course, he did act – by playing amateur football – but the *public* aspect of the sporting world – its deliberative dimension concerning the public issues it raised – was not one which afforded him an active role. This is our first hint, albeit in relation to an alternative definition of the mediated pubic world, of a disjuncture between orientation and action possibilities: we return to this theme in Chapter 6.

Conclusion

So far we have concentrated on the overall varieties of mediated public connection, and the elements that contribute to them, while bringing out, particularly towards the end of the chapter, the range of approaches to the public world that characterised our diarists. In the next chapter we look more closely at media consumption practices among our diarists.

Notes

1. Cf Couldry and Langer (2005) on the 'dispersed citizen'. On the relevance of practice theory generally to consumption research: see Warde (2005).
2. All quotations are from individual interviews, not diaries or focus groups, unless otherwise indicated.
3. 5 out of 12 diarists aged under 30.
4. Of the 24 ABC1 people who completed diaries, 7 were 'media world connectors', 9 'public world connectors', 3 'multiple connectors' and 5 weakly connected.
5. We did not systematically collect information on political orientation, and indeed avoided asking directly about this (cf Chapter 3); these particular diarists volunteered this information.
6. Our examples here are men over 50 (whereas all the diarists linked with a celebrity-related connection to media were women under 40), so age and gender probably intersect as causal factors.
7. Only one quote hints otherwise, and it is still generalised: 'perhaps I'll bring in my Heat magazine [to the office] and one of the lads will pick it up and be like "Whoah that's Kylie Minogue" and it will branch off into "Oh look she's getting married" . . . and then the whole office gets into a discussion about it, we have some quite good discussions at work really about the press and media' (Janet).

5
The Variability of Media Use

What type of media users were our diarists? We need to understand both basic media use and the quality of media use, including media literacy. First, however, we must comment on the type of data about media consumption we obtained and the interpretative issues it raises.

The nature of our evidence

People's media use is complex and multidimensional (Silverstone 1994; Livingstone 2002). We obtained a great deal of data about diarists' media use, and more than a chapter might easily be written on this alone. Here we must concentrate on what contributes to our understanding of the 'life-form' of mediated public connection.

The diary format

Because diaries were produced weekly, the evidence they provided was of a distinctive kind. Rather than tracking every day what media someone used and in what sequence, the diaries when produced (usually at the end of a week, although often on the basis, diarists told us, of notes or cuttings kept during the week) already involved a considerable amount of sifting by memory and subsequent reflection.[1] Even at its most report-like, diary-writing therefore involved a degree of generalization and typification:

> This week again has been mainly news items found in the *Mail*, *Metro Newspaper* (part of the Mail Group) and television. I've also read various articles from computer magazine *ComputerActive*. I've listened to various Radio Shows, mainly on Radio 2 and local shows, most of the "music and topics" variety. (Henry)

Indeed, our priority was to tap into people's processes of *reflecting on* use, rather than exhaustively tracking their media habits.

The 'indirect' style of this project's diaries nonetheless produced a rich sense of how differently people use media to orientate themselves to a public world. To illustrate this, let's take two diarists (Andrea and Patrick) whose degree of explicit reflexivity was in the mid-range of our diarists (they illustrate well the *overall* richness of the diary phase data). Both had a fairly terse diary style (each had limited time for the diary in very busy working weeks, as nurse and warehouse manager respectively; Andrea also had a young baby to care for). The two diaries largely overlapped in time (for 10 out of 12 weeks). However the implied pictures of how each diarist used media sharply differed; in Chapter 4's terms, Andrea was a weak media world connector and Patrick a clear public world connector.

Andrea's diary consistently took the form of brief comments on lead stories (often headlines), offering no link to an underlying issue; the interpretative context was almost always the media's latest framing of that story. While she followed media in general terms, in only one case did Andrea say in the diary that she was following a particular *issue* or story (a short-lived scandal involving local footballers). Andrea offered in her diary no criticism of the factual basis of media coverage, although she often commented on the moral appropriateness of a story being aired in public. Here is one of Andrea's diaries which illustrates her style (Figure 5.1).

Main topic of discussion with family, friends and work friends was programme 'The Foetus.' Very emotive topic of abortion, mixed views from people. Programme was made to show truth and because topic is supposedly so hush-hush, but I felt it was unnecessary. Did not change my own personal views but images shown were very unpleasant.

Outrage at American TV showing pictures of a dying Princess Diana. It's disgusting that after so many years they should do this and inflicting more upset on her family and 2 sons.

How wrong of football pundit to use racist term and silly excuse that he thought that microphones were turned off. If he is as anti-racism as he says he is, he should never use such names. Discussed with partner who feels it was right for him to lose his job.

Baftas seen on television and reports in newspapers and magazines – no surprise winners.

Sadness at grief of family at funeral of TV presenter Caran Keating. Such wonderful tributes from everyone who knew her.

Figure 5.1 Andrea's diary for week of 25 April 2004

Shock at uncovered bomb plot at Manchester Uniteds football club. Shows how vulnerable are as a country

Surprise that David Beckham's newly shaved hair cut made front page news!!

Other main news in papers is news of a referendum on the EU Constitution. My opinion is in majority vote I feel, I don't wish us to sign the EU Constitution. Don't feel that it would be in our interest to hand over power in major decisions on way our country is run, and would lose our national identity.

Admiration for the thousands of people who ran the London Marathon for such great causes.

Pleased to see more mention in news of St. George's day but still don't know of anybody who celebrated the day in anyway. Find it very odd that so many English join in celebrating for St. Patrick's day – only for the social side and alcohol – and probably do nothing for their own day?

Figure 5.1   (Continued)

Patrick's diary, by contrast, although even terser, always presented an item in the context of a preexisting issue about which he appeared to have a viewpoint or judgement to give. Media as such, and media sources, were rarely referred to: instead Patrick referred to 'issues', 'debates' and 'talking points locally'. He also criticised media bias underlying the factual basis of media stories. Here is Patrick's diary (Figure 5.2) from the same week as the Andrea extract just given (see Figure 5.3 below for our analysis of major news headlines at this time).

The contrast – between media use whose rhythms and interpretation appear shaped purely by media flows, and media use that appears directed by a preexisting stance towards external issues that media are presenting – persisted throughout both diaries and was fully corroborated in interviews. Andrea explained that because of her irregular work-shifts, her pattern of media consumption often involved 'catching up' on programmes she had missed. She said she did not track local or national news actively, and when asked in the second interview if there was any current issue she was following she couldn't name any. She relied on her partner to bring home the newspaper (the *Sun*) each day, and often it was her partner who tried to direct her news consumption:

> I mean as soon as I sit down to read the paper, like I say, my partner reads it at work and he'll come in flipping pages and say, look at that story and drive you mad cause I just sat down to try and read it myself and he'll say look at that.

Indeed her media consumption overall was not something either she or her friends ever considered ('I couldn't actually tell you what newspapers

Collapse of Sewer

The talking point locally and at work has been the collapse of a main sewer, which has been mentioned on local radio and TV. This had the effect of sewage coming up the main holes and fields and actually polluting the local river. (Large fine coming here me thinks). This is the third time this has happened in the last eight months and with planning permission for four hundred new homes on the adjoining recreational land. I wonder what the effect will be if Southern Water do not carry out major replacement work urgently.

Associated British Ports ([name]Bay)

A six berth deep water quay would have created around 1800 jobs and long term security [detail omitted for confidentiality], bas been rejected by the government on environmental grounds. This will effect not only [city] and local businesses but will also put a question mark on the existing container berth, which has reached saturation point. Local people are worried about their and their children's future.

Announcement by Tony Blair on European Constitution

There has been a lot of debate this week about the proposed referendum, people are drawing their own conclusions on how they are going to vote. Without any clear information about what they are voting for.

Clearly the media is going to have a large part to play, as they portray the details for us to make up our minds.

The majority of us are in a quandary because of the political bias of the media, with certain newspapers their allegiance is to certain parties. Therefore are we going to get an unbiased viewpoint, to enable us to form a considered opinion. The BBC's political editor is a classical example of biased views.

Figure 5.2   Patrick's diary for week of 23 April 2004

[my friends read] or if any of my friends read newspapers'); it was taken-for-granted *background* to the rest of life.

Patrick by contrast, while he too used television as a general relaxation in the winter when unable to work in his garden, had a more judgmental attitude to media. He disliked media that were 'far from reality' (soaps, crime), preferring 'factual' programmes (note that this was a common preference, and could be expressed by both men – Bill, Edward – and women – Kylie, Enid).[2] He always watched the TV news with local radio providing 'all the local news'; reading the national paper was also a taken-for-granted part of his personal routine, linked to his strong interest in local politics. While Andrea enjoyed writing the diary and always found a range of stories to comment upon, for Patrick the process became tedious because 'the news was predominantly about Iraq'. This frustrated his desire to give a report that was both varied and actual and he was specifically frustrated because the Iraq war was a major issue on which, as a long-time Labour supporter, he disagreed with the

New Labour government. Unlike Andrea, he had in advance a sense of what issues he would have liked to be covered more during the diary phase:

> the other interesting issue come out of it was Gaddafi and Blair meeting. And I was surprised it was that small in the news to be perfectly honest cause it was just sort of one day it was there and then Pow! It was gone. . . . That was one of the most significant moves I believe, apart from obviously the war, of news of that time.

The issue-orientation of his media use was clear.

Both diarists, if to varying degrees, were connected via media to a world beyond the private, but in very different ways. Not only did public issues play a different part in each diarist's 'public world' (for Andrea in a way that was completely subsumed in media narratives with a weak link to public orientation; for Patrick through a strong link to his broader engagement with the public world) but their media use was differently shaped and directed.

The broader news context

We decided that the data generated in the diary phase could not be analysed in isolation, and so sought to establish the news context in which it took place. The diary phase extended from February until July 2004, a period characterised by a series of themes and events in the news and elsewhere. What types of news item did our diarist sample *overall* select from the range of news stories available to them at the time?

Such a comparison, given the almost infinite expanse of contemporary information flows, is far from straightforward, but our comparison is based on a careful multi-path tracking of leading news items during the diary period (see Appendix ID), and then a tracking of the major patterns in the issues diarists followed.

Figure 5.3 represents the key stories covered in the press, while Figure 5.4 represents the prevalence of themes and events in the diaries themselves. Appendix 1D describes how these news timelines were constructed, and presents a key to interpreting Figures 5.3–5.5.

Since Figure 5.4 is complex, we also present, to facilitate comparison, a simplified diarist timeline (Figure 5.5) which includes only those issues recorded at substantial levels for three weeks or more. When this is compared to the news timeline (Figure 5.3), some interesting patterns emerge.

93

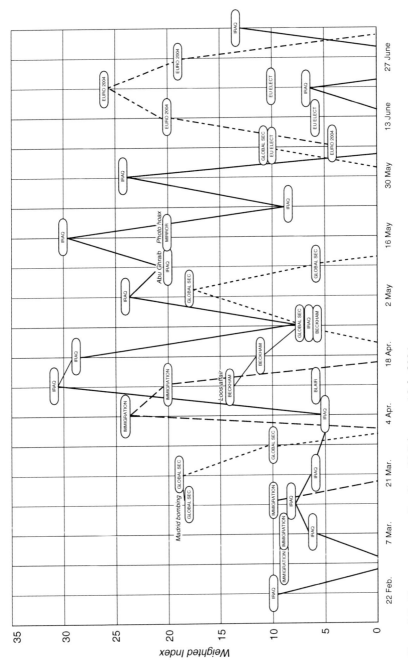

Figure 5.3 Newspaper news timeline: 22 February–4 July 2004

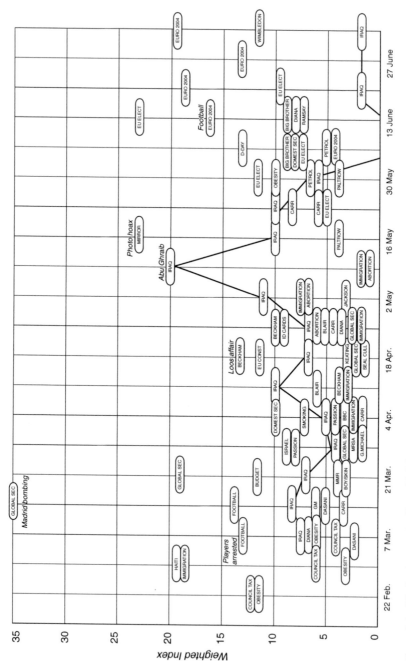

Figure 5.4 Diarists' news timeline: 22 February–4 July 2004

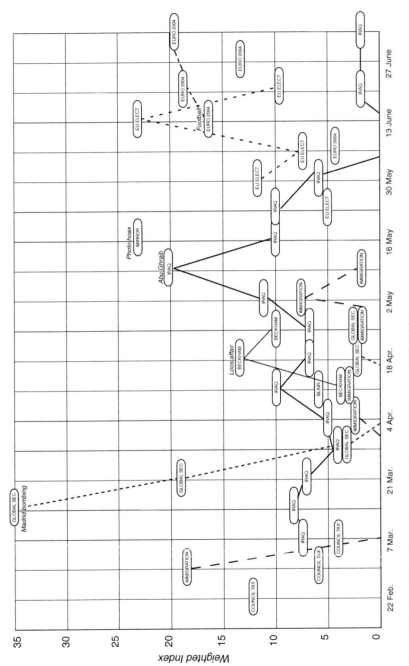

Figure 5.5 Simplified diarists' news timeline: 22 February–4 July 2004

The major events of the period, whether one-off or peaks of longer trends, were consistently represented across newspaper coverage and diary entries. These include: the Madrid bombings, the resignation of immigration minister Beverley Hughes (over asylum seekers), David Beckham's alleged extra-marital affairs, the revelation of prisoner abuse at Abu Ghraib in Iraq, the hoax abuse photos published in the Mirror, the local and European elections, and the Euro 2004 football tournament.

Some longer-term stories were represented strongly in the two 'samples': namely, events in Iraq and, to a lesser extent, immigration. There were some longer term trends which were fairly consistently represented in the press, but appeared in the diaries only when there were 'breakthrough' events: immigration, where it was only the resignation of a minister (Hughes) which resulted in diary references comparable to press coverage; and the EU constitution, which was referenced in the diaries mainly at the time when Blair reversed a decision on a referendum over the issue. It was also seen with regard to events in Iraq: while this was the most consistent news item referred to across the period, it was only at times of particularly sensational coverage that diarists wrote about it at overall levels comparable to its pervasiveness in the press, although there were some diarists who tracked persistent stories more regularly. A possible explanation is found in the interview data, in which some diarists explicitly commented that while they were aware of the continuing visibility of Iraq in the news, they *resisted* writing about it week after week (see below under 'attraction/withdrawal').

When we compare Figures 5.3 and 5.5, Westminster politics and immigration appear to be significantly less represented in the diaries than in the press. By contrast, there were news items which were more persistently present in the diaries than in the general news: including council tax rises, stories about Princess Diana (the circulation in the USA of videotapes and photographs of the accident in which she died),[3] and stories about childhood obesity and abortion. There were also two television programmes which sparked comment in the diaries (*The Boy Whose Skin Fell Off* and a programme which showed film of an actual abortion operation),[4] but did not register in patterns of overall news coverage.

It is not possible to draw from this comparison any definitive characterization (as news consumers) of our diarist sample relative to the general population. What we can suggest however is that, even with those of above-average engagement (the majority of our diarists had mediated public connection: Chapter 4), there remains a substantial difference between the peaks in *news coverage* (as represented by national press lead stories) and the peaks in detailed *audience attention* (as represented by items that diarists chose to comment upon in their diaries). Audience attention appears to select *from* persistent coverage of headline issues (whether Iraq or immigration) and select *for* other issues which have less headline prominence but more striking human or practical implications.

Patterns of media use

The diarist sample closely mirrored national trends in terms of access to different media. Unsurprisingly, all diarists had a television and radio. 57 per cent of our diarists had some form of access to the internet (in line with the national figure of 60 per cent in October 2004).[5] Of these diarists, six had broadband access at home (16 per cent of all diarists): this is also comparable with the then United Kingdom average for home broadband which in 2004 rose from 12 per cent to 24 per cent of all households.[6]

Levels of media use among the diarists varied considerably, but most diarists reported a consistent pattern of consumption. 14 diarists (38 per cent) appeared to be 'heavy' television consumers (saying they watched three or more hours per day on average), while 11 diarists (30 per cent) appeared to be 'light' television consumers (less than an hour per day).[7] This latter group was dominated by diarists with very little leisure time and low levels of all media consumption. Everyone, however, watched television news, although one diarist (Josh) appeared to do so only minimally: his diaries referred always to web or press news sources, not television (except occasionally television documentaries or sport).

Nearly all diarists listened to the radio to some extent (compare the RAJAR surveys which put overall audience reach at 90 per cent (December 2005)). Three of the four who explicitly said they didn't listen to radio (Edward, Stuart, Bill) were men, over 60 and in the AB socioeconomic group. As to newspapers, 23 diarists[8] indicated they read a newspaper every day (62 per cent),[9] with a clear age and gender stratification of those who didn't : all were under 40 (two-thirds under 30), and three-quarters were women. By contrast four described themselves as reading the newspaper from cover to cover, with two diarists (Susan and Bill) regularly reading more than one paper for the comparison. Eighteen of the diarists mentioned reading their local newspapers at least occasionally, while thirteen said they regularly read magazines.

Of 21 diarists who actively used the internet, 13 used it principally for personal information and only 8 (22 per cent of overall sample)[10] used it at all as a news source or site of debate. Interestingly, and contrary to our expectations, there was *only one* diarist (Josh) for whom the internet was the principal news source. While this might seem initially surprising (given some industry research suggesting that the internet is fast replacing television use: Johnson 2006), it fits well with a recent Ofcom finding that only 3 per cent of the UK population use the internet as their main news source (Ofcom 2006a: 66).[11] We also had non-internet-users in our diarist sample for whom the internet was well-known but simply considered by them irrelevant: for example Kylie who lost interest in internet talk ('you're talking to people that are so far away from you'). It is worth noting finally that there was no evidence of diarists using mobile media to a significant extent to obtain news (just one reference to being texted a news story on a mobile phone: Sherryl).

For our diarist sample, then, the traditional media – television, radio and the press – were overwhelmingly the key news sources from which they selected, and it is primarily in terms of those media that the quality of media use needs to be discussed.

Quality of media use

Everyone approaches their media use with a certain degree of instrumentality; we all need sometimes to relax with a film, or follow up a favourite TV series. But beyond this basic (purely instrumental) level, there are many subtle differences in the meaning of media use and the way it links with the rest of life.

Central or dispensable?

For some diarists (nine overall) media were, it seemed, an area of experience that could be switched off without major consequences. For these diarists media were not a central part of their personal 'world': some – Christine, Eric and Tyrrone – had a strong public connection through routes other than media, while others – the 'weakly connected' (see Chapter 4) – did not. For a larger group of diarists (probably 20 out of the whole sample), media (the aspects of media they selected) were an important and entirely regular part of their lifeworld.[12] This might of course be at home but it could also be in the media-saturated space outside the home (Pavarti, Gundeep and Samantha worked in retail outlets where media were crucial; Sheila worked in a professional job where media information needed constantly to be monitored). This phenomenological difference cuts across modes of use, since people may, or may not, value media's taken-for-granted presence in their lives but this is partly independent from how they use media.

Media could be central to diarists' everyday lives in contrasting ways: as a source of regular pleasure and entertainment or as an instrumental source of information, as a world of collective involvement (see Chapter 4) or as a space for popular debate on public issues. To illustrated the last possibility, take Alfred's appreciation of a local radio phone-in host:

> I'm an avid listener now. . . . He finds the alternative argument, whether he believes it or not, whether it's his thoughts on something or not, if somebody comes along waffling about certain issues he will very, very quickly find the alternative argument to it and argue it out with them and he very often wins. . . . yeah, it's quite informative.

By contrast, media's *dispensability* for some people is easily overlooked in media research, because of the strong element of routine that structures media use. Our second interviews with diarists were sometimes revealing: Mary told us that becoming a student away from home changed her from a regular TV and newspaper consumer to someone who rarely consumed either; Marie told us the opening of a fitness club near home meant that spare time, once spent with television, was now, more purposefully (in her view), spent on exercise.

Sometimes a sense of distance from media emerged subtly during the diary process. Abby had strong news-following habits, but noted in her diary a sense of dislocation from media, by contrast with her intense engagement at events like the London Marathon:

> Attended with the family the start of the marathon [in London]. As we stood there cheering on the charity runners – I started to think that this was the true meaning of 'public life'. Strangers from all over the country, even world, coming together for the sake of their charities, and ordinary people cheering them on, regardless of background, race, religion, etc. The diary has made me appreciate – *and at times view very cynically* – the news and how it affects me and my family in everyday life. (Abby diary, added emphasis)

She amplified on this in the follow-up interview:

> I like events. I go to quite a few events . . . you feel part of it.
> *So, with the media, do you think it's hard to feel part of it? Hard to feel connected to what's going on?*

Oh yeah yeah, you're not connected at all. No you're outside looking in . . . I don't feel connected to things that I watch on the television. . . . You're just thinking: I'm glad I'm not there. I'm glad my family's not there.

Not surprisingly, perhaps, Abby's viewing became disrupted during the overwhelmingly (for her) negative coverage of the Iraq war aftermath.

Directed or non-directed media use?

A key contrast was between diarists who used media in a *directed* way and those who used media in a *non-directed* way (as already noted, the difference is subtle, with some diarists showing both tendencies). Over-simplifying somewhat, the first group either had a general purpose in mind (to get information about certain broad areas) or a specific purpose (to find out about a specific issue) that shaped their particular trajectories of media consumption. The second group simply absorbed whatever reached them as news and reacted to it without seeking out specific stories. Whether a diarist was directed in their media use depended on whether they had a broader purpose in using media: for those who were public world connectors, their pre-existing public connection provided this. One of the clearest examples of directed media use was the following:

> If I see something at a glance, then I might go on the Guardian site and see if the story's been headlined on there, find the names or the key words and there's somebody else on-line's probably reported it, I can chase it from there. Usually Reuters [has] got stuff on it. Yahoo, I think they link quite closely with Reuters so if you follow a story, chances are that's where it came from cause I guess they're the biggest news agency. (Josh, cf Bill)

It was more common for diarists to be directed in their media use in a general way (as with Patrick, discussed earlier) rather than (like Josh) to regularly pursue specific information streams for interest: the latter requires the freedom to devote extra time to media consumption. Our two most directed diarists were Josh (a student, even if a busy one with work commitments) and Bill (retired).

Non-directed media use was often implied rather than explicit as we saw earlier from Andrea's account. It is often suggested that there are major generational differences here, with younger audiences being more likely to watch television, for example, by constantly switching between channels rather than watching a preselected programme, an argument intensified by habits of websurfing. Indeed the BBC is now concerned that 'clickers and flickers'[13] will come to dominate its news audience, requiring a major shift in how news is made available. There were clear signs of such a generational difference in our diarist sample, encapsulated in the word 'flicking'. While it has a more basic descriptive use ('flicking *on* a channel'), it was often used by younger diarists, and particularly women, to signal the way they use a range of media (Sheila was the only diarist over 40 to use the word in this sense):

> I tend to just flick through it [the paper] . . . I never read cover to cover. (Marie)
>
> We sort of just flick and just listen to songs [on the radio] (Mary)
>
> I'll just flick onto Ananova or flick onto nme.com or something. (Beccy)

It would be misleading to claim this type of non-directed media use was universal among younger diarists, as some were more explicitly directed (Jonathan, Josh) or made a point of saying they did not 'flip through the paper' (Tyrrone). Indeed 'flicking' can itself be partly directed ('I tend to find a song that I like and I flick until I do': Ross). But there is certainly an important generational and gendered patterning to consider here. Beccy provided an unusually self-reflexive example of non-directed use:

> I log on to BBC news and I get distracted by something that looks a bit more entertaining or a bit more like something I would read, from the local or the business section, or shamefully, from the entertainment section, and then I think I've been on the Internet too much and I go back off to do some work again. (diary)

Degrees of directedness of media use were reflected also in how people wrote about issues in diaries, and this has already been illustrated in detail for Andrea and Patrick.

Recent Danish research suggests that levels of education are crucial to whether people focus more on media story contents or have a broader critical perspective on media (Schrøder and Phillips 2005: 189–92). Is there any relation, then, between what we have called 'directedness' of media use and education? We also tracked education levels, but our picture is more complex: Patrick left school at 16 as did Bill, yet both were directed media users and had a clear sense of how media operated and a view on how media performed. In these cases, the resources and knowledge acquired through occupation (Bill as a managing director) and civic service (Patrick as a councillor) were as important, we suggest, as initial levels of education. So too with non-directedness: Beccy was *non*-directed in her media use, yet had a university degree from one of the most prominent UK universities. Directedness of use may be a more useful criterion here than having an explicitly critical perspective on media, since the former unlike the latter requires no specific level of articulacy; it is a matter of underlying orientation, and so can be found at any level of education.

Attraction/withdrawal

Even non-directed diarists could feel *attracted* towards exceptional events or issues which they might look at in a directed fashion (the significance they gave to this only brought out how non-directed their normal media use was):

> I can remember when Soham, the Soham story first happened [the internationally prominent murder of two young girls in the village of Soham, Cambridgeshire], we did actually watch you know, Sky News and things like that.... (Andrea)

But non-directed diarists, and to a lesser extent all diarists, might also feel a contrasting need to *withdraw* from, for example, particularly intense news coverage (such as the news coverage of the Iraq war aftermath during the diary period). There were many examples of this with varying degrees of intensity:

> Not listened to Radio 4 today, but had [name] our local radio station on instead, many because the world news is too depressing. So I had daft and light entertainment today. (Christine, diary)
>
> I am afraid that I am in danger of becoming bad news weary and developing an ostrich attitude. (Alfred, diary)

Greg Philo and Michael Berry (2004: 239–40) have noted the complexity of this pressure, as it often involves not apathy, but rather *caring* about what is happening and feeling powerless to do anything about it. Sherryl was a particularly interesting case of these contradictory pressures, in that much of her (spoken) diary involved reflections on the ambivalence of her relationship to news. She had strong views on many issues (for example, Iraq, Guantanamo Bay and US foreign policy generally) but also found the insistence of these news themes difficult to cope with: 'I have to say there's nothing really I want to talk about. It's all really depressing... I was gonna write about Iraq and that the Red Cross and I think the Government knowing of the abuse of prisoners around a year ago, but I can't be bothered' (Sherryl, diary).

Sometimes it was celebrity culture, not depressing international news, from which people wanted to escape (with women being particularly vociferous on this topic):

Have avoided newspapers, because as I predicted they are full of the Beckhams and real news is taking a back seat! (Abby, diary)

A very quiet Easter, have not really read the paper, mind you there was only the Beckhams, and the Beckhams' hangers on in the world this weekend, I am so sick of them I want to throw up, I have deliberately not read anything about them, but I'm sure you will understand!! (Christine, diary)

I really did think and hope that when Beckham went to Madrid, there wouldn't be as much news about him. But there seems to be more him and her than before they left England. Please give me a break. (Sherryl, diary)

Boredom or lack of knowledge created a different impetus to withdraw, particularly on issues requiring some precise background knowledge, such as a speech of Tony Blair's about a possible European Referendum (Marie).

Although media consumption is largely constituted by habit, it is clear that from these examples that habit by itself does not guarantee an *interpretative* context sufficient to sustain mediated public connection in the long run.

Media use and wider routine

Yet the wider routine patterns that structure media use remain crucial. Clearly there are personal or collective routines of media consumption: at home (reading the paper when it's delivered in the morning, watching or listening to news as you get up, watching a regular TV news bulletin in the evening) or on the way to work.[14] Older diarists in particular sometimes had a strong sense of personal routine around news gathering: Susan enjoyed sitting down with a bacon sandwich to read the

Sunday newspaper, while Christine insisted 'I won't go to work unless I've read the paper'. Increasingly important here, and socially stratifying (because uncontrolled access to the internet is only available to certain types of worker), is online consumption during work breaks. Diarists did this, for example, for individual news gathering (Josh, Jonathan) or for social use of online sources (Beccy: see further Chapter 6). Interestingly diarists could find they had overestimated the degree to which their apparently routine news consumption was regular. Kathleen realised (through doing her diary) that her claim in the first interview to watch the news every day was incorrect:

> It did bring out that I thought I watched the news more than I did. I was convinced that I thought I watched it everyday without fail at least once and it picked up that I didn't.

This illustrates the value of collecting data at multiple times, so that such corrections can emerge.

Other routines, however, *cut across* regular media consumption, whether an extremely pressured job with long working hours (Edward reflecting back on his past working life) or the rhythm of student life with its highly coordinated patterns of socialising as well as study (Mary; cf Andrea and Beccy reflecting back on their student days). A different routine, rather than constraining media use, generates an easy rationalization for limits to one's own media consumption; this is the sharing of media consumption 'responsibilities' across a family. Four women reported relying on their male partners to bring home a newspaper, while others relied on parents to have a local paper to hand when they saw them. There is no reason, of course, from the point of view of 'consumption', why in a family media tasks should not be shared.

It was rare for a diarist to have a strong practice of publicly oriented media consumption without a durable framework provided by domestic and/or work routine. Josh was perhaps the only exception, but had an exceptional will to keep up with the news, perhaps linked to his still being in the process of completing his professional education. Overall, routine, both positively and negatively, is crucial in shaping publicly oriented media consumption, even though, as we have just seen, some family routines relax, rather than reinforce, the pressures of media consumption for particular individuals.

Earlier discussion of how generations might differ in the directedness of media use raised the question of whether key habits of news consumption are destined to fade as younger media audiences grow older. As we saw, the evidence was a little more complex (indeed we did have younger diarists with clear news-consumption habits: Jonathan, Kylie, Crystal), and there is always the possibility that current shifts, which appear generational, will prove explicable by life-stage differences. We return to this point in Chapter 9.

Critical media use and media literacy

Our main focus throughout has been on people's degrees of orientation to a public world through media; that orientation (public connection) is only one precondition of effective democracy, another being that citizens use that public connection to give informed responses to issues that are put to them. In democracies that depend on mediated flows of information, *media* literacy crucially contributes, therefore, to democracy's effective workings. Media literacy is a large and growing area of research, stimulated in the UK by the new responsibilities of Ofcom to encourage media literacy.

Our concern was not, however, to track media literacy in all its aspects. Ofcom defines media literacy as 'the ability to access, understand and create media in a variety of forms' (Ofcom 2006a): for critical discussion of media literacy debates, see Livingstone (2004). We have already discussed access to media, while we found virtually no evidence of media creativity among our diarists. Our main interest lay therefore in people's understanding of media: not comprehension of media forms in general, but rather critical understanding of media that contributes to the sustaining of public connection. Some diarists offered no critical comments about media at any point, and we can only surmise that this is not how they interact with media. Others were regularly critical, although there were various distinct modes of criticism, as we shall see.

First, it is easy to overlook the media literacy implicit in people's basic consumption choices. Choice is not entirely habitual as the controversy during the diary period over the *Daily Mirror*'s use of fake photos of alleged UK soldier abuse of Iraqi prisoners brought out: at least two diarists stopped buying the *Mirror* as a direct result. One *Mirror* reader who it appears didn't (Kylie) illustrated this important form of media literacy in a different way when she distanced herself from her parents' choice of paper, the *Daily Star* or *Sun*: 'quite sexual papers [they are] I feel. It doesn't really give you a lot of news'.

Turning to more explicit forms of critical attitude towards media, most common were critical comments about media's balance and news priorities (at least 16 diarists). The simultaneous appearance as competing headline stories during the diary period of the Beckham/Rebecca Loos sex 'scandal' and disturbing news on Iraq (and on the general global security situation) provoked much comment and unease, for example:

> With all the important issues in the world such as war, terrorism, kidnapping hostages and trying to hold whole countries to ransom, isn't it a shame that the tabloid papers cover their front pages with lurid details of David Beckham's alleged affairs? (Jane, diary)

Such critical comments came from diarists regardless of whether they tended towards being public world connectors or media world connectors.

Less common (seven clear cases) was direct criticism of the facts or substance of a particular story (as opposed to broad news values) but when it occurred it was precise and vivid:

> there was an article the other day when the banner headlines in the newspaper were the fact that a dentist from Belgium had come over to set up practice in Scarborough and [he] was taking NHS patients and it said thousands queued and again it was repeated on the news, thousands, but... when we saw the local news, there were 300 hundred initially... when you see things like that, 300 to 2,000, you think well if they'll do something like that on a small story, how are they interpreting some of the other big things you know? (Stuart)

Sometimes detailed critique of media presentation of the facts was linked to consideration of underlying news values:

> Maxine Carr – is once again on the front pages of the newspapers.... why is she the one who's being vilified and shown on the front pages of newspapers? After all it was Huntley who murdered those poor girls. This is yet another situation and example where the "wicked woman" is the one on the front pages, incurring the wrath of the nation, whilst the man/murderer is given a relatively easy ride by the media. Look at Fred West who committed suicide, whilst his wife carried on, receiving the brick-backs along the way. Why should it be like this? Male Editors? Trying to create another Myra Hindley? (Henry, diary)

Relatively rare were cases where diarists reflected on media practice more broadly. We have already quoted Jonathan's general reservations about media balance which led him to become disenchanted with media, but these were reflected in his detailed choices about what stories to follow:

> Although some stories are worthy of reporting (terror, Iraq, economy etc) I do also feel as though there is not enough diversity, not enough representation of minority issues and also reporting positive issues. There seems to be a continued sidelining of other stories which should be getting reviewed. I am no longer reviewing stories on Afghanistan or Zimbabwe. (Jonathan, diary)

Such confidence in reviewing media coverage contributes to public connection, since it validates the diarist's status as a commentator on how media present the public world. Such confidence can have various sources, as we have emphasised: Jonathan had a degree in politics, but other diarists had acquired experience of observing media in various practical contexts (Patrick as a former councillor, Sheila as a senior public health nurse, Bill through frequent business and now leisure travel: Bill was perhaps the only diarist regularly aware of how different countries' newspapers presented similar stories).

A different type of critical perspective of media was based on values. Kathleen imagined a better life without media:

> The media is here to stay, love it or leave it, but I can't help wondering whether it was better to live in an age when you only knew what was happening in the next street or maybe village. We seem to live in an age now when we thrive on listening to other's misfortunes. (Kathleen, diary)

Tyrrone sharply criticised the wider social implications of the growth in celebrity culture and reality TV, and the forms of social surveillance they implied:

> I mean now you're even getting the contents of what goes in people's bedrooms... if that's going to be the case, then I mean there is no need for things like Eastenders, there is no need for the news, there is no need for anything because these are the celebrities... and we're just going to watch them live out their lives just like it's a 24-hour thing... a great Big Brother, we're just going watch them have sex, we're going to watch them eat their food, we're going to watch them have affairs and mess up their lives. So where do you draw the line? I don't know. (Tyrrone, diary)

Neither had particular experience of interacting with media, but both diarists had a sense of their values lying elsewhere, Kathleen in social networks built from bringing up children, Tyrrone in the implicitly ethnic community of musicians in which he worked (compare Chapter 4 on Lesley and Frank's alternative values). Jonathan implicitly linked a traditional evaluation of politics to his broader media literacy, reflecting on how what counts as public issues is itself shaped by media:

> I think the public issues very much vary. There's a differ-
> ence nowadays... between public... issues and agenda setting
> issues.... Because... you speak to most people... I mean you only
> have to look at the electoral turnout, 50%, that just shows you that
> people don't really give a shit about [voting]. That's only once every
> four years. It doesn't take that much effort to do. Yet more people are
> more interested in ringing up for bloody *Big Brother* or you know, *I'm
> a Celebrity, Get Me Out of Here*. So for me to say that public issues are
> politics, I don't think they are. I think they're [the result of] agenda
> setting as well.

What is particularly interesting here is that Jonathan's particular 'cultural capital' (Bourdieu 1984), that is, his degree in politics as well as his consumption of broadsheet as well as tabloid newspapers, allowed him to articulate a position outside celebrity culture which others, as we have seen, were only able to withdraw from. Tyrrone's critical stance on celebrity culture was similarly grounded in an alternative cultural perspective, linked to the community of music production to which he belonged. But critical orientations to media such as these cannot be fitted easily into the template of media literacy since they are concerned, in part, not with how to interpret media but with media's broader ethical and social consequences.

How, finally, does trust fit into this? We found that in most first interviews diarists' immediate response to questions about trust – both trust in politics and trust in media – was negative. However, if the subject came up spontaneously during the interview or in the course of the diary, there were frequent cases contradicting that initial response, or at least painting a more complex picture. In contrast to the survey (Chapter 8), it was sometimes higher status diarists who were more trusting of media (in part, because they trusted their ability to select more reliable media: Edward, Bill, Sheila), though we also found some low-status trusters (such as Kylie). This makes us not only wary of gener-alising about trust levels among the diarists, but cautious about how much the conventional and performative element in statements of trust/mistrust allows us to draw wider inferences about media literacy or critical orientation towards media.

Conclusion

In this chapter we have tried to give a detailed sense of how people's varied ways of orientating themselves (or not) to a public world through their media consumption are embedded in habit. A few broader points are worth noting. First, while the internet is important for some, generally younger, diarists, it is still habits focused on traditional media consumption that, for the time being at least, are crucial in sustaining public connection. Second, since habit is of major importance in stabilising mediated public connection, we will learn much more from studying the differentiation of citizens' habits than from an idealised model of the active information-seeking citizen. Third, for some diarists their media consumption was relatively detachable from the rest of their routines: they could live and orientate themselves to the world without media, or so they believed (to ignore this evidence would be to impose a mediacentrism). Fourth, critical orientation to media takes many forms, even if few of our diarists tracked specific issues through media in an active way (they lacked time and the direct benefits were far from obvious). Nonetheless there was a great deal of media literacy and sophistication among our diarists.

How far individual citizens choose to use their limited time and resources on following the public world through *directed* media use must depend not just on capabilities and acquired habits, but also on the wider contexts in which their daily practice have meaning. This is the topic of the next chapter.

Notes

1. A few diarists (such as Jonathan) started with a daily account but shifted over time to a weekly one.
2. See also Arvind's preference for 'a reality programme' (*Panorama, Question Time*) over 'fiction'.
3. References to Diana overwhelmingly comprised criticism of media coverage of these events.
4. Three references from diarists on each.
5. See www.statistics.gov.uk/cci/nugget_print.asp?ID=8. Of those 60%, 86% said they accessed the internet at home, suggesting a lower figure for home internet access.

6. www.statistics.gov.uk/cci/nugget_print.asp?ID=1367
7. The substantial difference in heavy television consumers from our survey (23 % watching television for three hours or more) may be due to some under-reporting in the more formal setting of a telephone survey.
8. Excluding two diarists who worked in retail outlets that sold newspapers.
9. This was higher than a recent British Social Attitudes survey finding of 49.5 % who 'normally read' a daily paper (National Centre for Social Research: 2006), but comparable to the Public Connection Survey finding of 61 % who read a national newspaper at least three times a week.
10. Cf the figure of 18 % in recent Ofcom research (Ofcom 2006a: 66).
11. According to the recent British Social Attitudes survey (National Centre for Social Research 2006), 8 % access internet news 'every day or nearly everyday' with 4 % doing so 2–5 days a week. These figures are not incompatible with ours, if we allow for those who access news websites as a supplement to other regular news sources.
12. Cf Hoover *et al.* (2004: 41) for the distinction between US households which are 'suffused' by media and those which have a more 'differentiated' approach to media.
13. Deputy Director General Mark Byford, quoted in Gibson (2006).
14. Six diarists mentioned reading a newspaper on the train or bus (now or in the past); three listened to radio driving to work.

6
Values, Talk and Action

What broader contexts stabilise mediated public connection? Three possibilities are discussed in this chapter: the values people bring to bear on their interpretation of events, the extent to which they have discursive contexts to talk about issues, and what sort, if any, of public and quasi-public actions they perform or can imagine performing. At the end of the chapter, we ask what links there are, for particular diarists, between action, talk and media consumption, and what significance such links (or their absence) have for diarists' sense of connection.

Values

In Chapter 4, we noted how people's values may be important in stabilising what they do: values may serve as a bridge between private and public worlds, reinforcing links between habits of media consumption (essentially a matter of private choice) and a broader orientation to the world.

Three diarists cited religion as an important influence on the views they hold. While this was on the whole uncommon, it was clearly linked not just to a specific issue but to a broader worldview. Angela, for example, was a Catholic and disparaged coverage of Catholicism in the media, while espousing values of tolerance around media stories (such as the media's treatment of former criminals and immigrants) which aligned with this orientation; another diarist, Eric, was a lay preacher, and some of his diary entries appeared to be sermons in which Christian interpretations of events in Iraq and elsewhere were weighed up in great detail. Other diarists expressed a counter-value, being concerned with the excessive influence of organised religion in the world (Gundeep, Sikh; Alfred, atheist).

Values such as privacy, diversity and tolerance for ethnic or racial difference were expressed more often by diarists without reference to faith. Sometimes this implied a sense of how the public sphere should be conducted: Kylie recalled telephoning a radio talkback programme to complain after hearing what she deemed racist jokes about Africans. Linked was a sense of the need for respect, or, more broadly, community. 'Community' was invoked as a value by eight diarists (interestingly the older term, 'society', was only mentioned by two). These were all, however, nostalgic views of what had been lost; in only one case were they linked to a sense of what needed to be done *in the present* (Christine, discussed later). A more common frame of reference was family. Many diarists saw the immediate family as a place where values are learned or sometimes undermined. This took many forms: sometimes criticisms of media (for the oversexualised content of pre-teen magazines or inappropriate images on television before the 9pm 'watershed'), and sometimes criticisms of parents and children reported in media (several diarists picked up on the story of a 14-year-old girl whose school arranged for an abortion without her parents' consent).

Of course a certain degree of moralising is inherent to media commentary and this was reflected in the style of some diarists, most notably Andrea, one of whose diaries was reproduced in full in Chapter 5. To quote her briefly again:

> Shocking pictures in papers of a photographer exhibiting naked pictures of daughter in the name of Art. I find this unbelievable and irresponsible especially at this time of so many horrible stories and crimes involving the problem of paedophiles. (Andrea, diary)

Here there is no sense of a larger frame of individual judgement, nor any broader moral context made explicit. The comments exist entirely within the moralising frame already set by media stories. What was missing, however, from our diarists were any cases where following media was *itself* understood as an active moral stance (this was a contrast with the parallel US study on public connection: Williams *et al.* 2006). Not only did the English diarists rarely articulate an explicit religious position, but those who did (Eric, Tyrrone) were among those who followed media least closely in our sample:[1] their public connection took other routes and forms.

The duty to keep up with the news

That is not to say that values were unimportant for diarists. Many diarists – both men and women, across the age range and the range from media 'poor' to 'media superrich' – recognised the specific value of 'keeping up with the news':

> I need the radio 24 hours. Like regular 24 hours because all the time in car, I listen radio news . . . every hour I have to listen to news just to find it out what's happening. (Gundeep)

> Yeah, I've always felt that anyway that you need to know what's going on all over the world. . . . Even though you can't always make a difference, but you try and do something and if you can't, just realise how lucky you are. (Kylie)

> Even if I'm not working, I'm watching the news pretty much constantly . . . I'll always watch the news. (Jonathan)

Sometimes this duty merged with taste and interest, but an interest that was seen as necessary: 'I'm compulsive, I have to pick up any paper that I see and have a look through it' (Enid). This covered not just news but current affairs and documentaries. Documentaries were picked out as important by a number of diarists: 'I love documentaries . . . they just give you different insights into the way people are, the way people live' (Kylie).

The value of keeping up with news might be expressed, in negative form, through shock at *others* who lacked that value, predictably by older people judging those younger but just as often by young people judging their peers:

> This is what I find quite astonishing really that most people I know really just don't care about what's going on. They're focused on their own thing and as long as they know that David Beckham's had a new hair cut and that they can go and get it done at the salon just like this, . . . they just carry on with stuff. (Josh)

Men were more likely to *express* judgments of others, but the sense of distinction was found across both women and men.

What of diarists who lacked this value? The evidence was generally only implicit, because framed against an acknowledged dominant value: 'I read *the headlines* and I read *the first few bits* and . . . I always get told

I should have more of an interest but . . . most stories are the government and things but it's something that's out of our hands. . . . I do tend to *go past* a lot of the stories' (Andrea, added emphasis). Beccy, one of the most reflexive diarists, explored this issue many times, explicitly acknowledging that her attention to news was sporadic (see also chapter 5). Her 'self-defence' was interesting:

> I think everybody would have their own line. My cynical friend would say that you know everybody should be obligated to know about politics and everybody should use their vote responsibly because he's really into that. . . . Whereas me . . . I don't know where my line would be because I know I look at a lot of celebrity news but that's not important and I wouldn't say people were obliged to know about that at all. But certain things in my head I think I should be obliged to know about I'm not.

Consumerist individualism, even if tinged with guilt, works here as an alternative value that rationalises the *separation* of media consumption from public orientation. It is possible that diarists underreported this because of their sense of our expectations as researchers.

Talk

Most accounts of civic culture, including Dahlgren's six-dimensional model, give some place to talk oriented to public matters. Avoiding a fixed definition of 'public deliberation', we systematically catalogued those instances where the diarists recounted speaking to others, particularly about the issues mentioned in their diaries. Could everyday talk be an important part of the taken-for-granted context for following public events through media consumption?

Forms of talk

Evidence of publicly oriented talk was widespread (our survey findings will be similar: Chapter 8), and only four diarists made no mention of it when asked directly in the first interview (all men). No diarist told us directly that they saw no point in talking about public issues with others: the idea that public issues are in principal *social* in their relevance seemed therefore to be universal. That twenty participants mentioned talk in their diaries, without direct direction to do so, suggests that most had a discursive context for the issues they discussed in the diary. But what type of context and with what consequences? Talk about issues could operate in many registers, from the instrumental to the passive, from the consensual to the conflictual, and from casual talk to talk intended to be informative. Sometimes however the informational status of what was discussed mattered less than the social purpose of talking:

> In the office today the only topic in the public eye that we have talked about is the Beckham story. Although nobody watched the interview last night. So we don't care that much! Nobody is particularly bothered about whether it's true or not, it's just something to chat about for 2 minutes. (Beccy, diary)

Most of the talk reported was face-to-face talk, although we have just seen how stories *sourced* online can provide an important discursive context. As to online conversations, only three diarists mentioned this: two had instant messaging exchanges with family and one took part in religion-related online forums:

> I take part in a number of Internet discussion forums, where people from any part of the world can meet in what some call 'cyberspace' to discuss matters of mutual interest. . . . When I take a short break from work I can get a cup of coffee, check what's happening in one or two forums and if there's something I find interesting or important chip in with a comment or a question. (Eric, diary)

Given that we encouraged participants to recount any form of discussion, the level of online talk registered is strikingly low. This suggests that the internet was less important to our UK diarists as a discursive context than current research (often dominated by a US perspective) would predict.

Location

As Nina Eliasoph persuasively argued (1998), we cannot understand talk about public issues unless we note the locations and contexts in which it occurs, since opportunities for talk are spatially patterned. Certain bounded, structured contexts for talk about public issues were shared across our diarist sample. First, the return home from work (14 diarists) generates talk with children or (more often in our sample) talk between partners. Sometimes such talk and its context was strongly gendered, as when a husband or boyfriend was reported bringing home the newspaper and starting conversation: 'if [name of partner] has seen something in the paper, and he's like – oh did you know about – you know, so and so – and he'll tell me' (Beccy). The second most cited context were nights out with friends at a pub or club, especially for diarists under 50. Many diarists recounted discussing issues while out with friends, and two – both women – describe satisfying nights out 'putting the world to rights', or 'just having a good old moan', as they self-deprecatingly described it.

A third, more complex context was work. When talk at work was limited to a shared tea or lunch break, media could provide a ready stimulus, whether as the material for casual chat with colleagues (for example celebrity gossip from websites: Beccy) or as a stimulus to a more focussed debate within a larger group:

> what else do you do when you're all thrown together in a room this size? . . . You get you know a few people sitting in the corner with the National Enquirer, talking about that . . . and you get other people talking politics, and you decide which group you want to go with. (Abby)

The context of news may supply material for talk more indirectly where people 'go and put the world to rights on a Friday lunchtime' (Henry). By contrast, one diarist (Arvind) who had been made redundant from a large factory felt keenly the loss of a work discussion context: 'then we had like a different group with different people, all sort of people. . . . I mean we used to get a hundred people around there on the table and everybody got their different opinion'.

Very different is public-oriented talk that is inherent to the work itself, as with three diarists who ran small retail or service outlets (hairdressing salon, petrol station). Pavarti ran a newspaper shop:

> Mine is the only shop on the road. So they all come and talk to me. They all [tell] what happened in their house and where they went and what they did and which cinema they been to or what theatre or what show they been, they always ask me – and how you are and how was your day. So it [is] like a – in a small community, small town shop.

Rarely, there are cases where what happens at work is *itself* the subject of discussion, because of its public relevance; here there is no need for a media stimulus. Clearly only certain types of paid or voluntary work (such as being a magistrate: Edward, Bill) afford such opportunities; less privileged were diarists whose work was crossed by public issues with a high prominence in media, requiring informed talk as part of daily work. We discuss in Chapter 7 our clearest case – Sheila, a senior public health nurse – but there were other examples (hospital nurse, teacher): 'obviously being a children's nurse, there would be things ... regarding the MMR for us to advise parents ... when it all came out initially, parents, if they were in with their children, would question us' (Andrea).

Finally, besides home and work, the diaries also gave us many incidental glimpses of talk in other casual contexts. It is striking, however, that only one diarist mentioned talking to a neighbour and it was this same diarist (Lesley, from a rural area) who more than any other mentioned talk outside the home or work situation (in shopping queues, or at the swimming pool). However, it may be that diarists underreported such casual talk, or did not see its significance.

Discursive constraints and opportunities

Situations of talk, as noted, involve constraints and these were often registered by diarists. First, people avoided depressing or serious topics when in social situations ('you don't particularly want to be sitting there talking about doom and gloom that's going on in the world': Marie) or in breaks during stressful work (teachers, nurses):

> we've got very limited time in the staff room so I mean it tends to be you know stupid things about what you've watched on telly or something light-hearted or fun. (Lisa)

Diarists also knew to avoid perceived sensitive subjects including both religion and politics ('I say well you have your own opinions, I have my own opinions that I don't push politics because I don't know that much about it': Frank). In all, five diarists said social conversations excluded talk of 'serious' issues and four male diarists (including Jonathan and Edward) commented negatively on the fact that serious topics were excluded.

Perhaps the clearest example of the *implicit* boundaries around talk on 'issues' came from Susan's story of how her involvement in the diary research allowed her, temporarily, to overcome those constraints. This diarist hiked with a group, where conversation was usually sporadic and light (holidays, the weather). On mentioning the diary, however, people's interest was triggered:

from walking like two or three abreast, it was like eight and nine abreast.... And then we were stopped for our lunch, they were all sat round me you know, when normally there's about four women who sit together.... so this diary...became quite a conversation piece.... it was incredible, it really was. (Susan)

But, when the diary ended, conversation of this sort on the ramble ended too.

It would be a mistake however to only mention constraints. Many diarists talked positively of the opportunity for debate. Some, all men, deliberately stimulated debate to help them with their diary (Harry, Nigel, Bill). Other diarists like Susan were pleased to find that bringing up their participation in the project in their social circle provoked discussion:

I remember...I think the first week I started doing it we went out to a pub...and then a party and we got talking about it and a few things came out there, it sparked a conversation.... It started off a whole sort of spiral of thoughts there. (Beccy).

Whether or not the diary was important here, seven diarists made it clear that they enjoyed substantive debate, for example Patrick:

I'm lucky in as much as my wife, my wife's sister and her husband [are] very much politically minded. So we have a lot of good debates (laughs) on...various topics...you're sort of sharing with people, like-minded people.

We would risk underestimating the significance of such debate, if we looked only for cases where 'issues' are the principal focus of conversation. For, if some diarists (seven) debated issues, a similar number (eight, particularly women) implied that 'serious' social or political issues were threaded throughout general conversations. Sometimes of course exchange among friends or family was motivated by a media story. One human-interest television programme (*The Boy Whose Skin Fell Off*) led two diarists to report calling others during the programme or afterwards.

Debate and disagreement

Against the assumptions of some political theory, Noelle-Neumann (1984) argued that face-to-face talk might close off real debate (the exchange of *differences* of opinion) because of a 'spiral of silence': a person is less likely to voice an opinion on a topic where they feel they are in the minority, especially if that minority view is not rendered visible in the news media. Our evidence only partly supported this, and we found considerable evidence of open discussion in diarists' daily lives.

One diarist artificially stimulated debate at work to generate the content of his diary: 'My staff quite enjoyed it because ... I picked out the topics out of the paper and then we discussed it as a sort of group sometimes.... it really was interesting ... different people's ideas on different things' (Nigel). Such an artificial case was, of course, rare, but there were plenty of other examples of 'naturally occurring' debate. Six diarists described situations of genuine, sometimes heated debate where opinions were contested, although diarists might see debates going on around them, for example in the workplace, but hold back from contributing because of lack of information or confidence. A remarkable case of someone leading debate was Enid who organised discussions about the news in her local women's group once or twice a year:

> we have a discussion night. We do it twice a year ... on a night like that you're all in your little groups of maybe eight people, here are all the papers and you're supposed to have a good look and say you know did you think that in this story that was right, that was wrong and you discuss it, right? And then you discuss that, that and that ...

We based one of our focus groups in this pre-existing social setting, recording half of the parallel discussions.

Some discussion may, however, simply confirm pre-existing opinions, so neither avoiding the risk of Noelle-Neumann's spiral of silence nor providing true deliberation. What were the outcomes of talk about issues, when recorded by our diarists? Agreement was certainly the most common outcome of talk about issues, for example in relation to the *Daily Mirror*'s 'fake' photos of alleged British soldier abuses of Iraqi prisoners: 'discussed with friends who agreed that if photos are genuine, then appropriate action should be taken by the army' (Abby). Three diarists said they had changed their opinions on the basis of a discussion. One diarist in particular, who had once been politically active, saw media as having a positive role to play in highlighting differences of opinion:

> No, I think, you do form your own opinions by discussion. I mean if I read one paper and [daughter] reads another paper and you know, if I

say to her this, this and this and she'll say, no, that's not right . . . then you form your own opinion or that's how it should be. You're not just taking what is said there. (Jane)

To summarise, our evidence does not overall support Noelle-Neumann's view that divergent opinions are suppressed in everyday social activity; potentially discussion remains an important route to deliberation and engagement, often stimulated by media.

For some diarists, however, talk's relation to their public orientation was problematic. Only one diarist (Jonathan) reflected in detail on the broader social conditions for satisfactory talk about public issues, but six diarists (both men and women) said they lacked a satisfactory social context for talk about public-type issues. Crystal was one example:

I talk about Iraq with my partner, with my mum, sometimes . . . but - you know, a lot of people around me are very materialistic and that's just not on their minds. . . . I'm one of those people, but I also like to concentrate on reality – things – but a lot of people around me are more into their own lives than others that they never knew and are now getting killed 500,000 miles away.

Four other diarists mentioned losing past social contexts for public-related talk. Sometimes this reflected personal choice (Patrick had stood down as a councillor, Nigel had stopped his long commute to London) but sometimes broader changes: the loss of doorstep politics, local clubs with declining membership. We see hints here of Putnam's narrative of civic decline but since social talk is already constrained, the implications for peoples' opportunities to discuss *public* issues very much depend on specific circumstances.

A number of diarists commented positively on media's role in providing spaces for debate (compare Alfred's appreciation of a local radio phone in, quoted in Chapter 5). But for some diarists the frustration of such media debates outweighed their benefits. Paul said he avoided the BBC programme *Question Time* '[be]cause I would go to bed feeling furious, kick the telly'. The interviewer asked if it would make a difference if he had the chance to ask a question himself:

no because I'd be so angry with the reply. . . . You see programmes like that are . . . so general . . . all they're doing is just scratching the surface to me . . . you're not allowed to expand anything . . . nothing actually gets resolved . . . and people's points of view are never really taken into account.

Emerging here is a wider concern about the absence of spaces *to be heard* to which we will return.

Talk and action: the missing link

What of more concrete, durable outcomes to talk? The most striking aspect of our diary phase data is *the almost complete absence of recorded links between talk and action*. We found only one case of discussion leading to action – Christine and her friends resolving at a party to start a local recycling drive.[2] This absence is certainly not caused by our diarists overall being apathetic or lacking opinions; nor, on the whole, were they reluctant to share them socially and subject them to disagreement in social contexts. Further, the next section makes clear that many diarists were involved in at least low-level public actions.

The explanation may be that diarists saw talk about public issues and action in relation to those same issues as independent zones of practice: a matter not so much of discursive constraints, but of the absence of any practical context that might *articulate* talk *to* action. Yet political theory implies that public engagement, deliberation and practical involvement should be mutually reinforcing.[3] The talk we have been examining, while often reinforcing mediated public connection, hardly guaranteed a link to active involvement in the public world. Is this evidence for Pattie's (2004: 278) suggestion of a decline in a deliberative culture in the UK? We return to this point in our conclusion.

Action

We were interested to track diarists' 'public' actions in a broad sense, that is, any signs of agency with regard to issues requiring common action or common resolution (cf Eriksen and Weigard 2000: 32).

Types of action

We avoided asking diarists directly about whether they had previously engaged in particular types of political action so as to avoid suggesting a traditional definition of the 'political' or 'civic': instead we waited for diarists to mention an issue, following up with a question about action, or else relied upon unsolicited evidence from diaries or interviews. Nonetheless, we gathered a range of evidence about 'public' actions across the sample.

Excluding voting for the moment (32 out of 37 said that they regularly voted in any case), the most common actions diarists said they had undertaken at some point were attending local community events and meetings (eight diarists), local council consultation meetings (seven diarists), party political involvement (six diarists), work-related public actions (six diarists), contacting their MP (five diarists), contributing to or working with charities (five diarists) and signing a petition (five diarists).[4] Individual diarists also referred to church-based activities and participation in online forums. Pattie *et al.* (2004: 134) distinguish three types of public-oriented action: individual, collective and contact. 'Individual' actions include signing a petition and consumer boycotts; 'collective' actions (which depend on others also acting) include public demonstrations and strikes, whereas 'contact' actions refer to sending a message to an MP, organisation or media outlet (Pattie *et al.* 2004: 135). The authors go on to compare different motivations for acting, ranging from self-interested to principled (Pattie *et al.* 2004: 138–50). In our data, 'self-interested' or inward-focused action included contacting an MP or local council to address a specific concern – twelve of the diarists had done something along these lines. Whether actions were outward-focussed and 'principled' was more difficult to measure, but (leaving aside voting) ten diarists, or just over a quarter of the sample, appeared to have engaged in 'principled' action. Overall, responsive (rather than self-instigated) actions – accepting an invitation to attend a local council meeting, signing a petition – were the largest category of actions, covering half of the diarists.

There were only a handful (five) diarists who registered no action at all, though justification for inaction was a theme also for a larger group (see below): the inactive were either young diarists with other commitments (university, sport) and a general lack of interest in matters of shared concern, or socially isolated, older diarists (we cannot tell if such diarists had been active previously). However, if we exclude action which involves no time or resources – such as signing a petition – then the number of diarists for whom we lack evidence of action rises considerably. Indeed, if we concentrate on 'collective' actions - those undertaken with others - very few diarists would be classified as active.[5]

Reasons and contexts for public action

Reasons given for public action varied from the principled to the self-interested, and from the instrumental to the passive or routinised. For political action, including voting, by far the most common reason given was right or obligation (10 diarists): 'yes, I really I feel very strongly that you should vote, and I do always go and vote' (Angela). Out of the avowals of civic action, four diarists referenced disposition including Susan:

> I'm really a very honest person and I hate to see somebody being victimised or something. You know I'd go all out to help.... And if I saw anybody you know kicking a dog, I would go up to them and I wouldn't think of my own self.... I would have to get involved.

Personal satisfaction and the sense of 'making a difference' were also important as well as a basic sense of reciprocity ('what if I needed help?'). As to explicit motivations for action on contentious public issues, only seven diarists overall invoked principle, and only one diarist had anything approaching a 'philosophy' of activism:

> yes, I'm still actively involved in you know basically just trying to see the way forward for the community. I mean there's so much that can be done for so little amount of money and I think it's just raising awareness really. (Christine)

Christine was very much an exception in our sample.

It is notable that no diarist mentioned media items as a trigger for any actions which were themselves not already mediated, and we found no link of any sort between online use (for example, to get personal information or contact family) and public action. But here we must note another important category of action which *is* mediated and which we call 'quasi-public' (cf Chapter 4): these are actions which are not based on any traditional notion of civic or public spaces, and are instead entirely mediated. One diarist, for instance, describes attending the final night of *Big Brother*:

> So we got five tickets for the final and we went down and we got there half ten in the morning and we queued all day (laughs) to make sure we got in ... we just got right down the front and made our banners and it was fantastic. It was like these people that go to, I don't know, cup finals or something, just the crowd atmosphere and the sense of, I don't know, camaraderie that was going on, it was fantastic. (Beccy)

The event is described in terms which make clear she is participating in something 'collective', not merely personal, but it is not 'public' in the sense of relating to issues for public resolution. Interestingly, Beccy also described a marketing conference related to her work in terms that suggested politics (her boss encouraging the conference audience to lobby government to show interest in her company's products), but again she saw no link here to her individual identity as a citizen. This suggests that the limits on involvement in public action are, in part, 'cultural', at least in the reverse sense, that a 'civic culture' is *missing* that would make sense of apparently public acts as linked to a public domain where individual citizens can and should act.[6]

Inaction and missing action-contexts

Illuminating, in terms of what might sustain or block a sense of public orientation's links to action, is how diarists rationalised inaction. One fundamental reason was not having an interest or motivation to act on a specific issues (cf Pattie *et al.* 2004). But there were other general reasons for inaction. The most common rationalisation was a lack of efficacy, with six diarists saying explicitly they didn't engage in particular actions – voting, contacting and MP or getting involved locally – because it would not make a difference: 'I always thought it was fairly futile writing to politicians about stuff because one letter won't get a response and I haven't got the time to go around collecting signatures and just leave it at that' (Josh). Cynicism must be cautiously treated here: a large number of diarists (twenty) expressed cynicism, though this could be purely conventional[7] and, as Thomas Janoski remarks (1998: 100), cynical citizens have a complex attitude whose action consequences are difficult to predict: it is dangerous therefore to use diarists' stated cynicism to explain inaction.

Other factors were more significant. First, life circumstances, predominantly a lack of time, were cited by seven diarists as their primary reason for not acting politically or civically. Lack of time was most often associated with diarists aged 30–50 (especially men), and (unsurprisingly) women with young children. Second, and perhaps more important, was disposition (six diarists), since this involved internalising reasons for inaction:

> If I wanted to be more active then you know I could be. I could sort like you know go sign up to Outrage. I could go flying banners every

weekend in London and throwing pink paint over priests...but I
don't want to do that. It's not me. (Frank)

A broader narrative could be involved that sharply separated one's
private world from the world of public action. Here fear emerged,
unexpectedly, as a factor justifying inaction,:

Yeah, fear.... Yeah, I don't want anyone else outside of my circle
of... friends, people who I can trust to know because [I might be]
penalised for it. (Lesley)

Only one diarist (Kylie) gave political *satisfaction* ('I'm quite happy with
Labour') as the reason for not acting – in this case, paradoxically, for
not voting! – although two other diarists (Harry, Albert) who did vote,
but were not involved in other public actions, expressed themselves
generally satisfied with how things had worked out for them. Some
diarists (Jane, Patrick) linked inaction, in part at least, to the loss of a
particular social and political context (the old 'doorstep politics' based
on working-class community).

This raises the question of what *would* stimulate diarists to public
action. For some diarists, their distance from the public world was
already taken-for-granted: nothing could motivate them, since they
were already disengaged and had grown used to rationalising inaction.
But some diarists discussed their thresholds for potential actions in
hypothetical situations which proved revealing. Two diarists imagined
a context where they might connect with others publicly (Crystal,
Bill) – interestingly in both cases, going into schools and talking to
students about their lives, in Crystal's case about the experience and
difficulty of becoming a 'teenage mum'. Three diarists said that while
they did not engage in public or civil actions, they would do 'if they
felt passionate enough' about an issue; three other diarists said they
would act if it did not take up too much time. Other hypothetical
reasons included if the issue, and action required, were close enough
to home, or involved protecting the personal or private sphere. We
see again here an individualism that rationalises inaction in all but
exceptional circumstances (where one's personal living space is directly
affected).

But what if your individual circumstances are threatened? Is all diarists
lack the individual motivation for specific public actions? This is not
what the testimony of diarists who *did* act suggests. Almost all diarists
engaged in actions with a principled or value component had some sort

of local or social network in which that practice could be oriented. The nature of that local or social context was quite heterogeneous; it varied from the Sikh ethnic and cultural community whose scale far exceeds the local (Gundeep) to the institutionalised context of voluntary work (Bill) – such opportunities are clearly class-stratified (Burns *et al.* 2001) – to the highly organised network of a particular church (Eric). The diarist who most explicitly identified herself as involved in principled action (Christine) performed small-scale 'political' actions (requiring the local council to have a more active recycling policy) while at the same time caring not just for her own mother but for other elderly people nearby who needed help on small matters.

What bridged the gap between the potential for action and action remained uncertain. One diarist, Abby, a local government worker in South London enjoyed taking part in her local Citizens Jury (potentially an action-context):

> Did I tell you I belong to the [borough of residence] Citizens Panel?... it can have any subject the one I'm going to on Monday, it's a two hour event... we're actually speaking about social housing in [borough of residence].... But that's just our views though, you know. I'm not an expert I don't know much about it. But like you do they just want our views on certain subjects.... It's... quite good fun. And it's all walks of life go there. You don't know who you'll be paired up with, and the rest of it... I've enjoyed them.

But Abby made no links between this experience of being addressed as a 'citizen' and possible civic or public actions on her part. It is a striking contrast overall with the parallel US study (Williams *et al.* 2006) how rarely in our diary data 'the local' provided an effective action-context for diarists. It is also striking, although perhaps less surprising, that it was rare to find in the diary data an explicit discourse of 'citizenship': an exception was Arvind, discussing the dangers of consumerism for young Muslim youth.

A hint of the larger problem came from one diarist, Edward, who was civically engaged, yet disengaged from any political action. While his cynicism about politicians was all-too-typical ('I don't think politicians inform or consult!... I have a very jaundiced view of politicians'), his main actual concern was not voters' standard complaint (politicians don't listen to the message voters give when they vote), but that his regular and active experience 'on the ground' in an area crucial to government policy (criminal sentencing) was not being taken into account in the formulation of that policy:

> the be all and end all is putting out the story. It isn't delivering anything. It's putting out the perception [on crime and crime prevention]. . . . It's all a top thing – it's not at the bottom at all. The reality at the bottom is still totally different. You still have the courts clogged up with police witnesses who have to wait forever in court for cases which don't go through for one reason or another. . . . You'll probably never see all of this, of course: nobody does. But it happens all the time. But that's of no concern to politicians. What the politicians are concerned with is that very top layer of presentation through the media of one sort or another to the public.

The disjuncture expressed by Edward is not between an isolated individual and a distant public world (a lack of connection); the disjuncture instead is between an individual's existing civic/ public engagement and the practice of governments (a lack of *recognition*).

Conclusion

How, finally, do talk and action link with media consumption? To explore this, we mapped for each diarist a diagram, showing at the bottom a diarist's scale of social interaction, in the middle the scale of mediated events followed by that diarist, and at the top the scale (if any) on which that diarist performed public actions. Two sample diagrams are shown as Figures 6.1 and 6.2

We were interested in what overlaps there might be for particular diarists between different dimensions of interaction (social, mediated and public). Did diarists operate on all three dimensions within a particular scale (say, the local)? If so, we can imagine (as in Figure 6.2) a vertical line being drawn in a diarist's diagram, indicating an overlap between their social interactions, media focus and public actions; in the case of Bill, this would be on both local and national scales, suggesting he is a 'three-dimensional' actor on both those scales. Or was there a disjuncture, so a diarist's dimensions of activity failed to overlap on a particular scale? The results of this analysis, while inevitably tentative, link back to the analysis of Chapter 4. All six diarists who were active on three dimensions in any one scale had clear mediated public connection; all six who came closest to being active on all three levels (failing only because the scope of their public action was arguably small)

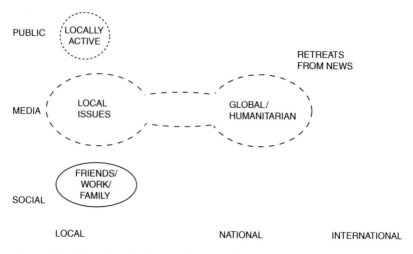

Figure 6.1   Scales of action/interaction: social/media/public: Christine

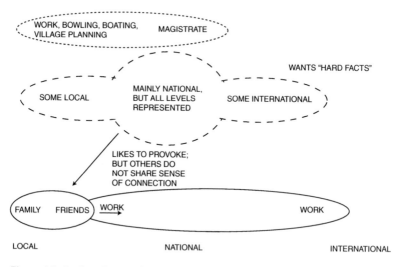

Figure 6.2   Scales of action/interaction: social/media/public: Bill

also had clear mediated public connection. Taking these two groups together, a majority of those with clear mediated public connection (11 out of 15) were diarists whose dimensions of action/ interaction (social, mediated and public) tended to overlap on one or more scales. This suggests that one fundamental precondition of democratic engagement (mediated public connection) is not understandable purely in media-specific terms. Certainly the principled practice of 'keeping up with the news' remains, as we have emphasised, of great importance, but mediated public connection is more likely to occur when people's disparate activities (as social being, audience member, and public actor) *intersect* in at least one common domain, whether this is local, national or, rarely, global.

At the same time we have found certain disconnections between talk and public action, and between civic engagement and a viable and supportive context for public action. Our inquiry is expanding inexorably to take in the wider conditions of democracy itself. It is to diarists' understanding of those larger issues – their overall orientation *as citizens* of a mediated society – that we turn in the next chapter.

Notes

1. Angela interestingly did not buy 'Catholic newspapers', 'as I feel that they are not particularly objective' (diary).
2. It is possible that the time-lack of some of the most civically active of our recruited diarists enhanced this absence: Eric was very active through his church on various civic and social issues, but his diary was brief and he only agreed to be interviewed once; another recruit, a community worker from the Southern Urban region, was too busy in his job to even start a diary. But the absence remains striking.
3. According to James Bohman the basic threshold of deliberative democracy is that 'each citizen [is] able to initiate deliberation and participate effectively in it' (1997: 333).
4. Some diarists had performed a number of these.
5. We would here exclude voting whose coordination with others is by convention.
6. Cf Couldry (2006a) for fuller discussion.
7. Cf Gamson on 'cynical chic' (1992: 82).

7
Democracy Seen from Afar

How did our diarists themselves describe their overall orientation to a world beyond the private? Specifically, how did they conceive of democracy in contemporary Britain and their position in it? In this chapter, we listen in more detail to diarists' voices on these fundamental questions.

In order to capture the range of diarists, we have selected five media world connectors (Henry, Kylie, Andrea, Samantha, Beccy), two public world connectors (Bill, Sheila) and one multiply connected diarist (Josh). The reason we have selected more media world connectors is because of the ambiguous relation their media connection may have to the public world (see Chapter 4): Beccy had no mediated public connection, because her media interests orientated her away from public issues, and Andrea and Samantha displayed this tendency in a weaker form.

Henry

Henry was a 52-year-old insurance underwriter living in a comfortable suburb of a major northern English city and married with teenage children. He described himself as a 'realist', whose expectations of the public world were limited because of low-level cynicism and general satisfaction with his own situation. He was, however, a heavy media consumer for whom media contributed importantly to the routine pleasures of everyday life.

Henry enjoyed both information and entertainment aspects of media, with regular television news-viewing complemented by film, comedies, the occasional soap opera and a little sport. Like many diarists, Henry could satisfy his appetite for media despite the considerable constraints of a busy work and family schedule (indeed habit was important in his media consumption: 'I suppose half your life is ritual, isn't it?'). But he went far beyond a superficial sampling of media, engaging fully (as his diary made clear) with the topics he encountered and actively seeking out sources of information on those in which he was interested. He demonstrated a clear sense of how the news media frame issues, and he was reflexive about how far into the multiple layers of available information he ventured: 'you can buy the *Sun* and read the headlines and then you can read an article that'll just be two or three lines. And you can go half way down with the *Mail* and the *Express*, and you can get more information'. Radio was particularly important for him in forming his opinions:

> I do listen to the radio a fair bit to be honest. Johnny Walker [drive-time talk and music show in Radio 2] . . . would chew the cud if you like with somebody for 10 or 15 minutes and get reasonably deep, so everybody could understand but they're throwing around opinions you see, and it's from these opinions that you form your own.

Sometimes he might also sample different newspapers 'to get a more balanced view or a different view' or to return briefly to 'the papers of my youth'. All this demonstrated a considerable degree of media literacy.

Henry also had an unproblematic socially-reinforced connection to a public world. He was loyal to his region – uniquely among our participants, he praised local hospitals – and had an awareness of how it fitted into the broader, national picture, to which he was also unproblematically oriented. He mentioned having debates about issues with family, friends and colleagues at work ('it's always a good debate').

Henry's mediated public connection offered him a consistent link to a public world, which fitted easily into his everyday routines and sense of enjoyment. He had no overbearing feeling of 'duty' to follow the public world; he did so because he liked to. Similarly, if he formed a view on an issue by weighing up media sources or debating it within his social network, what drove this was, it seemed, principally the pleasure of doing so. As a result, the absence of a link between Henry's mediated public connection and public action was simply not experienced by him as painful or problematic. Not that he lacked social capital or opportunities for action: he belonged to a photography club, and in his first interview recalled a situation where he could have been drawn into action in the context of a local interest group, but declined. His rationalisations of inaction appeared to mask no deeper disillusionment.

Henry was therefore a 'media world connector' whose connection took in both the entertainment side of media and the intellectual process of engaging with public issues from time to time. Henry's was an unconflicted form of engagement compatible with a traditional conception of the public sphere; he had an implicit sense that being engaged in a public world was both a good thing in general and personally satisfying, but without a practical conception of that world as a space in which he could personally act. Henry was more than able to present a subtle critique of contemporary democracy ('Yeah, a democracy where we're told what to do'), but this implied no impulsion to act nor any tension about missing possibilities for action. It would be misleading therefore to present his mediated public connection as anything other than satisfied.

Josh

Even more important than the distinction between those who thought British democracy was working well and those who perceived a democratic deficit is, within the latter category, the distinction between those who experienced this deficit as problematic and those who did not. Josh lived in the suburbs of another northern city, with his parents. He was studying architecture, and worked in an architectural firm alongside his studies. Whereas for Henry there was no obvious direction for developing his subtle criticism of British democracy, Josh was in no doubt about what would have to be different in order for democracy to work better.

Like Henry, Josh had a high level of media literacy and broad media consumption, from news to films, music, science- and design-related media. But Josh was closer to Jonathan in his highly directed use of the internet, skimming headlines on sites such as Yahoo or Reuters and following up through a variety of websites those stories which interested him. Josh used media to gather information to resolve contested issues in his own mind, self-consciously distinguishing himself from the average news consumer: 'don't really like it [Radio 1] because it's kind of news for idiots. I don't like the way they go and patronise you, break it all down'. More than just media literate, Josh had a sense of media as an industry: rare amongst the sample, he followed specific news agencies such as Reuters, which fitted with his overt goal of gathering information about subjects where he felt he lacked knowledge:

> I don't like being uninformed. . . . I was asked about the Euro and I didn't know. I felt stupid, although, you know, it's one thing out of many things that I get asked about . . . and I just hated, to not know. And I think that's the answer. I just don't like not knowing.

Reflected here is perhaps more than a sense of social pressure. He had, he said, recently developed a principled position, 'abandoning' his 'dream of becoming a millionaire and having a stupidly expensive car' and acquiring 'a bit more of a social conscience' which had forged his work interest in 'social housing and things like that'. Although expressed here in individual terms, this motivating principle was linked to his sense that opinion-forming on public issues should not be exercised in isolation. He felt the lack of a social context that supported his engagement with the public world: 'even down to my girlfriend actually and I can try and explain things to her . . . [but] she doesn't care, or she hates me watching the news, it bores her to tears . . . it frustrates me that people don't care what's going on around them'. In Josh's case we can justifiably talk of *disillusioned connection*.

Josh's disillusionment linked directly to his (frustrated) sense of how democracy should work. He defined democracy explicitly in terms of the public resolution of shared concerns: 'a democracy to me is when a decision needs making, you've got the balance between the speed of your response and . . . the quality of the response on the other side of it'. While understanding the restrictions in a representative democracy on the 'right to speak' on every issue, he distinguished between issues where that right is unimportant, and those – the Iraq war of 2003 – where not being able to speak up effectively mattered a great deal. Where, he said, 'we start losing family members', direct, immediate consultation (a plebiscite) is necessary: in having such an explicit account of how 'democracy' could function better, Josh differed from Jonathan, who shared the same concerns about 'the accountability and reliability of our own "democracy" ' (as Jonathan put it). Josh could articulate a practical perspective within which his frustrated mediated public connection made sense as a challenge to an unsatisfactory state of affairs, rather than remaining, like Jonathan's, merely frustrated. Significantly perhaps Josh completed his diary and met us for a second interview, whereas Jonathan did not.

Andrea

For other diarists, however, an absence not only of action but of strong public connection – mediated or otherwise – was not experienced as a source of everyday tension at all. Andrea was 25 and lived with her partner and their baby in an area of the Midlands in transition between being rural and suburban. Hardly alienated, Andrea was best characterised in terms of *satisfied disconnection*.

Andrea worked as a children's nurse, a role which gave her the potential for a public voice, or at least expert position, on health and related social/practical issues. For her, media was principally relaxation (she discounted her consumption of 'trashy' magazines and soaps, but saw herself as being 'as guilty as everyone else' in this). Andrea took in news on a regular but limited basis, seeing traditional politics as remote from her world in terms of both relevance and geography:[1]

> it just seems like it's a little bit of another world. You know, they're supposed to be making decisions on behalf of all of us but it doesn't generally seem that way. You know, they make the decisions, it doesn't matter you know, obviously they consider the consequences but other things sometimes generally happen... it seems like we're a long way away from it.

Note however the strong sense here of *collective* disconnection ('on behalf of *all of us*', '*we're* a long way from it') from institutional centres of power which does not imply an individual disconnection from the public at large. Andrea felt justified in her distance from 'the information *they* give us'. But this collective disconnection was not, for Andrea, linked to any positive frame within which public issues could be actively interpreted; Andrea had no stable, external frame of reference for making meaning out of the news.

Andrea's sense of distance was rationalised to some degree by her strongly and traditionally gendered domestic environment where men, but not women, had the principal role of keeping up with the news. Her partner brought a paper home from work and directed her to what he perceived to be important stories (as discussed in Chapter 5). News discussion in her wider family was similarly gendered:

> if I see my mum, [it's] have you heard this, have you heard that about local issues. Whereas my dad over the dinner table, if we're there for Sunday lunch or something... it's more likely to be political issues between him and my partner you know, just completely disagree and like most families.

Andrea's family – which across her diary and interviews provided her key frame of reference – offered a moral economy in which mediated public connection worked at a general level but without imposing an individual duty on her. If she followed particular news items, it was on the basis of personal motivation (for example, the debate over the MMR vaccine that linked to her work).

Andrea acknowledged opportunities for action (through her nursing union) but dismissed them: 'I've always kind of been in that mind, don't get involved.... if I did, I don't feel it would make any difference. [Be]cause... there's a wider issue there... with money and the government... all relating back to political issues'. Note that it was the *presence* of a wider issue – the presence, potentially, of 'public connection' – that in this passage seems to turn Andrea off. For Andrea, her weak mediated public connection was entirely unproblematic and consistent with her enjoyment from time to time of the collective dimensions of media (*Big Brother*, celebrity culture).

Kylie

Kylie[2] by contrast was distinctive for being disorientated in her mediated public connection, and in a way that was painful. Kylie was a 24-year-old single mother living on a run-down council estate in urban South London. She lacked Josh's ability to articulate what was wrong with her public connection, and indeed the 'problem' was subtle: for she operated within a strong moral framework that motivated her to care about public issues, but lacked the opportunity or knowledge to 'convert' this into any form of public action.

Kylie's media consumption, like Patrick's (discussed in Chapter 5), was motivated above all by the value of having 'the facts' about issues. She watched documentaries frequently, fitted regular television news into her childcare routine (her child was pre-school), and read both local and national papers. She had a clear sense of the media's responsibility to bear witness, regardless of how distressing a story might be:

> Yeah, I think it is important they make us aware of what's going on otherwise no one's gonna change... there's no point in putting all nice things in the paper if it's not the truth... you need to know the truth and that's it. Even if it's hurting and it's horrible you need to know.

In her diaries Kylie applied this position mainly to humanitarian issues or the war in Iraq, and strikingly drew a sharp line between these issues and her complete lack of interest in 'politics': 'I just don't really understand it and therefore it just doesn't interest me. I haven't really got an opinion on anything to do with politics.'

At the same time, she expressed the value of deliberation in forming opinions about issues:

> You would never [without discussion] see things in another, another opinion. Me and my friend got into a row the other day actually, we do a lot of that when we start talking...it was about the war and I said something and she said no [name] that's not...and afterwards I sat back and I thought, oh yeah, I suppose. As I say I don't really know much about the war but what I was saying was totally just wrong until she explained to me.

Similarly media news was implicitly social in its relevance to her. In an interview she vividly described her reaction to a *Daily Mirror* story some years before of an orphaned child abandoned in China, but it is her social use of the press cutting that was most striking:

> when I read it, it made me cry...I sobbed for days. And I carried this piece of paper around with [me], and everywhere I go, I showed it to people – it was so – so upsetting. And everyone that I show it to – they was disgusted with it.

Kylie had a strong moral sense of why 'public connection' mattered – 'I've always felt that anyway that you need to know what's going on all over the world' – linked to the 'global compassion' narrative of international news. Media were crucial in sustaining her public engagement in the face of personal isolation: without the media, she said, 'we'd never know anything of what's going on around us' (in this she was similar to another working-class diarist, Arvind, whose circumstances, in his case disability, restricted his movements). But the world to which media oriented her was not articulated to any possibilities of public action,[3] nor did she know where to turn to make those links; this is why we call her public connection *disorientated*. Strikingly also, she didn't vote; she saw no point ('can't change anything, can I?'). As a result her mediated public connection, although strong in itself, was frustrated in terms of its wider effectiveness and meaningfulness.

Beccy

Beccy shared Kylie's lack of involvement in public action but felt self-sufficient and largely untroubled by this. Beccy was 27 and worked in marketing; she lived with her boyfriend in a small house in a comfortable northern suburb. Media did not connect her to a public world, but for reasons quite different from those which made Andrea's public connection weak. Beccy was content with her distance from any form of public world, and that disconnection was individualised, not collective: the public world was simply marginal to her individual life.

Beccy's media use was broad, fairly superficial and fragmented. She watched television when there was nothing else happening, 'flicked through' a newspaper (though she wouldn't buy one herself), enjoyed magazines, and surfing news and enterntainment stories at Ananova.com and nme.com. Not surprisingly, she sometimes reported having no recollection of what news stories she had viewed or read the week before. Like Andrea, Beccy described her partner as encouraging her to be more interested in news. Much of Beccy's media consumption was social in purpose (for example surfing the Ananova website at work). Her attitude to celebrity culture was cynical but relaxed: 'the public are... always gonna want to know more and the public are going to buy *Heat* magazine no matter what trash is in it because you know you just get fed the stuff and you just take it in'.

At the same time Beccy was highly articulate and the context of writing the diary led her to become (within the space of the diary, although not more widely) troubled at whether her distance from the public world was justifiable. She described herself as unable to sleep one night during the diary period: 'I can't resolve it in my mind how, even how I feel about it, whether I want to watch something that I don't like [she had just been discussing famine in Africa], or whether I should or whether I turn it off and go and read a magazine, I don't know' (diary). Over time, and particularly in interviews, she came to articulate a justification for her distance in some interesting ways. One rationalisation was in terms of individual choice (already discussed in Chapter 6) based in a strong validation of the 'private' *over* the 'public' ('for me, and a lot of people I know, you only need to be motivated to do something if it encroaches in your own individual world'). In part, she could explain this in terms of pure practicality, given the stresses of her work life:

You need to be able to turn the tv off, as awful as it is... if you've had a bad day at work... you've got to do whatever, you know, it takes... to make you go back there the next day, you've got to go to the gym and help you wake up... you can't feel obliged to sit down and watch the news if it's gonna depress you if you're already a bit stressed. . . . I think you've got a responsibility to yourself to sort of pick yourself up but I don't know if that's right or not.

Most interesting here is the way that Beccy's sense of 'responsibility' was defined *against* any notion of public connection.

Not surprisingly that position was accompanied by considerable cynicism about the effectiveness of democracy ('I would suspect that we live in less of a democracy than we would like to think we do . . . it's all about the pretence of us living in a democracy'). But her position was not entirely cynical and could also be justified in 'rational choice' terms:

there's a certain route you have to follow, and you know, I'm so busy . . . to earn the money to pay for my house just to live, and you know - if I wanted to make a difference – there's what, a couple of parties you can choose from, and they're all offering the same things at the end of the day.

However an interesting but unresolved dimension of Beccy's (absent) mediated public connection was that at certain points she talked about situations completely unconnected to politics using language that was quasi-political, as discussed in Chapter 6. In spite of the enthusiasm she could feel for such actions, and in spite of the connections beyond the individual they implied (whether to a community of viewers or to a policy environment), Beccy nonetheless saw no connection between actions in her own 'private' (social, vocational) world, and the possibility of acting more 'publicly' as a citizen.

Samantha

If Beccy's disconnection was relaxed and stably embedded in everyday routine, Samantha's weak connection was very differently experienced. Samantha was a beautician living in a run-down part of a southern English city. She was married without children, and worked up to sixty hours a week in her salon (she was also studying for a part-time qualification related to her work).

Given her hectic schedule, Samantha's media consumption was understandably aimed at relaxation (films, comedy and music), though, as we have seen with two other diarists, her partner directed her towards particular news stories and explained political issues such as the Budget. Working in a salon, she either absorbed a good deal of media coverage indirectly, or had no choice but to be up on the latest celebrity gossip:

in the salon a lot of the ladies, oh did you see this on TV, or have
you seen this in this magazine, did you know Jordan's done this and
Jade's pregnant, things like that, so it's sort of building up something
to talk to with the clients as well.[4]

The issues covered in salon talk tended to the lighter side of the media
spectrum, though more 'serious' issues (such as local planning disputes
affecting clients) were by no means precluded. Her work space, while
not apparently giving her the chance to voice her own opinions much,
did at least expose her to current issues including local ones. However,
Samantha was acutely aware of the limits to the information that she and
the general public had available to them: 'we don't seem to be . . . aware
of everything we need, I don't think the message is put across. I think
we're sometimes fed what people what you to hear, what people want
you to see' (diary). She was conscious of her own lack of political knowledge, and as a result indeed did not feel *entitled* to vote. Samantha had
opinions about politics, but they were crossed by a sense of hopelessness,
especially in her diaries written in the run-up to the European elections
of June 2004: 'why should I have all these unanswered questions, I live
in this country and what Tony Blair decides to do does affect me so
therefore I should have the information' (diary). Unlike Beccy, then,
Samantha was consistently troubled by her own lack of connection.

Samantha commented frequently that she wished she knew more
about current events; her disenchantment from British democracy was
considerably more impassioned than Beccy's. In an interesting parallel
to Josh, she suggested replacing the party system with a more immediate
form of participation: 'we should have a big team of people selected
from the public every year that just voted' (with television providing the
key form of interactivity between those selected and those they represented: her parallel seemed to be *Big Brother*). Unlike other diarists such
as Lesley who simply took their disconnection for granted, Samantha
developed her thinking from first interview through the diary phase. And
while the diary encouraged her to present her views on certain issues,
the tension which increasingly emerged (over how far the quality of
her public connection mattered to her) was part of a longer trajectory:
she had, she said, been following public issues more closely since she
acquired new financial responsibilities after leaving home. The discussion in her salon provided a context for thinking about public issues, as
did media, but insufficient guidance ('we all seem to know a little bit . . .
but not enough'). Towards the end of the diary period her commentary

became intense and concerned, even if disturbingly lacking in secure information:

> Ah, voting week is drawing closer and I still don't know who to vote for. Very busy at work, so not much time to research therefore relying on TV and radio. I have seen a few broadcasts for the British National Party and quite liked the sound of them, it was simple and got the message across quickly, No to the Euro, No to European government and what a mess current government have made. All sounds good to me. My clients seem to be voting liberal, when the topic comes up at work, those seems to be where the vote lies probably due to local issues as opposed to National. (diary)

Samantha's trajectory was inconclusive, and the consequences for her long-term mediated public connection after the diary phase unclear (she didn't meet us again). But she illustrated well the distinction between disconnection which is more or less stable (Beccy) and weak connection whose strains may over the long term motivate people towards engagement in unpredictable political directions.

Bill

We have so far been concentrating either on different forms of disconnection (whether problematic or unproblematic) or various levels of media world connection (the exception was Josh who is best seen as multiply connected, although he was a complex case). Already in these cases, we have found some unease about the state of British democracy and the wider meaningfulness of mediated public connection. Such doubts were most acute among other diarists who were unambiguously public world connectors.

Bill was a retired managing director who lived in a comfortable rural village in the Midlands. Bill's relative detachment from the mediated public world was borne out of self-sufficiency rather than alienation. Like Edward, Bill's high occupational status and the opportunities for voluntary work (as school governor, magistrate, and so on) this afforded him in retirement enabled him to look on media's coverage of the public world from some distance. He relished engaging with issues and 'agitating' others into debate (for example, friends or colleagues at the magistrates' court): 'I don't think there are any subjects that I would not talk to my friends and colleagues about and in fact sometimes I think, not exactly mischievously but I perhaps at times I'm a little provocative in some discussion'. His media consumption was regular (a daily newspaper, at least one TV news bulletin, limited other television) and highly directed. Given the public context of his voluntary work, and these regular media habits, Bill's mediated public connection was very stable. His concern, however, was that others lacked this connection and (rather like Beccy!) were relaxed about that absence:

> there is this personal isolationism that I keep tripping over. My wife and I had dinner with some friends on Saturday evening and [name] is retired, a little bit younger than I am, does some part-time consultancy and I said to him, oh ever thought of being a magistrate. And he [said] no, I'm not interested. No, don't want to know anything about it. Okay, fine. But then the conversation developed and again, not interested in anything outside his personal sphere.

Implied here and elsewhere in his interviews and diaries was a conception of the public world in which the 'civic' was, or should be, connected to the public or the political. Indeed Bill linked the decay of civic participation just noted to a wider social and political failure:

> I actually believe we've got the society that, not that we necessarily deserve, but that we choose to have and I think a lot of people today are unhappy with the society that we've got. I'm unhappy about it. I choose to try and do something to alter it.

The possibility of public action was, for Bill, a given. His attention turned to the practical obstacles to action or deliberation. This was where, for him, media entered the equation, since, like others, Bill demanded of media, and government (when it interacts with media), transparency and the ability to make publicly available 'the facts'.

In Bill's view media were crucial because of other people's (not his own) dependency on them: 'the only real conduit that the vast majority of people in the UK have in obtaining information about government policies, government actions is either newspaper or television.' Distancing oneself from media (in our terms, 'weak connection') was simply not a responsible option, yet to Bill's surprise people were increasingly doing it: 'I take this from, only from the sort of casual conversation, I say . . . did you see so and so in the paper yesterday? Oh, I don't read the papers [any more] . . . I think, oh why's that? Or one hears the comment oh, I only read the sports page these days.'

Bill was particularly troubled by media's interplay with politics ('there is too much collusion between our political masters and some of the media') and uniquely among our diary sample was aware of and concerned about the adequacy of the British system for regulating the press. Bill was by no means the only diarist to criticise government 'spin' (a consistent theme of media debates about the New Labour government) but he was the most eloquent:

> essentially they [media] should all be reporting the facts in a manner that puts that particular subject in its true, honest perspective. By definition a spin doctor is trying to alter that. So the fact that we have spin doctors suggests to me that... it is now an accepted political ploy to take hard facts and to sharpen them or exaggerate them or blur them or diminish them or whatever... which is dishonest reporting.

Instead he wanted 'a greater, more transparent separation between' media and politics. The lack of this in his view encouraged people's general turn away from politics and current events.

Sheila

If Bill's highly secure mediated public connection was troubled, this was even more acute with Sheila. Sheila did not have Bill's sense of distance from the mediated public world, and exemplified well the tension that can develop in that relationship. She was 47 years old and worked as a senior public health nurse. Her news consumption was both broad and heavy: she took in several radio stations' bulletins, usually at least one television news programme daily, local news and multiple newspapers at the weekend. Sheila saw her media consumption as distinguishing her from others, by its breadth (her ability to start the day with either Radio 1 or Radio 4!) and her skill at negotiating different media sources: 'I can be quite discerning about what I take on from the media if I choose to be'. Her growing sense of sophistication in relation to media developed, she said, through her mid-life retraining in health education. Her reactions to media content tended to be both immediate and considered, based in pleasure at media but also a strong sense of media's social responsibility. The latter she linked back to watching the soaps with her children: 'we actually quite often had a family debate about the value of soaps to life in general and how they often deal with moral issues'.

Without Bill's distance from the news, Sheila was affected personally by disturbing or upsetting stories (the Abu Ghraib jail revelations,
beheadings and kidnaps in Iraq): 'I think in retrospect, I was getting too
involved and... I didn't like what it was doing to me but the whole
Iraq thing I just got, how can I describe it? I got too involved with it'.
This intense relation with news events during the project also ended
her diary after six weeks, although as she made clear later this was
certainly not because of lack of interest. When she reflected later in
2004 on her abrupt end to her diary, she criticised herself for having
been confused about an issue she had now resolved in her mind: she
had come to realise that she could both be highly critical of media
and accept that as a citizen she was dependent on media coverage of
important but distant events. She evolved towards the view, like Bill,
that withdrawal from media was not an acceptable response to this
contradiction.

Another reason for Sheila's intense reflexivity about her personal relationship with media's coverage of public events was the nature of her
work. Sheila's work as a public health nurse gave her immense personal
satisfaction and also status as an authority on health matters. Unlike
with Beccy, who saw no links between the media aspects of her job and
her own relationship to media, work intensified Sheila's mediated public
connection in two ways. First, at the practical level, the prominence of
a particular health issue in the media would influence how many calls
she received about it. Second, her own knowledge about health issues
covered extensively in the media allowed her to comment on the vera-
city of that coverage, and take a view on how far media fulfilled their
responsibility to report accurately:

I keep coming back to it but the MMR [vaccine scare]... was a good
example of the media giving half a story, people making a decision
which would affect their child's health and possible life on some, a
small amount of information. They [patients] sort of thought they'd
researched it because they'd seen another television programme or
they'd seen an article in the paper which agreed with that. Some of
them then went onto the Internet and found sites that supported
that argument. So they'd looked at different sort of media, but all
on the same thing.... And you know... I feel the media have some
responsibility for that. So that's an example I do know about because
I sort of dealt with it a lot in my work and have to sort of fight the
media as in fight the view they've left behind.

Sheila's concern was not at the absolute unavailability of health information ('[people] think there's information withheld. I don't believe there is. It is out there') but at people's lack of skill in finding and assessing accurate information. This led to some broader concerns with the media process that we want finally to consider.

Shared concerns

Both Bill and Sheila exhibited a high degree of reflexivity which meant that their position in relation to the 'public world' was subtle, complex, and always shaped by their questioning of their own public connection comprised and the quality of their relationship to the public world. Sheila's own view of democracy was informed by her own passion for countryside issues such as the hunting ban (then not yet law: she commented at length on the prospects for the countryside movement as a whole) but it was a bleak one nonetheless: 'I used to be quite a believer in democracy. I'm not so sure these days and I'm probably as suspicious of politicians as I am of the media I think. I think a lot of it is a game' (Midlands rural focus group).

While the sense that politicians did not deal with the issues that are most relevant to people was found more or less consistently across the diarist population, what was interesting in this and other cases ware the reasons given for what diarists perceived as the growing distance of politics from people's everyday concerns. Several diarists invoked increasing individualisation (the decline of 'community': Kathleen) or an increasingly 'selfish' society (Stuart, Christine, Jane). In the focus group they attended, Bill and Sheila also talked about the decline of party politics and the role of the media. While diarists such as Christine spoke about the negative effects of the media in terms of reducing the amount of time that people spend with their families and neighbours, for Sheila the principal effect of the media was broader, to contribute to distrust in all public figures:

> what is the truth? . . . I don't think I know any more, from either the media or the government . . . if we think they're an honest guy, what's the other story, what are they covering up or where are they trying to steer it.

For Sheila, this was related to a broader disconnection between the public and those in authority – she included media in this category – itself linked to a loss of a common frame of reference based on values:

'depending on which publication you're watching or reading or listening to, there seems to be very little in the way of ethics or morals'.

Bill's concerns, by contrast, were more explicitly in political terms, although they had moral implications too. Bill expressed concern at a widespread laziness in challenging the way politics and the public world had developed:

> We want to be entertained, we don't want aircraft flying over our backyard and we're happy to do something about that . . . but we're not as a nation I don't think really interested in correcting what to me are some of the greater evils like this too cosy relationship between government and the media. . . . There's an alarming degree of apathy I suspect and I don't see it getting any better.

He offered an interesting if alarming historical parallel with Germany's 1920s Weimar Republic from which Nazism emerged: 'this hedonistic, anything goes, no real rules or regulations [situation], so if a strong leader . . . a charismatic leader suddenly appeared there could be a flocking to him. Now hopefully it would be a benevolent dictator and not an evil dictator'.

When those who are intensely engaged with the public world are so pessimistic about the future of democratic engagement, we need surely to listen to their voices.

Conclusion

In this chapter we have opened up so far as possible the complex contrasts across our diarists sample. There are no simple ideal types of mediated public connection, but rather a set of overlapping patterns: patterns of both satisfaction and unease. An emerging theme with some diarists has been a concern at the relationship between media and democracy, and the extent to which British democracy is currently working effectively. In the next chapter we turn to a more classic means for researching political engagement: the survey, in the form of the Public Connection Survey conducted in June 2005.

Notes

1. Interestingly this sense of distance was shared by others from the same region, as became clear in the related focus group: for example, 'I have a suspicion

though that if I lived in Lambeth I'd still feel a hundred miles away from Parliament' (Bill).

2. For a more detailed analysis of Kylie, see Couldry *et al.* (forthcoming).

3. Cf Lembo (2000: 239) on working-class US television viewers who are situated within the logic of images but 'outside the logic of social action depicted in [those] images'.

4. Jordan and Jade (Goody) were in 2004 and remain in 2006 well known celebrities in Britain. Jordan raised and Jade acquired her profile through reality TV, by appearing in *I'm a Celebrity Get Me Out of Here* and *Big Brother* respectively.

8
Engagement and Mediation: Findings from the Public Connection Survey

Introduction

We have explored when, how and why people have an 'orientation to a public world where matters of shared concern are, or at least should in principle be, addressed' (cf. Chapter 1). People's diaries suggest that they are often oriented to the public or civic, variously defined, in ways that depend on the context. This orientation towards public connection is strongly embedded in media consumption, especially, but not only, of news. But the links to political participation – as addressed by political science, and as worried over by policy makers and governments, require further exploration, particularly given the 'missing links' identified in Chapter 6. The very scarcity and contextual sensitivity of such links, from daily routines to political interest, from civic engagement and talk about politics to public action, makes the identification of simple patterns difficult. In this chapter, we analyse the Public Connection Survey to examine these patterns further, relating media consumption to public connection defined broadly and to political participation more specifically.

Traditionally, public opinion surveys are used by political scientists to measure various indicators of participation: voting, other forms of civic engagement, trust (in political institutions and, sometimes, in the media), political interest and social capital. While surveys cannot easily capture the complex and contingent nature of public connection as explored in the everyday lives of our diarists, they can examine the patterns among multiple variables, and assess their distribution across the population. Statistical analysis permits systematic examination of any one variable – say, voting – while controlling for the influence of others (e.g. gender, age and socioeconomic status).

The Public Connection survey was administered by telephone to a nationally representative, quota sample of the population of Great Britain (18+) (see Appendix IIB). Conducted during June 2005, this was a few months after we completed the diary research and, it turned out, a few weeks after national elections in which Tony Blair's Labour Government narrowly won a third term in office. The survey questionnaire (see Appendix IIA) combined questions on public and political interest, knowledge and action with questions on media access, use and evaluation, so as to examine their interrelations: does the survey, we ask, shed light on the links between media consumption and public connection?

Declining public participation

Of various indicators showing declining public participation, electoral turnout is crucial. In the United Kingdom, this decline is evident in local, national and European elections. Turnout for the 2001 UK general election was 59 per cent, the lowest for any post-war UK general election, and at 61 per cent the turnout at the 2005 election was only marginally higher. The Electoral Commission (2005b) showed that age is a significant factor, with over 65s some 25 per cent more likely to vote than those under 35. Gender made no overall difference in the 2005 election (Electoral Commission 2005b), though women aged 18–24 have sometimes been regarded as the least likely demographic group to vote (Hansard 2001). In the USA,[1] national voter turnout at federal elections has fallen from 63 per cent in 1960 to 55 per cent in 2004. In the Netherlands, similarly, voter turn out fell from 96 per cent in 1959 to 80 per cent in 2003 (Statistiek 2003).

In explaining these trends, some question the public's interest in politics. The UK's Electoral Commission's (2005a) *Audit of Political Engagement* shows a slight decline in those who are very or fairly interested in politics from 60 per cent in 1973 to 53 per cent in 2004, though no subsequent fall is evident (Electoral Commission 2008). However, the British Social Attitude survey shows no real decline in interest over the past two decades.[2] More striking is the decline in public trust in established political institutions, both in the UK (Kavanagh 1989; Topf 1989) and elsewhere (BBC/Reuters/Media Center Poll 2006, Inglehart 1977; Norris 1999; Newton and Norris 2000). When asked, 'how much do you trust British governments of any party to place the needs of the nation above the interests of their own political party?', the proportion of respondents who 'just about always' or 'most of the time' trust British governments fell from 39 per cent in 1974 to 16 per cent in 2000,[3] before rising slightly to 24 per cent in 2005 (National Centre for Social Research 2006). Arguably, this distrust is restricted to 'traditional' or party politics, for there is evidence of growing participation in alternative forms of action. Political action increased from the mid-1980s to 2000, with a peak in political involvement in the early 1990s.[4] For example, in 1986, 34 per cent of people had signed a petition, rising to 53 per cent in 1991 before falling to 42 per cent in 2000. Just 11 per cent of people had contacted a member of parliament (MP) in 1986, compared with 17 per cent in 1991 and 16 per cent in 2000. Interestingly too, participating in a protest or demonstration steadily increased from 6 per cent in 1986 to 10 per cent in 2000, the international protest against the invasion of Iraq on 15 February 2003 being, perhaps, the most notable recent example of this.[5]

Political efficacy (Inglehart 1977), termed 'subjective competence' by Almond and Verba (1963), may also play a role, for people may be unlikely to take action unless they believe they can 'make a difference'. Mori's (2004) Rules of Engagement report showed that while 67 per cent of the population agreed that 'I want to have a say in how the country is run', only 27 per cent agreed that 'I have a say in how the country is run', pointing to a crucial gap between political interest and efficacy (see also Bromley *et al.* 2004; Electoral Commission 2008). Mori's multiple regression analysis identified the following predictors of the propensity to vote: efficacy (e.g. getting involved makes a difference), claimed political knowledge, age, passive involvement (signing a petition, boycotting a product, discussing issues), satisfaction with politics, being female, contacting an MP/councillor etc, and being in full-time work.

So, although voting is declining, it seems the public cannot simply be termed uninterested, naively trusting or apathetic. Sustained interest and political action but declining trust and low efficacy may suggest a shift in public preference from representative (or institutionally centralised) to a more participatory (or devolved) democracy. Or perhaps these different measures derive from distinct population subgroups – some being trusting, others lacking efficacy, still others taking action, for example. We pursue these and related questions in this chapter. But most significantly, we link these questions to everyday practices of media consumption. For, although often neglected in surveys concerned with participation,[6] a growing body of theory and evidence points to the importance of media in relation to public connection and political participation.

Traditional accounts of participation: voting, political interest, political trust

Beginning with the most conventional, and arguably the most important, measure of participation, we note that the Public Connection Survey shows a fairly high level of voting, with 82% saying that they 'generally' vote in national elections.[7] However, there is considerable variation, for voting is strongly associated with age, with younger voters being rather ambivalent about voting and the oldest groups being much more committed voters. Gender makes little difference to voting, although men claim more interest in politics than women. Socioeconomic status (SES[8]) has a curvilinear relation to voting, with the upper middle class (AB) and the lowest group (E) more likely to vote (see Table 8.1).

Almost as many (65 per cent) claim an interest in politics[9], and the relation between voting and SES is mirrored in the different groups' levels of political interest. Consistent with their greater likelihood of voting, older people also claim more interest in politics than younger people. Unsurprisingly, political interest is strongly associated with voting. Political trust,[10] by contrast, is evenly distributed across the

Table 8.1 Voting, interest in politics and political trust, by demographic factors (% agree/strongly agree)

		Voting	Political interest	Trust politicians do deal with what matters	Trust politicians to tell truth	Trust government to do what is right
Gender	Male	81	67*	45	22	43
	Female	83	64*	45	20	45
Age	18–24	63**	61**	45	20	43
	25–34	72**	61**	44	16	44
	35–44	78**	58**	51	23	46
	45–54	86**	62**	40	20	40
	55–64	93**	78**	46	22	46
	65+	94**	73**	45	24	43
SES	AB	86*	79**	41	18	40**
	C1	81*	63**	43	18	38**
	C2	78*	59**	49	24	50**
	D	77*	52**	40	18	41**
	E	86*	63**	52	29	53**

Note: Public Connection Survey (2005) of British adults aged 18+ ($N = 1013$). Asterisks indicate ANOVA significance of difference in means of five-point scales, **$p < 0.01$, *$p < 0.05$.

different social groups, with the average response indicating a fair amount of distrust overall – only 45 per cent trust politicians to deal with the things that matter and only 21 per cent trust them to tell the truth. Trust is weakly (but positively) associated with voting but, interestingly, not at all associated with political interest.[11]

Since there is growing – although contested – evidence that social capital plays a role in explaining participation (Putnam 2000; Hooghe and Stolle 2003; Field 2005; though see Fine 2001), we examined this in terms of measures of local involvement:[12] one in 5 (18 per cent) report playing an active role in local, voluntary or political organisations, and a quarter (28 per cent – more for older people) say they are involved in voluntary work. Further, political interest, political trust and voting are all significantly associated with social capital variables and political efficacy, supporting the claim that these variables are important. Although the interrelations among these variables[13] (see Table 8.2) afford several explanations, it is likely that the direction of causality is, in most cases, bidirectional: for example, political interest may sustain social capital, here measured in terms of local involvement, and local involvement may, in turn, generate political interest.

The measures of political efficacy[14] reveal some challenges for public connection, for there is a notable gap between feeling informed (with 81 per cent saying they know where to get the information they need – more older and middle class people) and feeling involved (with only

Table 8.2 Correlations among public connection variables

	Social capital	Political efficacy		
	Measured by a scale based on three items on local involvement	'You feel you can influence decisions in your area'	'You know where to go to find the information that you need'	'You can affect things by getting involved in the issues you care about'
Political interest	0.20 **	0.14 **	0.18 **	0.16 **
Voting	0.18 **	0.12 **	0.18 **	0.12 **
Political trust	0.07 *	0.14 **	0.07 *	0.18 **

Note: *Public Connection Survey* (2005) of British adults aged 18+ ($N = 1007$). Asterisks indicate the statistical significance of the coefficients with $p < 0.05^*$, $p < 0.01^{**}$.

39 per cent saying they can influence decisions in their area, and 55 per cent feeling that 'people like us' have no say in what the government does), though 68 per cent felt they could make a difference if they really got involved. Three quarters (73 per cent) say they sometimes feel strongly about something but do not know what to do about it, suggesting that the opportunity structures for action are lacking.

Since there is little variation in trust, we decided to examine further these two measures of political participation – one 'hard' (likelihood of voting) and one 'soft' (interest in politics). The analytic strategy was first to test the explanatory value of measures traditionally considered by political science – demographics, social capital, efficacy, and so forth and then, later, to test whether media consumption adds to that explanation. Thus, we conducted a series of multiple regression analyses, first entering the demographic variables as the first step in an explanation, then adding in subsequent variables in blocks.[15]

Some 11 per cent of the variation in likelihood of voting was explained by entering just the demographic variables, with age (older) and SES (higher) contributing significantly to the regression equation (see also Scheufele and Nisbet 2002), while gender played no role (see Table 8.3). In the next step, we added in measures of, trust and efficacy, along with our social capital measure (local involvement). This significantly increased the variance explained in voting ($R^2 = 16$ per cent), contra Henry Milner (2002) who claims not only that there is no correlation between interest and trust but also that trust is unrelated to voting.[16] In sum, demographic, social capital, trust and efficacy variables altogether account for about one sixth of the variance in voting, with the latter 'social cohesion' variables (see Misztal 1996) adding substantially to the explanation over and above a demographic/structural account.[17]

Arguably, political interest is itself in need of explanation. In a second multiple regression analysis (see Table 8.3), gender (male), age (older) and SES (higher) together accounted for only 7 per cent of the variance in political interest. In the second step, an additional 7 per cent of the variance was explained by adding social capital, political efficacy and social expectations.[18] This again suggests that social capital and political efficacy matter, perhaps resulting from but more likely also underpinning political interest. Moreover, while political trust plays no role here, by contrast with its role in voting, it emerges that social expectations – being expected by peers to 'keep up' and to 'be in touch' – are important in accounting for political interest.[19] In short, it seems that

Table 8.3 Regression equation, predicting voting and political interest

	Voting	Political interest
Age	0.33**	0.15**
SES	−0.10**	−0.14**
Political trust	0.10**	n.s.
Social capital (local involvement)	0.11**	0.18**
Social expectations	n.s.	0.19**
'You can affect things by getting involved in issues you care about' (political efficacy)	0.08**	0.10**
'You know where to go to find out the information that you need' (political efficacy)	0.08**	0.07*
R^2	0.16	0.14

Note: *Public Connection Survey* (2005) of British adults aged 18+ ($N = 1007$). Asterisks indicate the statistical significance of the coefficients with $p < 0.05^*$, $p < 0.01^{**}$.

political interest rests on social norms and practices as well as personal beliefs or motivations (see also Chapter 5).[20] Indeed, more than half say that their friends (66 per cent) and people at work (54 per cent) expect them to know what's going on in the world – men and older people particularly feel this.

All this points to the need for a broader approach to public connection, especially since, as our diarists have made clear, public connection is more complex than voting or other direct expressions of political interest. We have also argued in the previous chapters, that media have a central, if complex role to play in mediating public connection. This we examine next.

Linking media consumption to public participation

Do media undermine public connection, supporting what Pippa Norris (2000) terms the 'media malaise' thesis? Or can they facilitate it in one form or another? Commonly, television is blamed for filling the audiences' time and so distracting them from civic involvement, while newspapers are lauded for informing the public (or bemoaned for 'selling out' from their traditional role in the fourth estate). But this is a simplification, undervaluing the quality of television news (particularly in countries with a strong public service tradition), and perhaps overvaluing the quality of the press (particularly in countries with a strong tabloid tradition). As Neuman *et al.* (1992: 113) found, 'television was more successful in communicating information about topics that were of low salience to the audience, while print media were superior in conveying information about topics that had high salience' (see also Robinson and Levy 1986). Since the public sphere comprises a mix of topics of differential salience, different media must surely be expected to play differentiated roles. What about other news sources? Radio featured strongly in our diarists' daily routines, and the internet represents a new and potentially transformative source of information, though others express concern at its growing commercialisation and mainstreaming (McChesney 2000).

Thus we distinguish, first, the media conceived as a distraction or time-filler, preventing the activities required to sustain political participation, from the media as a shared source of civic and political information, setting the public agenda and ensuring an informed electorate (see Chapter 2). We would distinguish, second, overall media consumption from news consumption in particular. And last, we distinguish different forms of media – television, radio, press, internet. Together, this suggests several hypotheses. The time displacement hypothesis focuses on overall time spent with the media, assuming a zero-sum game in time expenditure (although see Robinson and Godbey 1997), and conceiving of media as displacing both direct political participation and the more informal activities that sustain social capital – as Robert Putnam (2000) argues, television is the 'main culprit' in the decline of social capital. The 'dumbing down' hypothesis instead points to a critique of the quality of media content (the commodification or infotainment values of news, for example, or the degradation of political into celebrity culture).[21] A third hypothesis, itself a version of the 'knowledge gap' hypothesis (Bonfadelli 2002) stems from Norris's notion of a 'virtuous circle' of civic information disproportionately benefiting the already-informed, the focus being less on overall media consumption than on engagement with news in particular (see also Ward *et al.* 2005 in relation to the internet).[22] These hypotheses may be combined, though they are not necessarily consonant – the same news is seen by some to undermine public connection (because it is commodified) and by others to enhance it (at least for the already-advantaged).

The Public Connection Survey disaggregated different aspects of media consumption into the following elements: (1) media consumption – measured as overall time spent with media;[23] (2) news consumption – measured as frequency of engagement with the news media;[24] and (3) news engagement – measured as people's motives or reasons for engaging or not with the news (as discussed in Chapter 5, see also Katz *et al.* 1973).[25] These three questions were asked of each medium in turn (see survey questions in Appendix IIA).

Undoubtedly, television is the most widely engaged with medium, watched every day by 96 per cent of people. It is also the most time-consuming medium, occupying, on average, 1–3 hours of people's daily leisure time. Radio, listened to by 4 in 5 people, takes up just half an hour, at least as a primary activity, a similar amount of time being spent on newspapers (by 3 in 4 people) and reading for leisure (by 2 in 3). The distinctive character of different media means that using one medium is not necessarily associated with use of another: interestingly, time spent watching television is correlated positively with reading the newspaper ($r = 0.102$, $p < 0.01$) but negatively with listening to radio ($r = -0.082$, $p < 0.01$) and going online ($r = -0.111$, $p < 0.01$).

Significantly, media use – like political participation – is stratified, with television watched more by older and working class people (see Table 8.4). Older groups spend longer reading the newspaper and books, but markedly less time on the internet.[26] Middle class people spend more time with radio and reading books, while lower SES households spend more time with television but less with the internet. Reading (but not broadcasting) is also stratified by gender, with men spending longer reading newspapers and women spending longer reading books for leisure. Despite widespread attention to the participatory potential

Table 8.4   Regular media consumption: 'do you do any of these things at least 3 times a week on average? if so – which ones'? (% respondents)

	Gender		Age			SES		All
	Male	Female	18–34	35–54	55+	ABC1	C2DE	
Read a local newspaper	58	55	54	57	59	55	58	56
Read a national newspaper	68**	55**	54**	57**	71**	62	60	61
Listen to the radio news	77**	66**	70**	77**	67**	74**	68**	71
Watch the television news	89	89	87	88	92	89	89	89
Go onto the internet for news	28**	18**	40**	25**	7**	31**	14**	23

Note: *Public Connection Survey* (2005) of British adults aged 18+ ($N = 1017$). Asterisks indicate the statistical significance of the coefficients with $p < 0.05^*$, $p < 0.01^{**}$.

of the internet, half the population does not access it at all, and those who do are more likely to be younger and middle class. Of those who do go online (in their own time), most spend half an hour to one hour, with men spending longer online than women.

News consumption represents a more distinct form of engagement with the media. If we look specifically at who uses a particular medium for the news at least three times a week, a rather different demographic and usage pattern emerges (see Table 8.4). A majority said that they use all sources at least three times per week, apart from the internet – only 23 per cent of people used the internet at least three times a week as a news source. Television was by far the 'main source' for everyone (89 per cent) (cf Robinson and Levy 1986; Ofcom 2005), 71 per cent listen to radio news (higher for men and middle class people), while 61 per cent read the national paper (more men and older people) and over half (56 per cent) read their local newspaper. Only 23 per cent use the internet to access the news, and this is strongly stratified – more men, younger and middle class people.

It seems that, for older people, the greater time they spend with television does not translate into a greater likelihood of being regular news viewers. Similarly, lower SES households are not more likely to watch the news regularly, though they watch more television overall. In other words, although younger and middle class people consume less media, they sustain an average level of news consumption. However, the greater internet use in higher SES households and among young people does result in greater use of online news. Further, while there are no SES differences for radio use overall, middle class households seem more likely to seek out radio news. Lastly, men's greater time with newspapers and the internet is also evident in their increased likelihood of following the news in the papers, online and, additionally, on the radio. Overall, men and middle class people draw on a wider range of news sources than do women[27] or working class people.[28]

While overall media consumption, time spent with one medium is not necessarily associated with time spent on another, suggesting that people make trade-offs in allocating disposable time, for news consumption, seeking news on one medium is positively associated with seeking news on another. However, these positive correlations for news consumption across television, radio and the local and national papers do not extend to seeking out news on the internet; rather, online news is, at present, part of a pattern of internet use rather than an extension of news-related practices.[29] In sum, it is misleading to talk of 'media use' to cover the range of uses of different media by different people.[30]

Media use is stratified – no great surprise, but this means that so too is the mediation of public connection, and the implications of this have been little pursued in the research literature.

Mediating participation

Most people say that they follow the news to understand what's going on in the world (90 per cent) and to know what other people are talking about (76 per cent). Thus most people (80 per cent) have made watching the news a regular part of their day, even though nearly half the population (44 per cent) considers that politics has little connection with their own life. Moreover, the Public Connection Survey shows that overall time spent on any medium is only weakly related to voting – those more likely to vote listen more to the radio in general, are slightly more likely to read the newspaper, and they use the internet rather less, partly a function of age (see Table 8.5). There is no significant correlation between voting and the amount of time spent watching television, and the same is the case for the news consumption variables.

Political interest is another matter. Although also not associated with overall time spent watching television, it is related to time spent with radio and newspapers and it is positively associated with news consumption (press, radio, television and internet). Political trust, however, remains puzzling, being associated only with less time reading books and more time reading the local paper; the media conceived generally, it seems, neither encourage nor discourage political trust. News consumption does sustain political interest (and, as shown by Scheufele and Nisbet, 2002, political efficacy), though it can equally be argued that political interest motivates news consumption.

Table 8.5 Voting and interest in politics, by media consumption and news consumption

	How many hours do you spend with . . .					Do you do any of these at least 3 times per week . . .				
	TV	Radio	News paper	Books	Internet	Local paper	National paper	Radio news	TV news	Online news
Voting	0.02	0.11**	0.07*	0.08*	−0.10**	−0.04	0.05	0.05	0.05	−0.06
Political interest	−0.06*	0.12**	0.17**	0.07*	0.01	0.03	0.16**	0.14**	0.10**	0.07*

Note: *Public Connection Survey* (2005) of British adults aged 18+ ($N = 1007$). Asterisks indicate the statistical significance of the correlation coefficients with $p < 0.05^*$, $p < 0.01^{**}$.

Overall, 70 per cent of the population considers it a duty to keep up with what's going on in the world, especially older and middle class people. Indeed, 81 per cent claim a pretty good understanding of the main issues facing the country (more men and middle class people). On the other hand, 23 per cent (more older and working class people) consider there's no point watching the news as it deals with things they can do nothing about, and 61 per cent feel that politics is so complicated they can't really understand what's going on (more women and working class people) or that it doesn't matter which party is in power since things go on much the same (55 per cent). Since political interest is higher among male, older and middle class people, one could conclude that the news media better stimulate political interest for these subgroups (and so, possibly, a different approach to the news would increase news consumption among younger, working class women, and so broaden political interest among the wider population).

One interesting complication is that the relationship between hours spent watching television and interest in politics is curvilinear (significant at $p < 0.05$, Base: $N = 1013$). Thus, for below-average television viewers (the 22 per cent who watch for an hour or less per day), the correlation is positive – the more they watch, the *greater* their interest in politics, *contra* Putnam's 'bowling alone thesis'. Most people (52 per cent) watch between 1 and 3 hours per day, and describe themselves as fairly interested in politics. However, for the 26 per cent who watch more than three hours per day, the correlation is negative – the more one watches, the *less* one's interest in politics. This suggests a certain level of television consumption may sustain political interest but that if viewed heavily, it may instead support disengagement by displacing other activities. Or, there may be a third factor at work, since people from lower SES households are both higher television viewers and more disengaged (Lembo 2000).

Do these various and distinct forms of media consumption explain political participation? We added a further step to the multiple regression analyses in Table 8.3, adding media consumption, news consumption and news engagement (see Table 8.6). For voting, a modest but significant additional 3 per cent of the variance is explained, adding in news engagement and time spent reading the newspaper and listening to the radio as influences on voting,[31] in addition to demographics, social capital, political interest, trust and efficacy. Not only does a motivated and habitual engagement with the news media contribute to voting but the absence of such an engagement, conversely, undermines the likelihood of voting. Time spent listening to the radio contributes to voting,

Table 8.6 Further regression equation, predicting voting and political interest

	Voting	Political interest
Age	0.29**	n.s.
SES	−0.06*	−0.12**
Political trust	0.08**	n.s.
Political efficacy ('You know where to go to get the information you need')	0.07*	n.s.
Social capital (local involvement)	0.08*	0.10**
News engagement	0.18**	0.37**
Time spent reading a newspaper	−0.07**	0.09**
Time spent listening to the radio	0.06*	n.s.
Whether listen to radio news regularly	n.s.	0.08**
Whether access the news online regularly	n.s.	0.06*
R^2	0.19	0.24

Note: *Public Connection Survey* (2005) of British adults aged $18+(N = 1007)$. Asterisks indicate the statistical significance of the coefficients with $p < 0.05$ *, $p < 0.01$**.

which is interesting since most UK radio news is presented briefly but frequently, and current affairs is often presented through public call-in shows, apparently sustaining a habitual concern with the public world.

Less straightforwardly, it seems that more time reading the news-paper reduces the likelihood of voting. Since the equation has already controlled for (i.e. taken out the variance attributable to) news engage-ment, trust and efficacy, along with demographic variables, this means that what is left in relation to reading the paper is negatively correlated with voting. One might ask, what is left after removing interest in news from reading the paper? Since the answer seems to be – the sport, the weather, the gossip, etc. we term this 'a tabloid effect'.[32] What Putnam hypothesised in relation to television we have, instead, identified for the press.[33] While the observed effect is small (we could hardly say that, once other factors are controlled for, the press undermines voting), the find-ings do not positively support the claim that newspaper reading sustains voting (there being no correlation between the two measures). Last, we note that time spent watching television plays no role in explaining voting – as also shown in the correlations in Table 8.5.

For political interest (see Table 8.6), the equation improves consid-erably in predictive power – adding a further 10 per cent to the variance explained when the media-related variables are added (compare with Table 8.3). As before, SES (higher) and social capital (higher local involvement) are important. The political efficacy variables are replaced by news consumption, specifically reading the newspaper, listening to the radio news and following the news online.[34] As for voting, news engagement proves influential. Once again, overall television consumption plays no role, positive or negative. It seems that political interest is highly mediated (Livingstone *et al.* 2005). The analyses show that political interest and news engagement go hand in hand: news engagement sustains interest in politics and also, no doubt, political interest sustains news engagement. For those who seek to explain variation in political interest among the public, news consumption offers a better explanation than political efficacy or social capital.[35]

How shall we understand news engagement? This important predictor of political interest seems to capture a motivated use of the news media precisely in relation to public connection (see Graber 2004). It is positively correlated with media trust,[36] as anticipated by Stephen Coleman (2001) when he suggests that a revival of media trust is necessary in a mediated political culture.[37] It is also associated with media literacy: those higher in news engagement are more likely to agree that 'different sources of news tend to give different accounts of what's going on' (overall, 79 per cent agreed with this), and that 'you generally compare the news on different channels, newspapers or websites' (59 per cent overall). Conversely, those higher in news engagement are less likely to agree that 'the things the media cover have little to do with your life' (40 per cent overall). Further, news engagement is correlated with social capital, political efficacy and social expectations from others to 'know what's going on in the world'.[38] But it is not significantly correlated with either socioeconomic status or gender, though older people tend to have higher news engagement ($r = 0.24$, $p < 0.01$). In sum, news engagement integrates a positive interest in the news agenda and a literate approach to judging sources and so determining trust in the media, none of which can be taken for granted by overall measures of media consumption.

Relating political participation and public connection

Although policy-makers hope to identify clear predictors of political participation, preferably amenable to intervention, research points to multiple but subtle routes to participation, each contingent on a range of factors and leading to rather different outcomes.[39] Hence, one main theme of this book is to examine the interesting, subtle and perhaps unexpected links between the private and the public evidenced through the practices of everyday life. What everyday practices might precede, contribute to, or otherwise frame political participation?

Keeping in touch with the public world

Informed by the diary findings, one survey question indexed people's general orientation towards the public world, inquiring into the deliberately-vague process of 'keeping up with' or 'being in touch with'. We asked, 'which of the following things, if any, do you generally follow or keep up to date with?', accompanied by a list of 18 possible 'things' (we deliberately did not label them 'issues' or 'concerns'). This included 'traditional' political issues (e.g. events in Westminster, crime and policing, etc) and life political or single issue politics (e.g. protecting the environment, religious questions, etc), as well as some more tangential themes in the public eye – these were generally mass-mediated (e.g. *Big Brother*, celebrity gossip, music, fashion, etc.).

The answers were interesting. Most commonly, people keep up the environment (70 per cent), crime (67 per cent), health (66 per cent) and events in Iraq (63 per cent). One in five (21 per cent) named *Big Brother* or other reality television programmes, more than named trade union politics (17 per cent). Men tend to follow Iraq, the UK economy, sports, Europe, international politics, Westminster politics and trade union politics more than women, who are more likely to follow issues relating to health, fashion, celebrity and reality television. Older people are more likely to follow the environment, crime, Iraq, third world poverty, the UK economy, funding for local services, local council politics, and Westminster politics. Younger people, on the other hand, are more likely to follow issues relating to fashion, celebrity, reality television and popular music. Issues also vary by class: 50 per cent of middle class respondents follow international politics compared to 28 per cent of working class respondents; middle class respondents are also more likely to follow issues relating to health, the UK economy, Europe and Westminster politics. So, people share overlapping, if not entirely common, public agendas. Is there a positive transfer from type of public agenda (e.g. celebrity matters) to another (e.g. life political issues)?

Beyond the political

Two non-traditional routes to participation have been proposed: following single issues politics and following celebrity issues.[40] To test these, we first added the degree to which people express an interest in single issue politics[41] into the regression equations in Table 8.6.

This showed that such interests make a slight contribution to the likelihood of voting (though the 0.4 per cent added to the R^2 is not statistically significant) and that they play a larger role in stimulating political interest (adding 2.3 per cent to the R^2, f-test significant at $p < 0.05$). Political interest is not simply, then, a matter of following such mainstream issues as European affairs, trade unions, international and Westminster politics – following single issues such as the environment, crime and poverty also contributes to political interest.

Second, we added the number of celebrity themes followed into the same regression equation in Table 8.6.[42] It turned out that an interest in celebrity bears no relation to the likelihood of voting and, as many have suspected,[43] has a negative influence on political interest (adding 1.3 per cent to the R^2; f-test significant at $p < 0.05$).[44] Thus, it seems that people choose whether to orient more to political issues (defined widely but not too widely) or more to celebrity issues.

Talking politics

Since it has been argued that talking about the things people think about stimulates their civic or political engagement (Wyatt *et al.* 2000; Eliasoph 2004; Cho 2005), in the survey, we asked if people 'like to discuss politics with other people', finding that the population is evenly divided between those who do (49 per cent) and those who do not (41 per cent). Further, following up on the question about 'things you keep up to date with', we asked how often they talked about these to other people, Some 55 per cent of people said they talk about these things either 'all the time' or 'quite often' (higher for younger people under 35). Further, 61 per cent of middle class people talk to others about things they follow at least 'quite often', compared to 49 per cent of working class people. Excluding the 5 per cent of people who said they don't talk about these things at all, friends are the most common people to talk to (85 per cent), while 73 per cent talk to their family and half talk to work colleagues. Men and middle class people are more likely to talk to others at work, while more women talk to family members.

We added the frequency of such discussions into the regression equations shown earlier in Table 8.7, finding that amount of talk made no difference to voting but significantly predicted the likelihood of having taken an action in relation to the issue important to the respondent; amount of talk also added a little to the prediction of political interest.[45] In short, people talk about the things they are interested in, the amount of such talk being unevenly distributed across the population. And while such talk is not related to voting, it is clearly linked to public action.[46]

Table 8.7 Further regression equation, predicting voting and political interest

	Voting	Political interest
Age	0.29**	n.s.
SES	−0.10**	−0.11**
Political trust	0.09**	n.s.
Political efficacy ('You know where to go to get the information you need')	0.07*	n.s.
Social capital (local involvement)	n.s.	0.06*
News engagement	0.18**	0.33**
Time spent reading a newspaper	n.s.	0.09**
Time spent listening to the radio	0.08*	0.06*
Whether listen to radio news regularly	n.s.	n.s.
Whether access the news online regularly	n.s.	0.06*
Issues	0.08*	0.18**
Celebrity	n.s.	−0.09**
R^2	0.24	0.27

Note: *Public Connection Survey* (2005) of British adults aged 18+ ($N = 996$). Asterisks indicate the level of statistical significance of the coefficients with **$p < 0.01$, *$p < 0.05$

What's on people's minds?

What's on people's minds reflects the news agenda, suggesting the media's mainstreaming of public opinion (McCombs and Shaw 1972; Gerbner *et al.* 1982). Overall, 72 per cent named an issue in response to an open-ended survey question, 'which public issue has been particularly important to you over the past 3 months?' The top issues were Iraq (13 per cent), crime (12 per cent), health (7 per cent), the election (5 per cent), Europe (5 per cent), and poverty (4 per cent). Women were more likely to identify health, education and poverty; men were more likely to name Iraq, Europe and the environment. Predictably, younger people thought more about education and older people about pensions. Further, middle class people were more likely to name Europe, while working class people were more likely to name taxes.

Nearly half said they considered the issue they named to be of national importance. 38 per cent said it was an international issue, while 12 per cent said it was local. Perhaps for this reason, but also for reasons of media trust, television news was the most common source of information for this issue (65 per cent). Half got their information from a national newspaper (higher among for men and middle class respondents), 27 per cent from a local newspaper, 24 per cent from the radio and 24 per cent from other people; interestingly, a fifth (22 per cent) said they gained their information from personal experience. The internet (21 per cent) varied most by demographics (more men, young and middle class people).[47]

From interest to action

What do people do and which practices do they engage in, given different patterns of interest, consumption and social positioning? Some actions are more informal or indirect, yet they may contribute to political participation and civic engagement. In addition to talk, addressed above, the research literature has identified various kinds of civic or political action (Norris 2000; Bromley *et al.* 2004; Pattie *et al.* 2004) We asked about 16 of these in the survey, including traditional actions (e.g. contacting one's member of parliament, or joining a political party) or activism (e.g. signing a petition, going on a public protest, joining a local group) as well as more media-dependent actions (e.g. contributing to a public discussion in the newspaper, by text, on a talk show or online) and, last, more informal actions (boycotting a product, contributing money to a cause, etc.). However, wary of asking about activities in general, we sought to understand how genuine concerns may translate into action by asking people what action they have taken in relation to the specific issue of importance to them that they named in the open-ended question.

Of those who named an issue important to them in the past three months, 55 per cent said they had taken some form of action in relation to it, leaving 45 per cent who did not, these being evenly spread across different demographic groups. When asked why they did nothing, even for issues they consider important, the main reasons (each 23 per cent) were lack of time (more men, young, and middle class people) and the opinion that it would not make any difference (more older and working class people). Those aged 35–54 were most likely to say they are 'not that kind of person'. In addition to perceived time pressures[48], therefore, political efficacy and social identity are also important.

Logistic regression analysis showed that those who take no action are more likely to be those low in political interest and political efficacy, who experience low social expectations to 'keep up', who rarely talk to others about issues, and who evince high political trust and media trust but low media literacy.[49] Also in the equation is watching television news as a predictor of no action (though listening to the radio and reading are associated with taking action). Trust in both politics and media may, therefore, be seen as passivising rather than encouraging, perhaps because they support the view that others will deal with things.

However, nearly a third (31 per cent) of those who named an issue had signed a petition, 21 per cent had contacted an MP or councillor (higher among those 55+), 19 per cent had gone to a local meeting, 11 per cent had made a personal protest (such as boycotting a company), and 10 per cent had joined a local group. Less common actions were contributing to an online discussion (9 per cent – rising to 19 per cent for those under 35), contacting a newspaper/TV/radio station (8 per cent – twice as many men as women), contributing to a public message online in a newsletter, etc (8 per cent), joined a national interest or campaign group (7 per cent), gone on a public protest (7 per cent), joined a political party (5 per cent), taken part in a strike (4 per cent – three times as many men as women), or joined an international campaign group (3 per cent). Moreover, most talked about the issue that mattered to them with friends (78 per cent), family (73 per cent) or work colleagues (51 per cent).

Those who take at least one action, by contrast, are likely to be more media literate, comparing sources and being sceptical of the media generally; they are also higher on political interest, efficacy and social capital. A multiple regression on the number of actions taken explains some 12 per cent of the variance with the significant variables in the equation being social capital (higher), talking to others about issues (higher) political trust (lower) and political efficacy (higher).[50] In predicting the degree of action (rather than whether or not any actions are taken), media consumption did not add to the equation. Media consumption, it seems, plays a role at the borderline between acting and not acting, with media literacy associated with action and media trust associated with inaction. However, media consumption plays no role in either enabling or undermining further actions.

Disengagement

The converse of public connection is disconnection or disengagement, something we also measured in the survey. Although not a strong scale[51], a parallel stepwise multiple regression analysis to explain disengagement showed that, in step 1, SES (lower) is the sole predictor among the demographic variables, accounting for 5 per cent of the variance. The adjusted R^2 jumps to 17 per cent when the next set of variables are included, with political interest (lower), political efficacy (lower) and also age (higher) adding considerably to the explanation.[52] The extent to which someone is disengaged can best be explained, in short, in terms of being lower socioeconomic status, lower in political interest and political efficacy, and older.[53]

Adding the media variables contributes a further 4 per cent to the variance explained, with reading books (less time) and seeking news from the local paper (more likely) adding to the explanation of disengagement ($R^2 = 20$ per cent)[54] – those who are more disengaged also watch more television,[55] though this does not enter the equation, being correlated with the variables included already. Some media, it seems, mediate disengagement – local newspaper (and, correlated with this, watching television) – while others mediate engagement (reading books and, correlated with this, the internet, the radio, the national press).

Contextualising participation

How do the formal and informal activities surrounding political participation fit into the diverse contexts of everyday life? Thus far, we have looked for patterns and trends across the population. But, as we have learned from our diarists, people fall into different, perhaps distinctive groups. We acknowledge that typologies can be problematic if unduly reified, but, in the spirit of seeking analytic more than real-world groupings, we now examine the patterns that link public connection and media consumption. The aim is to go beyond the binary of connected/disconnected or engaged/disengaged, partly responding to the argument that people may seek alternative routes to engagement through life style politics or popular culture and partly responding to the complexity of our diary data. Cluster analysis identifies statistical patterns in the data, finding the people (or the issues) that 'go together'. The analysis identified four clusters into which each survey respondent could be classified, based on their answers to the question of what things they 'keep up' with (see Figure 8.1).[56]

Table 8.8 shows the top things they keep up with named by each cluster. The 'traditional' cluster is so labelled because their interests match those traditionally identified as 'political'. This is the largest cluster, suggesting that many attempt to keep up with the mainstream political agenda, including the economy, the environment, crime, Iraq and Europe. A sizeable minority fall into the 'issues' cluster, for they keep up with a subset of the news agenda focused on specific, single issues: the economy and Europe drop out of their top five themes, and

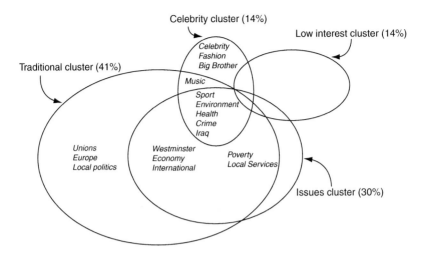

Figure 8.1 Survey respondents grouped by themes they usually follow

Table 8.8 The top five themes people keep up with, by cluster

Rank order (freq)	'Traditional'	'Issues'	'Celebrity'	'Low Interest'
1	Economy 89%	Environment 78%	*Big Brother* 80%	Health 45%
2	Environment 86%	Health 64%	Celebrity 79%	Sports 38%
3	Crime 85%	Crime 63%	Health 61%	Crime 35%
4	Iraq 85%	Poverty 59%	Fashion 61%	Environment 33%
5	Europe 82%	Iraq 57%	Iraq 58%	Iraq 16%
% who named < 2 issues	0%	4.9%	4.8%	38.6%

Note: respondents were asked to name as many items as they wanted from the list of 18 provided

health and poverty take their place. A smaller minority follow some similar issues (e.g. health and Iraq), combining this with topics such as *Big Brother*, celebrity news and the latest fashions. An equally small group professed little interest in any of these issues: when asked what they follow, 4 in 10 named only one, by contrast with the other clusters.

What makes the difference between these clusters? Drawing on the range of variables included in the Public Connection Survey, we characterise the clusters as follows.[57]

The 'traditional' cluster

More likely to be male (57 per cent) than female (43 per cent), older than the others (average 43 years) and with a tendency to be more middle class, this large cluster is the most likely to vote. They are also higher on political interest and political efficacy (though, interestingly, the clusters do not differ in political trust). Their social capital is high, with a greater sense of local involvement and social expectation apparently serving to sustain their interest in a broad but traditional set of political and public concerns. Thus they 'quite often' talk to friends, family or people at work about the things they keep up with. Notwithstanding debates about time spent with television, their overall television and internet consumption does not differ from the other clusters, though they spend more time with radio, newspapers and books. They are, however, the most likely to seek news across all media except the local paper; perhaps because they have most leisure time. Although their attitudes towards the media are fairly average, their news engagement is the highest and their disengagement the lowest. For them, it seems that social capital and local opportunity structures for participation work hand in hand with the media, particularly the news, to sustain a high level of political interest, efficacy and voting. They are, unsurprisingly, most likely to take some action in response to the issue on their minds, preferring an individualised action such as boycotting a product, wearing a slogan or walking out of a meeting to the more communal 'contributing to an online discussion' or 'joining a local group or organisation'.

The 'issues' cluster

This cluster contains slightly more women (53 per cent) than men (47 per cent) and is close to the average in age and SES. They are a little less likely to vote than the average, and are somewhat below average on political interest, social capital and political efficacy. Interestingly, their disposable leisure time is low, suggesting that lack of time encourages them to select a few issues to 'keep up' with. Or it may be that gender – there being more women in this cluster – is associated with both less disposable time and interest in these welfare-type issues. Their media and news consumption is average, though they spend a fair time reading books. Interestingly, their trust in the media is the lowest, and they tend to consider that the media address issues irrelevant to their lives (perhaps reflecting their relatively narrow agenda). So a rather time-pressured group with moderate political interest, their focus on specific issues suggests a strategic response to circumstances. While we cannot determine whether their lower interest in party politics or governmental processes leads to a lower trust in media or vice versa, it seems that their responses to media and politics go hand in hand.

The 'celebrity' cluster

Containing many more women than men (74 per cent versus 26 per cent), this is the youngest cluster (average age 32). They are the least likely to vote, their political interest is low, as is their social capital and sense of social expectations regarding public connection, though their political efficacy is average. They spend an average amount of time with the media in general and the news in particular, although their disposable leisure time is the lowest (again, perhaps because of the predominance of women). However, matching their low public connection is a low level of news engagement and a high sense of disengagement. Interestingly, their media trust is high, suggesting a willingness to accept the media's version of the public world along with a disinclination to challenge or engage with it. What makes them distinctive, then, is not their overall media consumption but their low news engagement,[58] high disengagement and high media trust, all going hand in hand with their interest in 'keeping up to date with' celebrity and popular culture, to the extent of prioritising this over both traditional or alternative public issues.[59]

The 'low interest' cluster

This cluster is the lowest in SES, although fairly average in age and gender. Contrary to popular expectation, their overall media consumption is lower than average, though their news consumption and news engagement is disproportionately lower still. Their level of voting is below average, their political interest and political efficacy are far the lowest, and so too is their perception of the social expectations upon them – from those at work and from their friends – 'to know what's going on in the world'. They rarely talk to others (especially, family and people at work) about those issues that they do keep up with. Since they do not lack disposable leisure time, their low public connection seems instead to be a matter of social structure – this group is not simply uninterested but they feel disempowered, as shown by their high sense of disengagement.[60] Their trust in the media is average,[61] but they have the strongest sense that the media cover issues irrelevant to their lives, and they make little effort to compare across media sources (a measure of media literacy; Livingstone 2004). Thus, compared with the 'traditional' cluster, for whom the media, especially the news, contributes to a high level of political interest, for this cluster the media seem to reinforce a sense of disengagement because of the issues covered (rather than the time occupied, since, relative to the other clusters, their disposable time is high and their media consumption low).

Conclusion

Analysis of the Public Connection Survey has shown that media consumption, along with demographics, trust, efficacy and social capital measures, contributes to public connection and political participation. Different media contribute in different ways, making a simple summary of 'the media's role' inappropriate (see also Livingstone and Markham 2009). Particularly, those engaged by the news are more likely to vote and to be interested in politics. So, news engagement feeds into a virtuous circle: the already-engaged become more interested, engaged and active; however, the opposite, 'vicious circle' is also indicated, with the unengaged becoming less interested, less engaged and more inactive.

Further, political interest is mediated. The media, particularly the news media (television, radio, internet), support and stimulate particip-ation. Interestingly, an interest in single issue politics adds to political interest in general, but an interest in celebrity undermines it. Media consumption generally, and news consumption specifically, play little role, however, in taking action or, conversely, in disengagement. The importance of other factors varies. Talking about issues, for example, and trust in media are, for some, part of the process of political engage-ment; but for others they are unrelated to engagement. Whether people take action about an issue that concerns them is more likely if they are less trusting of politics/media and watch less news. How much action they take, however, is unrelated to media consumption (instead, this is a matter of interest, social capital, efficacy, low political trust). Both taking an action, and the number of actions taken, is significantly related to whether or not people talk about the issue at stake. There are some signs that media consumption (including television viewing and news-paper reading) displaces the time that might otherwise be spent on participation – especially among heavy viewers and those low in media literacy.

The importance of political efficacy, social expectations, media literacy and everyday talk in stimulating political action suggests that the opportunity structures for some people enable participation, but that others lack the structures that mediate between interest and action. The disengaged are characterised by low interest and efficacy, and also by less news engagement, more celebrity interest. So, the media are part of the picture for both the more engaged and the disengaged, but in different ways.

The complexity of these relations was illustrated by the cluster analysis where we grouped people according to the types of issues they follow. This showed that some issues are followed by nearly everyone – health, the environment, crime, sport and events in Iraq. Other issues, however, mark some groups of people as distinct from others. The four distinct groups we identified point up the different life circumstances and choices that underlie different orientations to the public world. The clusters are also relatively easy to map onto our diarist samples, at least in broad terms: Bill, Janet and Marie fit easily into the 'traditional', 'celebrity' and 'low interest' clusters respectively, whereas the 'issues' cluster is perhaps best identified with Christine and Sheila, although they have perhaps higher social capital than might be expected for that cluster. The clusters, in a degree of detail that usefully complements the diary analysis, show how differently media consumption can mediate public connection.

Notes

1. US Census Bureau (2004) and see Chapter 1 note 2.
2. Office of National Statistics (2002).
3. Bromley *et al.* (2004); Electoral Commission (2005a: 18–22); MORI (2004).
4. Bromley *et al.* (2004).
5. National Centre for Social Research (2006).
6. For example, Evans and Butt (2005) chart relations between political parties and public opinion over time but treat communication from the former to the latter as unmediated. Similarly, Bromley *et al.* (2004) explain declining political trust in relation to the perceived responsibilities of governments, post materialist values, declining social trust and/or party identification etc, but do not consider the media's role in representing Government or parties to the public.
7. Voting refers to the question, 'You generally vote in national elections' (measured on a 5 point scale where 1 = strongly disagree, 5 = strongly agree). This figure may be high because the survey was conducted just one month after the 2005 General Election, though note that this figure does not represent those who always vote. In the 2005 BSA, 70% of respondents said they voted in the 2005 general election (National Centre for Social Research 2006).

8. Throughout this research, we use the market research categories ABC1 ('middle class' households) and C2DE ('working class' households) according to standard market research categories set out in Appendix IIB.

9. Political Interest refers to the question, 'You are generally interested in what's going on in politics' (where 1 = strongly disagree and 5 = strongly agree). In the 2005 BSA survey, 68% of respondents said that they had some, quite a lot or a great deal of interest in politics (National Centre for Social Research 2006).

10. Political Trust is a scale (Cronbach's alpha = 0.76) constructed following a factor analysis of three questions: 'You trust politicians to tell the truth', 'You trust politicians to deal with the things that matter' and 'You trust the government to do what is right' (1 = strongly disagree to 5 = strongly agree).

11. Correlation between voting and trust ($r = 0.12$, $p < 0.01$), between interest and trust ($r = 0.04$, n.s.), and between interest and voting ($r = 0.34$, $p < 0.01$).

12. Three Social Capital questions were combined, following a factor analysis, to form a scale for Local Involvement (Cronbach's alpha = 0.61): 'You play an active role in one or more voluntary, local or political organisations', 'Being involved in your local neighbourhood is important to you' and 'You are involved in voluntary work' (1 = 'strongly disagree' to 5 = 'strongly agree').

13. All correlations in this chapter use Pearson's coefficient, unless noted otherwise.

14. The Political Efficacy questions (1 = 'strongly disagree' to 5 = strongly agree) were analysed separately as they did not form a reliable scale.

15. This method allows an examination of the effect of a predictor variable (e.g. political interest) while controlling for the effect of other variables (e.g. demographic variables). Thus one can determine whether variables added later add to the explanatory value of the equation constructed using only the earlier variables (Hays 1988).

16. An f-test of the sums of squares of the demographic and more complex models indicates that the increase in variance explained by the more complex model is significant at $p < 0.05$.

17. These findings are similar to other research in stressing the importance of socio-structural factors (Kwak *et al.* 2004; Pattie *et al.* 2004) and efficacy (MORI 2004).

18. An f-test of the sums of squares of the demographic and more complex models indicates that the increase in variance explained by the more complex model is significant at $p < 0.05$.

19. Scale constructed from responses (1 = strongly disagree to 5 = strongly agree) to the questions: 'People at work would expect you to know what's going on in the world' and 'Your friends would expect you to know what's going on in the world'.

20. Gender drops out on this second step, not because it ceases to play a role but because the newly added variables are themselves correlated with gender (men are slightly higher on political efficacy and social expectations).

21. Prior (2003) observes that the benefits of 'soft news', if any, have yet to be demonstrated. Another version of this hypothesis is that the news excludes, confuses or alienates the public by failing to explain (BBC 2002) or talking only to the already-expert (Schlesinger and Tumber 1994).

22. A more optimistic version of this hypothesis suggests that the media could help the less-advantaged 'catch up', but we have not found recent sources that support this.

23. 'In a normal day, on average, how many hours do you spend doing each of the following?' Asked for television, radio, newspaper, books, internet.

24. 'Do you do any of these things at least 3 times a week on average? If so, which ones?' Asked for local newspaper, national newspaper, radio news, television news, online news.

25. Based on a factor analysis, the questions grouped in the 'news engagement' scale (Cronbach's alpha = 0.71) were: (1) 'It's a regular part of my day to catch up with the news', (2) 'I follow the news to understand what's going on in the world', (3) 'I follow the news to know what other people are talking about', (4) 'It's my duty to keep up with what's going on in the world', and (5) 'I have a pretty good understanding of the main issues facing our country'.

26. The correlations with age were, for TV viewing, 0.16 ($p < 0.01$), reading the newspaper, 0.20 ($p < 0.01$), reading books, 0.13 ($p < 0.01$) and time online, -0.39 ($p < 0.01$). Base: $N = 997$.

27. Possibly these gender differences reflect women's lesser interest in the news, or it may be that news has a masculine bias that excludes their interests (*van Zoonen* 1994). Possibly too, women's daily lives leave less time for keeping up with the news (Gauntlett and Hill 1999; Pew 2002a). Our survey shows that women report fewer leisure hours than men. Last, it is also possible that women have positive reasons (e.g. a focus on family or social activities) that explains a relatively lower engagement with news.

28. The Spearman product-moment correlations with SES were, for TV viewing, 0.17 ($p < 0.01$), for time online, -0.29 ($p < 0.01$), for radio news, -0.12 ($p < 0.01$), internet news, -0.23 ($p < 0.01$) and for national newspaper news, -0.07 ($p < 0.05$). The correlations for gender (with male = 1, female = 2) were, for daily newspaper reading, -0.13 ($p < 0.01$), for reading for leisure, 0.21 ($p < 0.01$), for time online, -0.12 ($p < 0.01$), for national paper news, -0.14 ($p < 0.01$), for radio news, -0.12 ($p < 0.01$) and for internet news, -0.12 ($p < 0.01$). Base: $N = 997$.

29. The Spearman correlations for reading a national newspaper at least three times a week were, for radio news, 0.097 ($p < 0.01$), and for television news, 0.164 ($p < 0.01$). The correlations for reading a local newspaper at least three times a week were, for national newspapers, 0.333 ($p < 0.01$), and for television news, 0.164 ($p < 0.01$). Base: $N = 997$.

30. A factor analysis on the media consumption variables did not identify a reliable factor for overall consumption (Cronbach's alpha = 0.35); consequently different media are analysed separately.

31. The significant political efficacy variables change when the media variables are added (they are inter-correlated).

32. Thanks to Peter Lunt for this point of interpretation.

33. This finding appears to contradict that of Scheufele and Nisbet (2002), but the difference is that they entered only demographics and then media consumption into their regression, while we first entered other variables associated with news consumption (social capital, efficacy etc) which

provide a sufficient explanation, leaving no further variance to be explained (positively) by the press.

34. Reading a newspaper now contributes positively, adding to political interest over and above the effect of news engagement. This complicates our earlier suggestion of a 'tabloid effect', a point we leave for future research.

35. Since age and news consumption are correlated, this may explain why age dropped out of the equation.

36. The media trust scale is the mean of four variables ($1 =$ strongly disagree to $5 =$ strongly agree): 'You trust the television to report the news fairly', 'You trust the press to report the news fairly', 'You trust the internet to report the news fairly', 'You trust the media to cover the things that matter to you'. Overall, 68% expressed trust in television news, 40% in the press and 36% in online news.

37. Note that for some, it is distrust (in media, in political elites) that is positive, suggesting healthy scepticism rather than a loss of social cohesion: Dalton and Wattenberg (2000), Tarrow (2000).

38. News engagement correlations were as follows: 'Different sources of news tend to give different accounts of what's going on' ($r = 0.173$, $p < 0.01$), 'You generally compare the news on different channels, newspapers or websites' ($r = 0.364$, $p < 0.01$); 'The things the media cover have little to do with your life' ($r = -0.138$, $p < 0.01$); Social capital (0.224, $p < 0.01$); 'You can affect things by getting involved in issues you care about' ($r = 0.240$, $p < 0.01$); Age ($r = 0.236$, $p < 0.01$).

39. See Pattie *et al.* (2004).

40. See Bennett and Entman (2001), Coleman (2003).

41. These issues – Information on health and nutrition, Local council politics, Crime and policing, Funding for local services, Protecting the environment, and Poverty in developing countries – were grouped using factor analysis (Cronbach's alpha $= 0.68$).

42. 'The latest celebrity gossip', 'The latest fashion in clothes', 'What's number one in the charts', '*Big Brother*'.

43. Although Keum *et al.* (2004) show that entertainment consumption need not undermine civic uses of media, Scheufele and Nisbet (2002) claim the opposite for the (increasingly commodified and entertainment-oriented) internet.

44. It may be objected that 'political interest' is perceived by celebrity fans precisely as 'not for them'; yet the point remains that an interest in celebrity, though it does demand that one 'keeps up with' some portion of the public agenda, does not appear to facilitate a wider engagement with civic or political concerns.

45. Talk predicts political interest with beta $= 0.09$, $p < 0.01$. The model adds 0.6% to the R2, significant at $p < 0.05$. Talk predicts taking at least one action with beta $= 0.40$, $p < 0.01$.

46. Also, as other research has shown, political discussion aids political knowledge and understanding (Dutwin 2003; Eveland 2004). Further, it has been argued that political discussion encourages political activity only if it occurs within certain settings - those organised to ensure civic activities or outcomes (Scheufele *et al.* 2004).

47. Similar findings, of public trust in television news, especially compared with internet news content, were also reported cross-nationally by the recent BBC/Reuters/Media Center Poll (2006).
48. There is no statistical relation between actual disposable time and the likelihood of taking action.
49. Political interest beta $= -0.18$, $p < 0.01$; 'You generally compare the news on different channels, newspapers or websites' beta $= -0.17$, $p < 0.01$; political trust beta $= 0.16$, $p < 0.05$; social expectation beta $= -0.18$, $p < 0.01$; talk to other beta $= -0.40$, $p < 0.01$; media trust beta $= 0.28$, $p < 0.01$; 'You know where to go to get information you need' beta $= -0.19$, $p < 0.01$; TV news beta 0.63, $p < 0.01$; radio beta $= -0.08$, $p < 0.05$; reading beta $= -0.12$, $p < 0.01$. R-squared $= 14\%$.
50. Social capital beta $= 0.49$, $p < 0.01$; talking to others beta $= 0.40$, $p < 0.01$; political trust beta $= -0.20$, $p < 0.01$; 'can influence local decisions' beta $= 0.17$, $p < 0.01$; 'can affect things by getting involved' beta $= 0.17$, $p < 0.01$.
51. The disengagement scale (Cronbach's alpha $= 0.59$) was constructed from nine variables ($1 =$ strongly disagree, $5 =$ strongly agree): 'You don't like to discuss politics with other people', 'You don't get involved in political protests', 'There's no point in watching the news, because it deals with things you can do nothing about', 'Politics has little connection with your life', 'It doesn't really matter which party is in power, in the end things go one pretty much the same', 'Sometimes politics seems so complicated that you can't really understand what's going on', 'You often feel that there's too much media, so you need to switch off', 'People like us have no say in what the government does', 'Sometimes you feel strongly about an issue, but you don't know what to do about it'.
52. Political interest beta $= -0.29$, $p < 0.01$; 'You feel that you can influence decisions in your area' beta $= -0.11$, $p < 0.01$; 'You know where to go to get the information you need' beta $= -0.09$, $p < 0.01$; 'You can affect things by getting involved in the issues you care about' beta $= -0.09$, $p < 0.01$; socioeconomic status beta $= 0.15$, $p < 0.01$; age beta $= 0.18$, $p < 0.01$.
53. This may seem surprising but recall that the levels of political interest and efficacy typically more associated with older people have already been partialled out, making it likely that the further effect of age here is due to a sense of disconnection from today's world.
54. Local newspaper beta $= 0.12$, $p < 0.01$; reading beta $= -0.05$, $p < 0.05$.
55. $r = 0.148$, significant at $p < 0.01$.
56. The cluster analysis was conducted using SPSS (Wards' method, using squared Euclidian distance) Before arriving at this solution, several methods were tried, with converging results indicating the validity of the solution selected. The decision on number of clusters balanced parsimony (fewer clusters preferred) with validity (meaningful clusters preferred).
57. Differences among clusters are only noted if statistically significant, using ANOVAs and Chi-squared tests, as appropriate.
58. The rank order of preferred 'types of entertainment' for each cluster shows that, for the 'traditional' and 'issues' clusters, the news enters at rank 6, whereas for the other two clusters it is ranked 13th.

59. The issues named were grouped by factor analysis, and scales were subsequently constructed grouping 'celebrity', 'traditional political' and 'issues-based' themes. Across the whole sample, there was a positive correlation between the number of celebrity issues named and disengagement ($r = 0.114$, $p < 0.0005$) ; and negative correlations between disengagement and the number of traditional politics ($r = -0.344$, $p < 0.0005$) and issues-based ($r = -0.123$, $p < 0.0005$).

60. This is also evident in a comparison of the clusters likelihood of taking action. Of those who named an issue of importance to them, only 35% of the 'low interest' cluster took some action, compared with 47% of the 'celebrity' cluster, 63% of the 'issues' cluster and 68% of the 'traditional cluster'.

61. We suggest media trust – like political trust, which also does not distinguish among the clusters – can be an unhelpful measure, for it is unclear how high media trust should be evaluated in terms of either media literacy or public connection.

Part III
Conclusion

9
Conclusion: The Future of Public Connection

> we are witnessing the end of the close correspondence between all the registers of collective life – the economic, the social, the political and the cultural – that were once unified within the framework of the nation. (Touraine 2001: 103)

> why should citizens enter into the hard work of education, discussion, deliberation and choice? They must understand that when they go through that hard work, their choices and judgments will be used. (Morrisett 2003: 30)

> in a deliberative democracy, there must be constant interaction between the media as institutions and the public to whom its messages are addressed. (Bohman 2000: 57)

We began with a question: what can media, and the organisation of communication, contribute to democratic engagement and so to the long-term sustainability of democracy? Today, we must answer this old question in the age that Alain Touraine dramatically tries to depict. This is an age of declining participation in the electoral process (Sussman 2005: 162) and declining institutional legitimacy[1] in many democracies. It is characterised also by the increasing pluralisation and segregation of lifeworlds and transformations in our sense of what 'politics' and 'public' life should be and where, and by whom, they should be conducted. It is marked, finally, by transformations in media – the forms through which media reach us and the habits by which we absorb media in our daily lives – leading to an intensified fragmentation of audiences. Three decades ago in the original German edition of *Legitimation Crisis* (Habermas 1988, orig. 1973), Jürgen Habermas famously diagnosed a

legitimation crisis for 'developed' societies and their democratic institutions. That late modern crisis remains unresolved while the 1920s crisis
which preoccupied Walter Lippman and John Dewey hardly found an
acceptable solution in the mass politics of the 1930s. The continuing
legitimation crisis of the early 21st century surely requires us to imagine
new solutions.

Nor is the problem going away. The 2006 British Social Attitudes
survey (conducted around the same time as the Public Connection
Survey) finds that in the UK as many as 60 per cent agree that 'people like
me have no say in government' (with only 25 per cent disagreeing); a
remarkably low *8 per cent* trust 'any politician to tell the truth' always or
most of the time, while 52 per cent trust them 'almost never'; and only
14 per cent and 4 per cent respectively have ever contacted their MP or
media institutions (National Centre for Social Research 2006). If we turn
to media consumption, the same survey finds that only 49 per cent of the
UK population now 'normally read a daily morning paper' (important
if as Neuman *et al.* argue (1992: 113) written, not visual, media are
important for 'information about topics [of] high salience'). Yet only
12 per cent used the internet – the newspaper's promising long-term
substitute – as a 'regular' news source, that is, between two and five
days per week. These figures confirm the UK as an 'elitist democracy',[2]
characterised by almost universal mistrust of the professionalised political elite on which it relies, low levels of citizen interaction with both
politicians and media, and a sizeable proportion of the population who
are not in the habit of using media that might provide more detailed
information on public issues salient to them.

What, specifically, does the Public Connection research add, by way of
complication, doubts, or confirmation, to this bleak picture? In this final
chapter we review the larger picture that emerges from our investigation
of whether and how people are oriented to a world of public issues of
shared concern. Focussing particularly on the extent to which public
connection is mediated, we note the implications of our research for
an international comparative perspective, and we suggest some ways
forward for renewing democratic engagement.

Review of our findings

The public connection diary phase

Analysis of people's diaries showed that there is no single ideal type of
mediated public connection; that is, no single way in which people use
media to orient themselves to a world of public issues beyond purely

private concerns. Rather, there are many individual forms along a broad spectrum from 'media world connectors' – whose public orientation is driven principally by their practice as media consumers – to 'public world connectors' whose public orientation is driven principally by their sense of themselves as agents in a public world (see Chapter 4). Further, different forms of mediated public connection are vulnerable in different ways: media world connection is vulnerable to a sense of overload and the need to withdraw from news; public world connection is vulnerable to specific disillusions with aspects of the public world or to the loss of action-contexts which motivate people to follow a public world beyond the private. Nor is an underlying *media* connection universal. We found both the fairly rare cases of people whose public connection is largely independent of their practice as media consumers (the lay preacher, Eric; the musician, Tyrrone) and also the more frequent cases (the 'weakly connected') of people who regard media as relatively dispensable yet lack public connection through other routes.

Mediated public connection, then, however important, cannot be taken as a given. It must be actively sustained by individuals and effectively facilitated by the wider social, cultural and governmental context. The nature of our diary-based research (and the considerable commitment it called for from participants) selected to some degree, however hard we tried to counter this, in favour of those more likely to have clear mediated public connection. As a result we may have *underestimated* disconnection within the wider population, especially if, as our survey data on the disengaged suggests, they are most likely to be of lower socioeconomic status (we noted at the beginning of Part II that people from Class D, those in unskilled manual work, were particularly difficult to recruit).

We have shown also that the dynamics of mediated public connection are complex, moving in more than one direction at once. A number of stabilising factors were important for different diarists: particularly important are work contexts which enhance public orientation, by providing motives or contexts for displaying knowledge of a public world. Habits of news-gathering also stabilise mediated public connection overall, and important in stabilising such habits is the value of keeping up with the news, found right across all diarists. What is unclear, however, is whether historically dominant habits of news consumption – the daily newspaper, the nightly TV news bulletin – will over the longer term be undermined by generational change. We found clear signs of the daily newspaper declining as a salient reference point among younger and particularly female diarists (Chapter 5) but there are only limited signs of internet news consumption generating stable habits to replace it (only two male diarists used the internet regularly in that way). A Guardian/ICM poll (Gibson 2005), suggesting that while 31 per cent of 14–21 year-olds in the UK have their own weblog or internet site, only 10 per cent use the internet to keep up with news and current affairs, does not give cause for confidence here.

There may be further dynamics undermining mediated public connection. Regular media consumption often reflects an orientation towards media as a form of collective involvement, not a means to access public issues. Broader orientations to social networks and family (positive, of course, in themselves) are more likely to be associated with such a non-public media connection: in other words, people may have *positive reasons for being disconnected*. A particular case here is an orientation towards celebrity culture (as in reality TV, celebrity magazines). We found no cases where discussion of celebrity culture was linked by diarists to any issue requiring public resolution, contradicting the claims of some researchers that celebrity culture may provide an alternative route into politics, particularly for the young. We had one striking case of an alternative conception of the public world (Ross, a design student). But, while he spoke about sport in public sphere-style language, he too made no links from sport to any other aspects of the public world. We suggest, therefore, that writers who have celebrated popular culture for democratising an old-fashioned and elitist political culture underestimate a fundamental divide in how audiences orient themselves to the world, namely distinguishing public from leisure spheres.

In Chapter 5 we looked more closely at what type of media users our diarists were. We found a clear distinction between directed and non-directed use of media, with the former being linked as much with work status and experience of civic and political involvement, as with levels of education (contrast Danish research by Schröder and Williams 2005). There were also signs of a generational and gendered shift with diarists' accounts of themselves as 'flicking' through media in a non-directed way much more common among those under 40. Our timeline analysis – which compared patterns in the issues diarists selected against overall peaks in press news coverage during the diary period – suggested that audiences select to a considerable degree from the news, often foregrounding human interest stories (with relatively low news prominence) and downplaying Westminster coverage and persistent serious topics such as Iraq or immigration. In terms of news sources, the internet proved much less important as a primary news source than recent hype about the internet replacing television consumption would suggest;[3] few diarists used the internet that way, while mobile media barely registered as a significant news source.

Turning to the quality of media use, an attraction/withdrawal dynamic is a significant factor, sometimes seriously destabilising people's news consumption habits because of an overload of 'serious' news or (also common) of celebrity coverage. Yet habit in media consumption remains of particular importance, with almost all of those with clear mediated public connection having regular habits of media use and news consumption. Turning, finally, to critical media use, cases where diarists criticised the detailed facts of media stories or had a detailed view on how media operate were relatively rare. Most diarists were, however, broadly media literate, while diarists' general unease about media's news values and the broader ethical consequences of media coverage cannot easily be fitted into any simple account of trust in the media.

Chapter 6 analysed the broader factors that might shape people's mediated public connection. The principal value relevant here was media-specific: the value of 'keeping up with the news' found across both genders and all ages in our diarist sample. There were however some signs, particularly among women diarists, of a rejection of that value on the grounds that news was of limited relevance to their lives. We found no trace, by contrast, of religious or other strong moral values motivating either media consumption or a turn away from media consumption, by contrast with US research (Hoover *et al.* 2004) including the results emerging from the parallel US project on public connection (Williams *et al.* 2006).

Some have diagnosed lack of talk contexts as one source of democratic disengagement, but our findings did not support that fear. Most diarists had *some* contexts in which they could talk about public issues. Indeed there was substantial evidence of people enjoying debate, even if social occasions sometimes constrain this; and some people, particularly but not exclusively men, found they lacked contexts for discussing more 'serious' issues. More striking was an almost complete lack of evidence among our diarists of links between the talk they recorded and any public action. This supports the concerns of other researchers that there is a lack of a deliberative culture in contemporary Britain (Pattie *et al.* 2004).

Turning to action about public issues, there was similarly no fundamental problem of our diarists' being inactive, although when we looked for actions involving at least some minimal effort or time, only a minority of diarists were publicly active. While many rationalisations for inaction were present – some expected, such as lack of political efficacy; some less expected, such as a sense that public action would expose one's private world to threat – what was most striking was the lack, in all but two cases (Christine, Eric), of a clear and stable context for public action. For only one diarist (Christine) was there any trace of a *local* civic sphere as a context that motivated action, another contrast with the diarists in the parallel US project. More disturbingly, we also found cases of civically active diarists (such as Edward) who did not see their civic action as linked effectively to the world where public issues get addressed, not because of their own disconnection but because their engagement, as they saw it, was not taken into account by governments. There is here an echo of the gap between civic activism and political disengagement which the high-profile Power Report (Power 2006) recently highlighted.

In Chapter 7 we developed these themes through the voices of individual diarists. As one might expect, some individuals are satisfied with their connection (Henry) or dissatisfied with their disconnection (Samantha). There are, however, more complex possibilities: diarists such as Andrea or Beccy who were fundamentally *satisfied* with their *disconnection*; or, by contrast, diarists such as Josh, Bill or Sheila who were *troubled* by aspects of their *connection*, in particular its relation to the disconnection of others or wider problems with British democracy. Kylie was a particularly interesting case because she showed mediated public connection based on strong emotional commitment, yet she had few if any opportunities to act publicly in relation to that commitment: nor did Kylie exercise her one formal right (to vote). An emerging theme through Chapter 7 was unease at how British democracy is currently working, whether from a perspective of minimal political knowledge (Samantha) or from a position of considerable political knowledge (Bill) or practical understanding of how media affect public agendas (Sheila).

It is clear then from the detailed qualitative research of our project's diary phase that mediated public connection exists in the daily life of contemporary Britain: most diarists had such a connection, at least to some degree. A key difference overall of our data from the parallel US project on public connection (Williams *et al.* 2006) is that in our study the internet was not as important a stabilising context for political/civic engagement, or indeed as a focus of media consumption – in spite of our diarist sample matching current averages in terms of online and broadband access. We must disagree therefore with Caroline Haythornthwaite and Barry Wellman (2002: 34): in the UK at least, and for the time being, 'the person' has *not* become 'the portal' to public information flows.

These conclusions stand even if we have emphasised the necessary complexity of any account of what mediated public connection involves for particular citizens. This is where our commitment to the framework of 'practice theory' developed recently in the sociology of consumption (Reckwitz 2002; Warde 2005) becomes important. For such an approach looks for the subtle order in everyday actions, but in certain cases ('dispersed practices': Schatzki 1998) it acknowledges that this order may not be readily articulable in explicit rules. Mediated public connection is just such a dispersed practice: real and important, but not reducible to, or embodied in, any straightforward 'ideal types'. At the same time, however subtle the patterns, it is still regularity, and the special embedding in social structure which *habitual* practices have, that we have been examining. In looking at 'habit', we have found order not just in the things people do and link with other things they do, but in the things people *don't* do, or do but *don't link up* with the other things they do (see further below).

Given the importance of understanding habit, including habits of media consumption, it is all the more important to consider the continued relevance of *traditional* media, and the links between everyday media consumption and wider *social* contexts. If we are concerned about the links between mediated public connection and wider democratic engagement, what matters is the extent to which once stable habits of news consumption remain stable and, if not, are being replaced by new forms of stable habit (including especially online news consumption). Without this, there will be a long-term and growing gap between the connected and the disconnected. That gap may be reinforced by the more subtle disarticulations we discovered in our diarist data: between everyday talk about public issues and opportunities for public action; between practices of civic engagement and a sense, nonetheless, of political disengagement; between many people's strong sense of collective involvement through media and their lack of orientation to a domain of public issues. Alain Touraine was perhaps right: certainly we cannot *assume* that all the 'registers of collective life' converge any more to sustain the framework of democratic nations such as the UK.

The Public Connection Survey

Our survey broadly confirmed and extended the main finding of the diary phase, that something like mediated public connection exists and is important for the British population. This emerged most clearly when we analysed what explained people's propensity to vote and their political interest. We found that political trust was low across all demographics and, as a result, it was not generally useful in predicting of variation in political interest. More predictably demographic and social capital factors contributed importantly to explanation, but so too did the variable of *news engagement* – providing evidence of both attitudes and a potentially stable news-consuming practice. This helped explain political engagement (itself a major determinant of voting propensity) in our multiple regression analyses.

Interestingly, news engagement is evenly spread across the socioeconomic groupings, and is equivalent for men and women. However, since it is higher among older age groups, these findings add to the picture of long-term decline in young people's participation. Just as the opportunity structures that have traditionally drawn youth into civic and political engagement – particularly, early entry into work and contact with community and workers' organisations – have changed for young people today compared with previous generations (Kimberlee 2002; Prout 2000), more informal social practices associated with regular news engagement may also be in decline. Further, just as young people turn away from the traditional concerns of national politics, seeking alternative agendas, the same may apply to their interest in the traditional concerns of the news agenda (it is relevant here that young people are less likely to read a newspaper regularly but more likely to follow online news).

Looking over the whole population, however, and notwithstanding widespread fears, the media do not simply, or only, act to undermine public connection, not least because different media are used in different ways, the effect being sometimes to enhance and sometimes to undermine political engagement in systematic ways, as mapped out in Chapter 8. Aggregate media consumption figures have limited usefulness, even for specific and familiar media such as television. Notably, the variable, 'numbers of TV hours watched', did not behave in a straightforward linear fashion in relation to interest in politics since, for low-to- average viewers, the more one viewed the *greater* one's interest in politics, while for high viewers this relation was reversed. Overall, our findings only partially support the 'media malaise' thesis. This is partly because media consumption, for both familiar and new media, is strongly stratified by demographic factors, and partly because for a substantial proportion of the population, particular practices of media consumption act to enhance public connection.

The mediated public sphere is not uniform. Our survey analysis revealed the overlapping density of the mediated public sphere for different groups. Having discriminated these groups simply in terms of the various things that people make an effort to keep up to date with, we found that these groups were also distinct in terms of demographic variables, social and domestic contexts and a host of other factors – political efficacy and trust, social capital, and so forth, including, significantly, distinct practices of media consumption. A large proportion of the public does follow traditional issues as represented in the mainstream news agenda, though an equivalent proportion instead singles out a few specific issues to follow, these tending to be more welfare-type issues. Smaller groups of people instead make a point of keeping up either with celebrity or popular culture news or, the fourth group, with nothing very much at all. Neither of these last groups showed much interest in politics of any kind, being broadly disengaged from the public world.

For the different groups, their public connection is differently mediated. For the 'traditional' group, the news especially seems to mediate their civic engagement in a positive manner. The 'issues' group is less trusting of media, and their pursuit of specific issues seems more motivated by circumstances from the public, not the media world. Interestingly, the 'celebrity' cluster is rather trusting of the media, though their news engagement is low, and there is little evidence that following celebrity leads them, indirectly, to a more generalised interest in the news agenda. This confirmed our scepticism from the diary phase data about arguments that celebrity/reality TV followers can potentially be brought back into public connection through this route: 'collective attention', as we argued in Chapter 2, is not the same as, and not necessarily even linked to, 'public orientation' or 'public connection'. Lastly, we note that the 'low interest' group must surely represent the target of renewed policy efforts, since they are disengaged from national politics, local communities and, as part of this picture, the media world.

People's levels of public action on issues that they nominated as important to them were relatively low, and were not correlated significantly with levels of news engagement, although news engagement did help explain whether someone took any action at all (compared with those who did nothing). This suggests that other factors – not related to media – are crucial in structuring political/civic action. As to talk, a clear association emerged in our survey between having opportunities to talk about public issues, and taking at least some action on that issue. Since in our diary data, we found little evidence of people's talk directly leading to, or indeed being a deliberation about, action, we conclude that it is general opportunities for talk (and the conditions that sustain them) that are important in facilitating public connection. However, this is not the same as saying that talk is directly articulated to action in the way that notions of 'deliberation' in political theory propose: such evidence was singularly lacking from our diary findings.

Summary of empirical findings

Media consumption, we have established, is an important factor in stabilising people's public orientation. Public connection is substantially mediated, although in many distinct ways and not for everyone. Whether the habits that underlie current forms of mediated public connection in the UK will remain stable in future decades remains uncertain, yet it is the social and personal embedding of habit - not simply the availability of new media technologies – that matters in the long run.

There are, however, crucial missing links between mediated public connection and any opportunities for effective deliberation or public action. While both diary and survey data indicated that a social context (and social expectations) are important in sustaining news engagement, we found little evidence of UK citizens having had access to 'communities of practice' (Wenger 1998) through which they could act together in the public world; the result must be to make it more difficult to build what Stewart Hoover (2006: ch. 4) has called 'plausible narratives of the self' that link citizenship to the rest of everyday life. Over the longer term, this calls into question whether current forms of mediated public connection in Britain are sustainable, particularly as habits of media consumption are destabilised.

Where do we go from here?

The nature of the problem

Just as one response to fears of declining engagement in traditional political parties is to argue that they look for politics in the wrong place (see Chapter 1), so one response to fears for citizens' supposed declining engagement is to say that they look in the wrong place for the *problem* with contemporary politics. For one thing, they tend to blame media institutions too readily and too indiscriminately (see Chapter 2). More broadly, the real problem may lie less with citizens' attitudes and practices, including their uses of media, and more with the availability (or not) of bridges between what citizens and governments do. The ambiguity of citizen engagement (and its ambiguous, because rarely if ever redeemed, links to government action) is something our research was designed to track. The Canadian novelist Carole Shields captured this ambiguity well through the voice of a narrator who runs a female discussion group:

> We don't have a name; we're not a club; there's no agenda. We prefer not to think of ourselves as holders of opinions, that is, we do not 'hold forth' on our opinions because such opinions are arbitrary and manufactured in an unreal world with only fifty per cent participation. (Shields 2002: 119)

The problem may then be not so much an absolute decline in political interest, or indeed public connection, but rather the lack of articulation between what governments and other public bodies do or think and what citizens do or think.

Although our argument has given a special priority to media consumption, a factor neglected in existing debates, it is clearly not enough to say that media and other institutions should encourage more people to follow politics (however defined). Under current conditions there may be *good reasons why* many people lack the inclination to pay attention to politics. We do not mean to point to a short-term political disillusion but rather to the longer-term sense that people are not listened to (Buckingham 2000: 34). Political systems where participation is highly stratified raise the possibility – as Robin Leblanc (1999: 91, 94) forcefully argued for Japanese housewives in an intensely patriarchal political system – that a disjuncture between public life and 'politics' may, from some perspectives (perspectives not taken into account within that system), be perfectly *legitimate*. If so, then ways forward must be multiple, paying attention both to changing dynamics of media consumption and to citizens' actual opportunities (or lack of opportunities) for interacting effectively with political and media institutions.

We emphasise here possibilities of inter*action*. The problem with a democracy such as Britain is not a 'motivation crisis' – expressed formally by Habermas (1988: 75) as a gap between the motivations required by the social system and the motivations supplied by the social-cultural system – but rather a *recognition crisis*, a gap between what citizens do, or would like to do, and the state's recognition of what they do. It is symptomatic of this recognition gap that, while the UK government's e-government initiative has certainly encouraged local authorities to develop an online interface with which their citizens can interact when using their services, only 11 per cent of local authorities in 2006 were found to have general discussion forums online where their

citizens could participate (Socitm 2006). If so, the problem, paradoxically, may be more amenable to practical solutions than the fundamental
break between system integration and value pluralisation diagnosed by
Habermas and Touraine. We want to suggest some routes towards solutions under three headings:

- fully integrating an understanding of media consumption (as a
  socially stratified practice) into the analysis of (declining) democratic
  engagement;
- practical steps by governments to take fuller account of not just
  citizens' choices but also their reflexivity;
- given the close interplay between the media and political processes,
  practical steps by media institutions to take fuller account of what
  citizens think about what media do, in particular how media interact
  with the political process.

Taking media consumption seriously

Debates about political disengagement need to focus much more consistently than they have before on understanding the quality of people's
uses of media – not just of the main news media but other media
that contribute to the formulation and expression of public issues
(such as documentaries, mentioned by many of our diarists and survey
respondents). Even important recent research (the Power Report 2006,
the Electoral Commission's 2004 and 2006 Audits) gives only limited
consideration to the everyday realities of people's media consumption.
Yet media consumption plays a subtle role in shaping both engagement with, and disengagement from, a public world. To put it more
bluntly, how can policymakers seriously hope to address disengagement
from politics *without* considering media's potential positive contribution? Encouraging a broad range of public-oriented media consumption,
and the growth of related media literacy, should be central to wider
strategies for reversing political disengagement.

Taking media seriously means much more than thinking loosely about
the 'consequences' of this or that new media technology, or worse
still the consequences of 'the media' as a block. As argued in detail in
Chapter 2 and developed in the empirical chapters, we must disaggregate
media in our analysis. Of course people have views about media in
general, and rightly so, but their *habits* of media consumption may be
different for particular media, and the particular constellation of media
on which one individual draws may be quite different from another's.
It is at the level of habit – routine consumption practice embedded in a

range of other routines, some social, some individual – that media come to make a difference, or not, as the case may be.

Habits of news consumption and news engagement, as well as media use generally, are socially stratified to a significant degree, which it would be misleading to ignore. They are heavily stratified by age, and the habits of an older generation (watching the evening TV news, regular radio updates, reading a daily newspaper) remain important, although less prevalent among those under 30. Regardless of industry hype, television remains overwhelmingly the most used medium (Ofcom 2006a), although the under-24s are distinctive in that they are the only age-group for whom TV is not the medium they would most 'miss' (Ofcom 2006a: 74). While we cannot ignore the argument that 'the foundations of traditional media' are potentially under challenge (Thompson 2006), there is a danger of exaggerating the likely extent of change. It is possible certainly that the nature of internet use will change radically in the UK as broadband access becomes taken-for-granted among the majority of the population. What matters most, we repeat, are transformations of habit.

As we saw in Chapter 5, there are signs that older habits of news consumption tied into domestic routine are more associated with those over 40, while the 'norm' of non-directed media use (or 'flicking') is more common among those under 40. But even if the internet comes to dominate media consumption habits in general, that does not mean the internet will generate habits of *news* consumption as stable as those associated with traditional media. In any case, basic internet access and internet literacy (Ofcom 2006a; cf Livingstone 2004) remain heavily stratified. A media-responsive policy on reversing democratic disengagement therefore needs to continue to think about *traditional* as well as new media and to look at the details of what media practices are, or are becoming, habitual and for whom.

Habit is inseparable from place; we do certain things in particular places, not others (cf Eliasoph 1998). The habit of websurfing in your lunch-hour at work *may* be the start of an important new type of news-gathering habit, one that is (potentially) social in a different way from reading the newspaper over the breakfast table or on the train to work, or indeed from watching a prime time TV news as a family. We need to think about how new habits of news-oriented internet use can be encouraged: what are the conditions which might make them not just practicable, but also *valued as social activities*? We saw in Chapter 4 that feedback loops for mediated public connection are of two kinds, some social and some value-related (and values may themselves be social or individual): underpinning both types of feedback loop are the conditions which make a practice meaningful. What conditions are there that currently *encourage* people not just to consume online news in social settings but to link that practice to other aspects of civic engagement – opinion-expression, deliberation, debate? Few, if any – and this absence is something policymakers, if concerned about long-term change, need to address.

Policy discussion will, we suggest, be better focused, if we drop the alibi provided by some populist accounts of changes in political culture[4] which argue that new forms of entertainment provide new ways of engaging people in politics. These arguments are fundamentally patronising (Williams 2006) because they assume that some citizens don't care about the difference between things they follow for pleasure (even those they value because they share them with others) and things they follow because they need to be collectively resolved. Our research has confirmed that people are well aware of the difference (see Chapter 4 on the public/private distinction), which is not to say that under current circumstances they will all decide it makes sense for them to spend scarce time on the latter. It is the factors which affect the rationality of that choice – for example the conditions that *generate* the underlying disengagement from politics of followers of celebrity culture (who come from all classes, but are more likely to be young and female: Chapter 8) – that need to be addressed, not simply issues of how media present politics, important though those may be.[5] The route to sustaining mediated public connection leads in the end to considering the underlying conditions of politics itself.

Citizens and the political process

Our diaries offered disturbing evidence of civically active people who doubted whether their experience was being taken into account by policymakers, while our survey found a gap between people's sense of being informed about civic issues (broadly they were) and their sense that they were able to influence local decisions (broadly they weren't). Important here is not just the well-known point about political efficacy, but a more subtle point about how efficacy in *one* setting (the civic) may not translate into efficacy in *another* setting (the political). This suggests that mediated public connection in itself is of limited value unless the wider context in which, as citizens, we follow the public world through media is transformed.

It is here, we suggest, worth recalling Leon Mayhew (1997)'s argument that citizens need regular opportunities where the day-to-day trust they, inevitably, place in public representatives (politicians but also, we would add, media professionals) can be 'redeemed' through face-to-face questioning and dialogue; dialogue that is seen to influence what those representatives do.[6] The question, in other words, is not just about trust – although as our research confirmed trust in politicians in the UK is generally low – but about *voice* (knowing, through being heard, that your trust is not being taken-for-granted). As our diaries brought out, many citizens have a great deal to say about the conduct of public life; their voices need to be heard and, more than that, recognised as valuable. Yet chances for 'ordinary' citizens to redeem such trust as they have in the political system are rare.

The online world will be important in extending the contexts and networks that can facilitate such opportunities for dialogue with public representatives: interesting initiatives are under way, such as the BBC Action Network, to use the legitimacy of traditional media organisations to build online spaces for the exchange of civic and political resources (although disappointingly such initiatives didn't register in the practice of our diarists). Traditional media forms (news, current affairs) also remain important as facilitators of such opportunities.[7] But it is crucial also that such opportunities are sometimes face-to-face. There is, as yet, no evidence that interactivity online, while useful for many other purposes, is sufficient to *restore* belief in a political system where it has been damaged for decades. This is especially the case where the links between deliberation and action are themselves frayed. As the opening quote from Lloyd Morrisett emphasises,[8] people will not invest the time in deliberation, or perhaps even in following the news, unless they believe that some account will be taken by governments of their commitment.

Citizens and the media process

An analogous argument applies, if perhaps less urgently, to media institutions. Our survey showed a reasonable level of trust in media institutions, although different media fare differently. But as our diary data brought out, citizens are well aware of the close interrelations between media and government, and are troubled by them. Media institutions cannot in the long run ignore the threats to *their* institutional legitimacy that these close interrelations generate. As the political philosopher James Bohman has recently argued, regular interaction between citizens and media professionals is as important as regular interaction between citizens and political representatives. That interaction should cover many aspects of media, 'both the ways in which the public is addressed and how its opinion is represented' (Bohman 2000: 56), as well as general questions of media ethics and media institutions' overall contribution to the health of democracies (cf Couldry 2006a, ch. 7).

We need, as Bohman puts it, 'to widen the circuit of influence over the means of communication' (2000: 60). Why should it not be normal for citizens to have the opportunity to attend public fora – not just in central locations but relatively near to where they live – communicate to media professionals their views about how media present public life? Why should it not be normal for media professionals to be seen to be accountable to such fora, and not just to their shareholders, advertisers and (in the special case of the BBC) the highly abstract figure of the 'licence-fee payer'? And why should it not be normal for politicians also to take serious account of the implications of such discussions for how *they* conduct their relations with media and the electorate?

Public broadcasting organisations could, we hope, take the lead in this area. Indeed, in the UK the BBC has been active in recent years in considering how its news and current affairs coverage can reach audiences more effectively and, most recently, in acknowledging the need to for more intense and genuinely two-way forms of interactivity with audiences (Thompson 2006). But no major media organisation is exempt from these expectations. If media organisations are, as we are always told and as the argument of this book confirms, vital to the fabric of democracy, then *all of them* need to be accountable to citizens as directly as other democratic institutions. For this to happen, however, media organisations may need to counter journalists' tendency (noted by some researchers)[9] to discount the value of the public's interactions with them.

Conclusion

What we are implying in these suggestions is, we realise, a partial rethinking of both the political and the media process. We have argued that media consumption plays an essential role in sustaining public connection, the basic orientation to a world of public issues that underlies democracy as a participative social form. Yet the elements of mediated public connection – habits of consuming media, including news, a broad orientation to a world of public contention beyond the private – cannot be taken for granted; each is subject to complex instabilities. What will sustain mediated pubic connection best in the long run is citizens' sense that if they follow the public world, that knowledge may contribute to their agency in that world, and that agency may in turn make a difference.

It is this underlying issue that underpins other research too: research that looks at the media consumption of those already active in the public domain (Dahlgren and Olsson 2008), but not necessarily through conventional political parties; and research concerned with the already disengaged (Eliasoph 1998). Our primary focus has however been elsewhere: on the many people, as it were, 'in the middle', who sense they have a social responsibility to engage, yet are gradually losing trust in political institutions and, especially, losing faith that their contributions to issues they themselves consider require public resolution will be adequately taken into account by governments. From that perspective, what matters most is sustaining the broader *action-contexts* in which paying attention to the world of public issues through media seems a useful thing for citizens to do. Nothing less perhaps is required if the legitimacy of the democratic process is to be maintained under today's conditions of increased complexity and uncertainty.

Notes

1. Recent debates on the general decline in trust in UK institutions (Toynbee 2005 discussing private MORI research) only echo longer-term research on 'the erosion of institutional legitimacy' in many countries (Inglehart 1997).
2. Conover *et al.* (1991: 814).
3. Johnson (2006) reporting recent Google survey. We are sceptical about that survey, since it did not appear to distinguish between different types of time online, particularly time for work versus time for leisure.
4. For example Pels (2003).
5. This is not to deny that some of the mechanisms of interactive participation popularised in such media (such as voting by text message) are potentially useful indicators of what *mechanisms* may be useful for involving people in other settings (as the Power Report (2006: 247–8) suggests).
6. Cf Eliasoph (1998: 20–21) on the need for recognised places of political debate by citizens.
7. Cf Power Report (2006: 247–8).
8. Cf Bryan (1998: 162).
9. Wahl-Jorgensen (2002); Lewis *et al.* (2005): cf earlier work in the sociology of journalism (Schlesinger 1978).

Appendix IA: The Public Connection Diarists

Pseudonym	Region	Age	Gender	Family status	Profile (SES)	Ethnic	Diary medium
Harry	Suburban London West	69	M	Married, adult children	Retired Bank Info-Systems Manager (B)	White	Written
Pavarti	Suburban London West	51	F	Married, teenage children	Shop Owner (C2)	Asian	Written
Jonathan	Suburban London West	23	M	Lives with parents	University administrator (C1)	White	Email
Angela	Suburban London West	29	F	Married, no children	Teacher (B)	White	Email
Gundeep	Suburban London West	48	M	Married, adult children	Garage Manager (C2)	Asian	Tape
Kylie	Urban London Southeast	24	F	Single mother	Unemployed (E)	White	Written
Eric	Urban London Southeast	47	M	Married, teenage children	Computer Analyst (C1)	Black	Email
Sherryl	Urban London Southeast	39	F	Single	Unemployed (E)	Black	Written/Tape
Crystal	Urban London Southeast	22	F	Single mother	Unemployed (E)	Black	Tape
Abby	Urban London Southeast	45	F	Married, teenage children	Admin. Officer (C1)	Mixed	Email

Name	Location	Age	Gender	Family status	Occupation	Ethnicity	Mode
Nigel	Rural Midlands	54	M	Married, adult children	Premises Officer School (C2)	White	Email
Marie	Rural Midlands	34	F	Married, young child	Accounts Clerk (Part-Time) (C1)	White	Written
Lesley	Rural Midlands	39	F		Secretary, Education (B)	White	Written/Tape
Andrea	Rural Midlands	25	F	Married	Children's Nurse (C2)	White	Written
Paul	Rural Midlands	55	M	Married, teenage children	Company Secretary (C1)	White	Written/Tape
Mary	Northern Suburb 1	18	F	Lives with parents/university	Student (B)	White	Written
Edward	Northern Suburb 1	64	M	Married, adult children	Retired Chief Exec., Financial Services (A)	White	Email
Lisa	Northern Suburb 1	30	F	Cohab, no children	Teacher (B)	White	Email
Henry	Northern Suburb 1	52	M	Married, teenage children	Insurance Underwriter (B)	Black	Email
Stuart	Northern Suburb 1	61	M	Married, adult children	Retired Bank Manager (B)	White	Written
Beccy	Northern Suburb 1	27	F	Cohab, no children	Marketing Executive (C1)	White	Email
Frank	Northern Suburb 2	37	M	Cohab.	Catering Manager (C1)	White	Email/Written
Susan	Northern Suburb 2	62	F	Divorced	Office Manager for a Retirement Home (C1)	White	Written
Alfred	Northern Suburb 2	67	M	Married, adult children	Retired Printer (C2)	White	Email

(Continued)

Pseudonym	Region	Age	Gender	Family status	Profile (SES)	Ethnic	Diary medium
Christine	Northern Suburb 2	46	F	Divorced	Events Co-ordinator (C1)	White	Email/Written
Janet	Northern Suburb 2	29	F	Single	Pre-Ops Controller (B)	White	Email
Jane	Urban South	52	F	Divorced	Supermarket assistant (part-time) (D)	White	Written
Kathleen	Urban South	34	F	Married, young children	Mature Student Part-Time (C1)	White	Written
Patrick	Urban South	52	M	Married, adult children	Warehouse Manager (C2)	White	Written
Samantha	Urban South	33	F	Married, no children	Beautician – Manager of Shop (C2)	White	Written
Ross	Urban South	25	M	Single	Student, Graphic Design (C1)	White	Written
Bill	Rural Midlands	61	M	Married, adult children	Retired Managing Director (A)	White	Email
Sheila	Rural Midlands	47	F	Divorced	Senior Health Protection Nurse (B)	White	Written
Tyrone	Urban London Southeast	23	M	Single	Musician (C1)	Black	Tape
Enid	Suburban London West	63	F	Married, adult children	P/T Assistant At Local School (C2)	White	Written
Josh	Northern Suburb 2	23	M	Single	Architecture Student (C1)	White	Email
Arvind	Urban South	40	M	Married, teenage children	Disabled, Former Bakery Worker (E)	Asian	Written

Appendix IB: Regional Profiles

Introduction

We wanted to recruit a sample of diarists which was spread geographic-ally and properly representative of the population, from urban to rural and suburban. Diarists for the project were recruited from six regions around England contrasting in socioeconomic status and closeness to, or distance from, the capital London. This section profiles each region, based on statistics relating to ethnicity and home ownership from the 2001 Census and employment and crime figures from local authority sources.

Suburban London West

Diarists: Harry, Pavarti, Jonathan, Angela, Gundeep and Enid.

This region comprises two types of area in West London, with some vari-ation in socio-economic character, but both identifiably suburban. Type (1) is largely residential, consisting of a number of old villages joined by housing developments in the inter-war period. Levels of owner-occupation are high and the number of council houses correspond-ingly low; there is little in the way of industry. More than half of the working population here can be classed as professional or managerial, and incomes are a little above the national average. Older families are the most common type of household here, and the population is ethic-ally mixed (Asians make up 14%). Crime is slightly above average here, while unemployment is low. Type (2) is closer to the industrial centres of West London, with fewer detached houses, and its character has been shaped by successive waves of Welsh, Scottish, Irish, Asian and Somali immigration. Incomes are above average and unemployment low in both areas. Politically type (1) was Conservative until 1997 since when it has been broadly Labour but with a conservative council; the type (2) area is mainly Labour. Harry, Pavarti, Jonathan and Angela live in the former, while Gundeep and Enid live in the latter.

Urban London South East

Diarists: Kylie, Eric, Sherryl, Crystal, Abby, Tyrrone

Though there is some variation in terms of affluence and accommodation types, this region is dominated by council housing estates and is characteristically inner urban. Home ownership rates are considerably lower than the national average, as are incomes. Unemployment is very high, although it has been falling recently, and crime is double the national average. The population is very young (the 20–34 age-group is particularly large) and ethnically mixed, with a large Afro-Caribbean representation. In more detail, this region can be broken into three types of area: type (1) borders a more affluent area of London and has seen its economic fortunes improve since the 1980s, with higher rates of owner-occupation than elsewhere in this region; type (2) neighbourhoods are characterised by large estates, with a high proportion of run-down council-owned flats; type (3) areas consist of newer housing developments on reclaimed industrial land, better maintained than in type (2) areas and with higher rates of car ownership. Politically, this region has been almost entirely Labour for many decades. Kylie, Eric and Sherryl live in type (2) areas. Abby and Tyrrone live in type (1) areas; Crystal lives in a council estate flat in a type (3) area.

Northern Suburb 1

Diarists: Mary, Edward, Lisa, Henry, Stuart, Beccy.

This region is made up of several distinct suburban areas of a major northern city. All are middle class and affluent but can be divided into two types: type (1) areas are on the outskirts of the city, often in sight of rural land with some pre-First World War housing, a comfortable but not elite area; the type (2) area is more conspicuously affluent in appearance, and concentrated in the historic towns which have since been subsumed into the city, populated by senior managers and professionals, with many detached houses almost always occupied by the owner. Both areas have a low proportion of manual workers and income well above the national average. The region is mainly conservative, although there have been some Labour gains since 1997. Lisa lives in a type (1) area, as do the parents of Mary. Henry and Stuart live in a more exclusive type (2) area, as do Edward and Beccy (although Beccy's is a smaller starter-home).

Northern Suburb 2

Diarists: Frank, Susan, Alfred, Christine, Janet, Josh

This region comprises suburbs of a major northern city, consisting of several market towns which have been absorbed by suburban sprawl. In some cases, among the traditionally more affluent suburbs, the urbanisation of the area is long-established. In others, development of what was rural land occurred only in the last twenty years, and these areas retain something of their separate identity. Uniformly the region is comfortable, with fairly large, detached houses – almost all owner-occupied – quiet streets and a preponderance of high quality vehicles. The population is overwhelmingly white and middle-class, and principally professional, managerial and technical. Average income is above-average, with a high proportion of retirees. The area has been solidly Conservative for the last century. All this region's diarists except Frank live in quiet, suburban streets typical of this area. Frank lives in a poorer suburb of terraced housed and industrial estates, but this was a recent move, prompted by a business difficulty (otherwise his profile, history and aspirations were broadly similar to the rest of this region's sample).

Urban South

Diarists: Jane, Kathleen, Patrick, Samantha, Ross, Arvind

This region can be characterised as urban and working class and comprises 2 areas: area (1) is a low-income satellite town of a southern city and area (2) the inner centre of that same city. The region is historically industrial, with housing consisting of council terraces. Local industry is now in sharp decline. Income levels are considerably below the national average, though crime and unemployment are broadly average. The region has been broadly Labour in its council representation until recently (when Liberals and Conservatives have been more successful), although some parliamentary seats here are traditionally Conservative. All diarists except Arvind and Ross live in the formerly-council-owned terraces of area (1); Ross is a student living in the city (his parents live in a more comfortable part of area (1)); Arvind lives in the inner urban sector, area (2).

Rural Midlands

Diarists: Nigel, Marie, Lesley, Andrea, Paul, Bill, Sheila

This region is sharply distinct from our other regions, comprising a number of rural locations within 10–20 miles of a Midlands city. This is an area where the rural/ urban divide is complex, as rural areas steadily get absorbed into urban and suburban areas; Bill and Sheila were recruited later to ensure the 'traditional' rural was represented in the sample. The region comprises: area (1) which is fully rural (small to medium size villages, linked to old market towns); area (2) which is old industrial small towns (and the villages around them) which retain some rural employment, to area (3), rural villages in the course of being over-taken by urban expansion. There is a wide range of incomes and facilities in this region. Taken together this region well illustrates the *complexity* of the 'rural' in a contemporary England where actual farming employment is very low (2 per cent of national employment compared to 5 per cent in France and 9 per cent in Spain)[1] and ties to local towns and cities often very strong. Unemployment is generally low, with senior managerial and professional occupations dominating in the higher income villages, while professional commuters to the nearby city make up the bulk of the population in the other areas. Crime rates are about average. There is a high proportion of retirees, with high rates of home ownership. This region is solidly Conservative with the only competition recently being from the UK Independence Party. Nigel, Marie and Paul live in areas of type (2); Lesley and Andrea live in villages of type (3); Bill and Sheila live in more obviously rural villages of type (1).

Note

1. European Commission, 'Employment in Europe 1996', *World Competitiveness Yearbook*, 1997.

Appendix IC: Interview and Focus Group Schedules

First interview

A. Introduction

B. Opening questions as warm-ups

1. [ask about occupation mentioned in info received from marketers.] How much of your time does that take up each week? what about family demands, domestic chores and so on?
2. How much time, if any, does that leave you with free for yourself? [*follow-up briefly if appropriate*]
3. What do you like to do with your free time?
4. Is there anything you always make time for in your week? [*suggestions – TV show, news, going out to something local . . .*]
5. Is there anything you'd like to do more of if you had more time?

C. Moving onto questions on media consumption

6. [ask re media access reported by marketers] In a typical week, how much time would you say you spent on media? [*prompt if necessary – TV radio press internet novels magazines – if asked, say exclude internet or other media purely for work purposes*]
7. [depending on what media they use *most*] What sort of [newspaper-reader] [TV viewer] etc would you describe yourself as?
8. Is there a particular form of media you couldn't do without?
9. How have the media *themselves* changed in your view over the past five years? [i.e in a way relevant to your choices . . .]
10. Would you say your use of media has changed much over the past five years? If so, how?

[*Note:* if don't mention Internet/ Web and we know has online access at home, prompt . . . since may not include 'internet' as 'media']

D. Questions on public world/ related media use/ civic involvement

As intro to this section, begin with brief recap of project description given by recruiters and then informally (in conversational way) explore with participant his/her idea of public/private boundary, for example:

> We're interested in how the public world looks *to you* – what sort of things and issues you think of as public, what sort of things and issues you think of as private – and where you would draw the line. So something may arise in your private life, but for you it raises issues or questions of public significance . . . so with that in mind can you give me an idea of what type(s) of things you think of as public, rather than private [if necessary, invent people and scenarios to give idea of what form responses might take]

11. If we take the type of public issues or themes that interest you (and it could be anything that *you* consider is of common concern, rather than of just private concern), where do you generally get your information about it from? [if mention only media, ask re non-media – or vice versa . . .]

12. Are these things something you'd make a special effort to get information on [eg watching a TV programme, reading a press article, checking a website]?

13. Are these things you talk about with other people? Who with? [family, friends, people at work, people at college etc] Where do you talk about this and when, in what sort of situation?

14. Do you belong to any group or organisation linked to these issues ? [prompt: any charity, self-help group, national organisation, political party, online chatroom or newsgroup]

15. You think this issue is important – do you feel that your view of its importance is reflected in the media or not?

16. Do you think that your focus on these types of issue, rather than others, might tell other people something important about you?

17. Have you ever got involved in public discussion on such issues, for example written in to the newspapers, phoned-in to a radio or TV phone-in, taken part in a poll for a TV or radio programme, voted in an online poll? [if say no, prompt – eg so you've never voted on anything like Big Brother?]

18. Obviously, it's no business of ours *how* you vote in elections, but can you tell me *whether* you vote in elections? [if react negatively to questions, explain: we're not being judgmental about whether

you should vote, we're just trying to get a sense of the public things that matter to you]

19. If you had to name one recent issue that's been important to you, what would it be? [this allows for issue that they may be unsure whether sufficiently 'public' or not]

20. Did you/ do you talk to colleagues/ friends/ family about *that* issue? [also come back to Qs 12, 14 and 17 here if time]

21. Looking back, do you think you're more or less involved with public issues than in the past?

22. Are there things which would connect with public issues like this that you would *like* to do, but don't? What are they and what is it that prevents you doing them?

23. We'd like to finish off today's *questions* with a broader question on which we'd really like to know your views: we're often asked to think of ourselves as members of a democracy. . . . is that how you think of yourself? If so, do you feel you have the information you need to play a part in that democracy? [Explore: if not, why not? What else do you think you need? If yes, which media are most important here?]

E. Introducing the diary

We've touched on the type of public issues and activities you're interested in and think important (and it's *your* sense of what's important that we're interested in, not necessarily other people's) . . . . the diary we'd like you to produce for the project should be about these sorts of things – the issues and activities from time to time that are of public importance in *your* view. Specifically we're interested in knowing:

- Things significant to you that you think of as having public significance
- what sources of information you have on these issues and activities (including media)
- Whether you've talked about them to other people and what has come out of that
- Any activities you've been involved in relating to them
- How those public issues links with your choices of media to watch/ read etc
- *Plus* your general reflections about doing the diary

Explain format of diary

F. For interviewers to keep in mind throughout . . .

- Questions should allow for multiple publics, possibly conflicting – majority/minority, local/global etc.
- If there are issues or groups which the interviewee cares about, ask: how did you first get involved in this? What made you interested? How do you keep up your interest? Will you always be concerned about this issue, do you think?
- Discussion. If interviewee does talk about issues with others, ask: are these talks with people you agree or disagree with? If agree, do you seek out people you disagree with? Or do you see them in the media, and if so, how do you respond?
- Emphasise that we are *not* assuming 'everyone's connected' – we're interested also in feelings or thoughts about disconnection, or different views about how much 'connection' matters.

Second Interview Schedule

[NB here and in focus group protocol, some questions specific to the US presidential elections (2004) asked on behalf of the University of Illinois have been omitted]

A. Preliminary

A1 how have you been since the diary?

A2 explain purpose of second interview (to receive feedback on diary process; to discuss issues coming out of doing the diary)

B. Warmup questions

B1 How was doing the diary for you? Did you enjoy it, did it get you down, etc.?

C. Doing the diary

C1 The time when you were doing the diary – what sort of time was it for you? Completely normal? Busier than normal? Quiet period?

C2 How was it finding time to do the diary – difficult? easy? depended on what was going on each week?

C3 Were there any other difficulties in doing the diary which you experienced?

C4 Did anything make you angry doing the diary?

C5 Did you find yourself commenting on things you wouldn't have expected to comment on?

C6 What did other people say about you doing the diary?

D. Media use as reflected in diary

D1 [interviewer should comment on sort of media use reflected in this diarist's diaries, ie what the diarist's key media are, and ask any necessary follow-ups – this is good place to raise issues about gaps between account of media use in first interview and diaries]

D2 [coming out of discussion on D1] Is there a particular type of media you take in right away when you get up each morning?

D3 Looking back, do you think there was anything unusual for you about your media use in that period?

D4 Has your media use changed for any reason since doing the diaries for any reason?

E. Issues/themes specifically raised in diary

E1 [raise questions about specific issues commented on in diary eg]

– have you continued to follow this issue in the media?
– Is it [still] [not] something discussed with your [friends] [family] [workplace]?
– Has your view on this issue changed at all over the past few months? How?

E2 [mention themes raised in diary – invite to comment on these]

F. Current issues

F1 what issues are you following closely at the moment?
[follow-up questions about social context for this, how links back to what said in diary and first interview about issues and media coverage – try to get discussion going]

G. Media responsibilities

There are some broader issues coming out of your diary and also other people's diaries which we're interested to know your thoughts on:

G1 Do you think media have responsibilities to inform you of certain things?

G2 How do you feel about the role media play in keeping you in touch with things that matter – Satisfied? Dissatisfied? Bit of both? [Follow-up: do media have their priorities right in your view?]

G3 Do you trust media? [in follow-up, ask if makes a distinction between newspapers/ TV/ radio/ Internet/ local]

G4 Do you sometimes want the media just not to be there? Do you ever want to get away from media?

G5 Do we maybe give too much importance to media – i.e. are other things (apart from media) just as important, maybe even more important, in keeping you in touch with what matters? [work, friends, church, other activities?]

H. Politics/civic action

H1 Do you think politicians have responsibilities to inform you of certain things and to consult you on certain things?

H2 How do you feel politicians fulfil those responsibilities? Satisfied? Dissatisfied? Bit of both?

H3 Do you trust politicians? [in follow-up, ask if it makes a difference which sort of politicians – local, national, international?]

H4 [if social discussion of issues mentioned in diary] You told us about how you discussed issues [at work] [with friends] [with family] [at church] [others]. Is it important to you – to be able to talk about things like this? If you couldn't do that, would it matter to you?

H5 Did you/ were you tempted to take any action on any of the things mentioned in your diary? [e.g. join a group, write to newspaper, join/leave political party, contact MP/ council, take action through group/ church] [Follow-up: if yes, details; if not, why not?]

H6 Do you expect to follow the next UK national election [if so, how much]?

I. Larger reflections

I1 Has doing the diary changed your view about [eg]:

– The role media play in your life?
– What public issues are important?
– How much politics and public life matters to you?
– Whether we live in a democracy?

I2 Has doing the diary changed your media use at all, do you think?

J. Closing

J1 Any other feedback you wanted to give us about doing the diaries/ should we have arranged things differently etc?

Focus group schedule

A. Preliminary

A1 Purpose of meeting: to talk about (1) some issues raised in people's diaries and also (2) about the more general question of people's sense of what types of thing really matter, what types of things it's important to follow outside our day-to-day life and those it isn't – which is the main question this project is trying to raise. . .

A2 Confidentiality: as always we will preserve this, so suggest use first names in the discussion.

A3 Go round room asking people to introduce themselves by first name (to help transcriber identify the different voices in the room).

. . . [Lead-in to B: people's diaries talked about lots of types of issues – national, local, international and global . . . since everyone here is from the area of [details], shall we start by talking about local issues, which might be ones you all share?]. . .

B. Local issues

B1 have there been any issues this year of major importance or concern to this area? [if necessary, prompt with mention of local issues mentioned by these diarists] [try to pick up if anyone disagrees about whether these issues are important]

B2 Has it been easy or difficult to get the information *you need* on these issues?

B3 Do you see any opportunities to take any action on this issue? [Follow-ups: If yes, what sorts of things? If not, why not? And does this matter or not?]

B4 Among all the different public issues you think about, how important are local issues like these compared with other types of issues ie national, international?

C. Other issues raised by diarists

C1 Perhaps we can move onto some of those other types of issues that many people raised in their diaries [NB important to link initially into what people wrote, rather than purely open-ended issues of the day at the time of the focus group]. One interesting thing was how varied people's choices of what to talk about in the diary were . . . [then introduce the following three issue areas in following suggested order] – [NB these should be the three issue areas we identify in our survey questions]

   (i)   Crime

  (ii)   Iraq war

 (iii)   Celebrity stories [Beckham, George Michael, others?]

On each issue, encourage people

(a)   to give their views

(b)   indicate how important (or unimportant) they think the issue is relative to others and

(c)   if discussion gets bogged down, suggest links to other issues made in diaries [viz Iraq War to general security issues; celebrity not just around Beckham/sport (sport being mainly of interest to male diarists) but also George Michael (mentioned by a number of female diarists)...; crime to quality of life, asylum, education]

C2 Don't lead people to discuss media coverage, but if there is significant consensus/ disagreement emerging on media coverage of any one issue, follow up and clarify...

D. Civic action

D1 Taking these issues we've just been discussing [recap], what do you see as our options for doing something about them? [Prompt if necessary – Write to MP/ council? Contact media? Visit website? Sign Petition? Go on protest? Consumer boycott? Join group?]

D2 Have you ever done any of these things?

D3 [If not,] What is your image of the types of people who do take such action?

D4 How much of a difference do you think doing these things would make?

D5 [If none or little difference], how do you feel about this? [explore people's feelings or thoughts on this]

[bring out any contrasts with discussion on B3]

E. Public awareness

E1 Are there things which *all of us*, no matter what our interests, should follow/ keep up with? Or is this purely up to our personal interests/taste? [Follow-up: does this link to the question of where you draw the line between public and private that we raised when we first met you?]

E2 Some people in their diaries wondered about the *point* of keeping up with public issues – one person said 'My opinions won't count anyway – it's already been decided', so why follow the news and politics? Did you ever think that? [follow-up if people say yes – did this make doing the diary more difficult? – important for question of artificiality]

E3 If Britain's a democracy (and we discussed this with everyone in the first interview), how do you feel about the part you're able to play in this democracy? Are you clear about what your role is? Do you have the time to do this? Do you have the resources?

E4 The project's also raised questions about the importance to us of media and media's role in democracy . . . some might say (and people did in their diaries) 'The things the media cover have little to do with my life' – would you agree with this, disagree etc?

E5 Some people feel quite disenchanted with politics or with media or with both of them – do you any of you feel like that?

Appendix ID: Technical Note on Timeline Construction

The timeline was constructed so as to represent the relative prominence of news stories both in the press and in the diaries, rather than absolute levels. For the diaries, each mention of a news story was recorded and dated, and references to new items across the sample were added up and calculated week-to-week. In some cases the specific date of diary entries was not clear, and had to be inferred by previous and subsequent entries as well as the content of the entry. These totals were then weighted so as to control for the number of diarists writing in any given week. The maximum number of simultaneously active diarists was 20; in the weeks where there were fewer (say n), the total number of references to each story was multiplied by the factor 20/n:

$$\text{Weighted value} = \text{Observed counts} \times \frac{20}{\text{No. active diarists}}$$

This led to some oversimplification in the last few weeks in which only two diarists were writing, but gives a good indication of the relative prevalence of news items in the diaries across the five month period.

To establish the representativeness of the diarist news timeline, a parallel timeline based on newspaper coverage of stories was constructed. For the period of the diary phase, the main stories in the *Sun*, the *Daily Mail*, *The Times* and the *Guardian* were collated using LexisNexis. Due to format differences, the top 15 stories each day were selected, and any with under 100 words was excluded, while in the broadsheets all front page stories were catalogued.

To compare the diary and newspaper timelines, a news reference point was chosen in a week (weighting = 1) where we had the maximum number of diarists the Madrid bombing. The number of diary references to Madrid that week was divided by the number of newspaper stories on that issue in that week, and the resulting ratio (2.3) was used to weight the number of press articles. This weighted figure is represented in Figure 5.3.

As well as these timelines, two of the research team kept their own track of the main news stories of each week, while the Guardian's weekly table of word counts across the press was also collated. These supported the timeline constructed on the LexisNexis search, and highlighted some interesting differences between press coverage and diarists' focuses, discussed in Chapter 5.

Table ID.1 Key to timeline 22 February–4 July 2004

Abbreviation	News item
Council Tax	Annual council tax rises
Obesity	Reports about increasing obesity in children
Haiti	Haitian coup
Immigration	Immigration and asylum items
Football	Off-pitch offences involving football players
Iraq	Iraq war
Diana	Airing of Diana tapes and US television showing pictures of accident
Dasani	Coca Cola bottled water brand revealed as tap water
GM	Genetically modified crops/foods
Carr	Maxine Carr/Ian Huntley
Global SEC.	Madrid bombings and other global security issues
Budget	Budget
MMR	MMR Vaccine
Boy/Skin	Channel 4 programme 'The Boy Whose Skin Fell Off'
Israel	Israel/Palestine – assassination of Sheikh Yassin
Passion	Film 'The Passion of the Christ'
MRSA	Hospital 'superbug'
G. Michael	Pop musician George Michael makes music available free
Domest Sec.	Domestic Security
Smoking	Smoking ban in Ireland, debate in UK
BBC	Michael Grade named as new head
Blair	Specific items relating to PM Blair – flour bomb, resignation talk
Beckham	Footballer David Beckham (all off-pitch)
ID Cards	ID Cards
Abortion	Underage abortion case; Channel 4 programme
Jackson	Singer Michael Jackson child abuse allegations
Paltrow	Actress Gwyneth Paltrow (statement on motherhood; birth of child)
EU Elect	EU and local elections, June 2004
D-Day	D-Day 50th anniversary

Table ID.1   (Continued)

Abbreviation	News item
Big Brother	Reality television programme
Petrol	Petrol prices
Euro 2004	Football tournament
Ramsay	Chef Gordon Ramsay
Wimbledon	Tennis tournament

Appendix IIA: Survey questions

Q1 *In a normal day, on average, how many hours do you spend doing each of the following? Watching TV, Listening to the radio, Reading a newspaper, Reading a book for leisure, On the internet or sending emails for yourself rather than for work.*
Response values: 1: No time, 2: Less than 15 minutes, 3: 15-30 mins, 4: 30 mins–1 hour, 5: 1–3 hours, 6: 3–6 hours, 7: 6–12 hours, 8: More than 12 hours

Q2 *Do you do any of these things at least 3 times a week on average? Read a local newspaper, Read a national newspaper, Listen to the radio news, Watch the television news, Go onto the internet for news*

Q3 *In a normal day, on average, how many hours would you say you have for yourself? By 'time for yourself' we mean leisure time you can spend as you want.*
Response variable values: 1: No time, 2: Less than 15 minutes, 3: 15–30 mins, 4: 30 mins–1 hour, 5: 1–3 hours, 6: 3–6 hours, 7: 6–12 hours, 8: More than 12 hours

Q4 *Please say to what extent you agree or disagree with the following statements: You generally have enough time to do what you want in the day; In general you are satisfied with your life at the moment*
Responses: 1 = strongly disagree, 2 = disagree, 3 = neither agree nor disagree, 4 = agree, 5 = strongly agree

Q5 *How safe do you feel living in the neighbourhood you live in now?*
Responses: 1 = not at all safe, 2 = not very safe, 3 = fairly safe, 4 = very safe

Q6 *To what extent do you agree or disagree with the following statements? You play an active role in one or more voluntary, local or political organisations; Most of your friends live nearby; You don't like to discuss politics with other people; Being involved in your neighbourhood is important to you; You don't get involved in political protests; You generally vote in national elections; You are involved in voluntary work; You are generally interested in what's going on in politics.*
Responses: 1 = strongly disagree, 2 = disagree, 3 = neither agree nor disagree, 4 = agree, 5 = strongly agree

Q7 *Which of the following are your top 3 favourite types of entertainment?*
News, Sport, Soaps, Celebrities, Documentary, History, Religion, Drama, Action–Adventure, Comedy, Music, Reality TV, Science Fiction, Arts, Romance, Crime, Science

Q8 *Which of the following things, if any, do you generally follow or keep up to date with?*
Trade union politics, What's number one in the charts, Sports news, International politics, The latest celebrity gossip, What's happening in Iraq, Ups and downs of the UK economy, Religious questions or debates, Information on health and nutrition

Q9 *And which of these things, if any, do you generally follow or keep up to date with?*
The latest fashion in clothes, Local council politics/elections, Events in Westminster, Crime and policing Big Brother (or other major reality TV shows), Funding for local services, Protecting the environment, Poverty in developing countries, Debates about Europe

Q10 *Taking these things that matter to you, by this I mean the things you have just mentioned – how often do you tend to talk to others about these kinds of things?*
Responses: 1 = not at all, 2 = not very often, 3 = quite often, 4 = all the time

Q11 *Do the people you tend to talk to about these issues tend to be . . . ?*
People at work, Friends, Family, Other

Q12 *To what extent do you agree or disagree with the following statements? People at work would expect you to know what's going on in the world; You follow the news to understand what's going on in the world; You follow the news to know what other people are talking about; Your friends would expect you to know what's going on in the world; It's* your duty to keep up with what's going on in the world; There's no point in watching the news, because it deals with things you can do nothing about; It's a regular part of your day to catch up with the news; Politics has little connection with your life; You have a pretty good understanding of the main issues facing our country; It doesn't really matter which party is in power, in the end things go on pretty much the same; Sometimes politics seems so complicated that you can't really understand what's going on; You often feel that there's too much media, so you need to switch off

Responses: 1 = strongly disagree, 2 = disagree, 3 = neither agree nor disagree, 4 = agree, 5 = strongly agree

Q13   *To what extent do you agree or disagree with the following statements about the media? By media, we mean television, newspapers, radio, internet, etc. The things the media cover have little to do with your life; Different sources of news tend to give different accounts of what's going on; You trust the television to report the news fairly; You trust the press to report the news fairly; You trust the internet to report the news fairly; You trust the media to cover the things that matter to you; You generally compare the news on different channels, newspapers or websites*

Responses: 1 = strongly disagree, 2 = disagree, 3 = neither agree nor disagree, 4 = agree, 5 = strongly agree

Q14   *Now thinking about politics, to what extent do you agree or disagree with the following statements?*
You feel that you can influence decisions in your area; You know where to go to find out information that you need; People like us have no say in what the government does; You trust politicians to tell the truth; You trust politicians to deal with the things that matter; You can affect things by getting involved in issues you care about; You trust the government to do what is right; Sometimes you feel strongly about an issue, but don't know what to do about it

Responses: 1 = strongly disagree, 2 = disagree, 3 = neither agree nor disagree, 4 = agree, 5 = strongly agree

Q15   *Which public issue has been particularly important to you over the past 3 months – this needn't be an issue covered in the media, but can be any issue you think of general importance?*

Q16   *Would you describe this issue as:* local, national, international

Q17   *For that issue, where have you got your information about it from?*
TV news, Other TV, Radio, National newspaper, Local newspaper, Magazine, Internet, Personal experiences, Other people, University, Friends/family/colleagues, Local government, Media, Church

Q18 *And which of these sources was MOST useful in providing you with relevant information?*
TV news, Other TV, Radio, National newspaper, Local newspaper, Magazine, Internet, Personal experiences, Other people, University, Friends/family/colleagues, Local government, Media, Church

Q19 *To what extent would you agree or disagree that you were satisfied with the media coverage of this issue?*
Responses: 1 = strongly disagree, 2 = disagree, 3 = neither agree nor disagree, 4 = agree, 5 = strongly agree

Q20 *Still thinking about the issue you have just mentioned, have you done any of these things in relation to it?*
Joined a national interest or campaign group; Joined a political party; Joined a local group or organisation; in a strike; Contacted an MP, councillor, etc; Got in touch with a newspaper/TV/radio station (e.g. letter to the editor, phoned a talk show, sent an email or text to a programme); Contributed to an online discussion; Gone on a public protest; Contributed to/created a public message (e.g. website, newsletter, video, etc); A personal protest (e.g. boycotted a product, worn a slogan, left a meeting); Contributed to them financially; Researched the topic; Discussed with family/friends/colleagues

Q21 *If not, why have you not taken any of these actions regarding the issue?*
No time; Don't know anyone who has; It won't make a difference; Not interested; Not that kind of person

Q22 *Still on that issue, have you talked about it to other people?*
Not talked about it, Talked to people at work, Talked to Friends, Talked to Family, Other

In addition, standard demographics questions (including socioeconomic status, gender, age, last full time education, ethnicity, religion) were asked plus additional questions concerning home ownership of digital TV or computer and internet access.

Appendix IIB: Demographic Breakdown of Survey Population

We commissioned a reputable market research company to conduct the survey for the Public Connection Project, following the design and piloting of the questionnaire (as described in Chapter 3). ICM Research interviewed a random sample of 1017 adults aged 18+ by telephone between 3 and 5 June 2005. Interviews were conducted across Great Britain, following quotas set by age, gender and socioeconomic status. The results have been weighted to the profile of all adults.

Socioeconomic status was categorised according to the following scale: A – Upper middle class (Higher managerial, administrative or professional occupations, top level civil servants), B – Middle class (intermediate managerial, administrative or professional occupations, senior officers in local government and civil service), C1 – Lower middle class (supervisory or clerical and junior managerial, administrative or professional occupations), C2 – Skilled working class (skilled manual workers), D – working class (semi- and unskilled manual workers), E – those at lowest level of subsistence (all those entirely dependent on the State long term, casual workers, those without regular income).

The demographic breakdown of the survey population (before weighting) was as follows:

Table IIB.1 Demographic breakdown of survey population (before weighting)

	Gender		Age						Class				
---	Male	Female	18–24	25–34	35–44	45–54	55–64	65+	AB	C1	C2	D	E
N	488	529	112	173	203	173	152	203	254	295	213	85	170
Survey (%)	48	52	11	17	20	17	15	20	25	29	21	8	17
2001 Census (%)	48	52	10	19	20	17	14	20	22	30	15	17	16

Comparison of the survey sample against the 2001 Census demonstrates that the sample is statistically representative for age and gender, though there is a slight socioeconomic bias built into it. Specifically, the sample over-represents the AB and C2 socioeconomic categories, and under-represents the D group, to a statistically significant level by chi-square analysis at $p < 0.01$. Rim weighting was applied to correct for this imbalance. The sample is representative in terms of ethnic make-up and residential status. There is a slight under-representation of those with avowed Christian beliefs and a slight over-representation of employed persons in terms of working status. The sample was again rim-weighted to redress these small imbalances. Such small divergences from the most recent census are of the same order as those in comparable surveys.

References

Reports

BBC (2002). *Beyond the Soundbite: BBC Research into Public Disillusion with Politics.* http://www.trbi.co.uk/trbipolitics.pdf. Last accessed 5 Oct. 2004.

BBC Press Office (2005). Press Release 15 Sept. 2005 'World Service/ Gallup International Poll Reveals Who Runs Your World'. http://www.bbc.co.uk/ pressreleases/ Last accessed 10 Oct. 2005.

BBC/Reuters/Media Center (2006) Press release 4 May 2006 'Media More Trusted Than Governments – poll'. http://www.bbc.co.uk/pressreleases /stories/2006 /05_may/03/trust.shtml Last accessed 8 May 2006.

Center for Social Media (2004). *Youth as E-Citizens.* Available from www. centerforsocialmedia.org/ecitizens/youthreport.pdf.

Dutton, W.H., Helsper, E.J. and Gerber, M.M. (2009). *The Internet in Britain: 2009* Oxford Internet Institute, University of Oxford.

Electoral Commission (2004a). *An Audit of Political Engagement.* London.

Electoral Commission (2004b). *Gender and Political Participation.* London.

Electoral Commission (2004c). *Political Engagement Along Young People: an Update.* London.

Electoral Commission (2005a). *An Audit of Political Engagement 2.* London.

Electoral Commission (2005b). *Election 2005: Turnout. How Many, Who and Why?* London.

Electoral Commission (2005c). *Election 2005: Engaging the Public in Great Britain.* London.

Electoral Commission (2006). *An Audit of Political Engagement 3.* London.

Electoral Commission (2008). *An Audit of Political Engagement 4.* London.

MORI (2004). *Rules of Engagement?: Participation, Involvement and Voting in Britain.* London.

National Centre for Social Research (2006). *British Social Attitudes: the 23rd Report.* Aldershot: Gower.

Ofcom (2004a). *The Communications Market 2004.* Available from www.ofcom. org.uk.

Ofcom (2004b). *Ofcom Review of Public Service Television Broadcasting (PSB) – phase 1.* Available from www.ofcom.org.uk

Ofcom (2005). *The Communications Market 2005.* Available from www.ofcom. org.uk

Ofcom (2006a). *Media Literacy Audit: Report on Adult Media Literacy.* London.

Ofcom (2006b). *Current Affairs: Qualitative Audience Research.* Presentation by Alison Preston 28 March 2006. Available from www.ofcom.org.uk/media/ speeches/2006/03/CA_qual_presntation.pdf Last accessed 20 Apr. 2006.

Ofcom (2008). *Media Literacy Audit: Report on UK Adults from Ethnic Minority Groups.* London.

Ofcom (2009). *Citizens' Digital Participation.* London.

Office of the E-envoy (2002). *In the Service of Democracy.* http://www.edemocracy. gov.uk, Last accessed 16 Aug. 2002.

Office of National Statistics (2002). *Social Trends 32*. London.
Oxford Internet Survey Report (2005). *The Internet in Britain*. Oxford.
Pew (2000). *Internet Sapping Broadcast News Audience*. Available from http://people-press.org/reports/pdf/
Pew (2002a). *The Rise of the E-citizen*. Available from www.pewinternet.org
Pew (2002b). *The Broadband Difference*. Available from www.pewinternet.org
Pew (2002c). *Pew Research Center Biennial News Consumption Survey*. Available from http://people-press.org/reports/pdf/
Pew (2003). *The Internet and the Iraq War*. Available from www.pewinternet.org
Pew (2004) *Pew Research Center Biennial News Consumption Survey*. Available from http://people-press.org/reports/pdf/
Power Report (2006). *The Report of Power: An Independent Inquiry into Britain's Democracy*. London: Joseph Rowntree. Available from http://www.powerinquiry.org/report/index.php
Socitm (2006) *Local Government Transformation and the Council Website*. Report dated Mar. 2006. Available from www.socitm.gov.uk
Election Statistics 1945–2003 (2003). *House of Commons Library Research Paper 03/59*.
US Census Bureau. (2004). Voting and Registration in the *Election of November 2004*. Washington, DC.

Other references

Abercrombie, N. S. Hill and B. Turner (1980). *The Dominant Ideology Thesis*. London, George Allen & Unwin.
Abercrombie, N. and B. Longhurst (1998). *Audiences*. London, Sage.
Alasuutari, P. (ed.) (1999). *Rethinking the Media Audience*. London, Sage.
Almond, G. and Verba, S. (1963). *The Civic Culture*. Princeton, Princeton University Press.
Almond, G. and S. Verba (eds), (1989). *The Civic Culture Revisited*. Newbury Park, Sage.
Althaus, S. and Tewksbury, D. (2000). 'Patterns of Internet and Traditional News Media Use in a Networked Community'. *Political Communication*, 17: 21–45.
Anderson, D. and Levin, S. (1976). 'Young Children's Attention to Sesame Street'. *Child Development*, 47: 806–11.
Ang, I. (1996). 'Ethnography and Radical Contextualism in Audience Studies'. In J. Hay, L. Grossberg and Wartella, E. (eds), *The Audience and Its Landscape*. Boulder, CO, Westview.
Ankersmit, F. (1996). *Aesthetic Politics: Political Philosophy Beyond Fact and Value*. Stanford, Stanford University Press.
Arendt, H. (1958). *The Human Condition*. Chicago, Chicago University Press.
Aristotle (1981). *The Politics*. Harmondsworth, Penguin.
Arnheim, R. (1943). 'The World of Daytime Serial'. In P. Lazarsfeld and F. Stanton (eds), *Radio Research*. New York, Duell, Sloan and Pearce.
Bader, V. (1995). 'Citizenship and Exclusion: Radical Democracy, Community and Justice'. *Political Theory* 23(2): 211–246.
Bakardjieva, M. and Smith, R. (2001). 'The Internet in Everyday Life: Computer Networking from the Standpoint of the Domestic User.' *New Media & Society*, 3(1): 67–83.

Ball-Rokeach, S. (1985). 'The Origins of Individual Media-System Dependency: A Sociological Framework'. *Communication Research*, 12: 485–510.

Barbalet, J. (2000). 'Vagaries of Social Capital: Citizenship, Trust and Loyalty'. In E. Vast (ed.), *Citizenship, Community and Democracy*. Basingstoke, Macmillan, 91–106.

Barber, B. (1984). *Strong Democracy: Participatory Politics for a New Age*. Berkeley, University of California Press.

Barber, B. (1999). 'Clansmen, Consumers and Citizens'. In R. Fullinwider (ed.), *Civil Society, Democracy and Civic Renewal*. Lanham, MD, Rowman and Littlefield, 9–30.

Barnett, C. (2003). *Culture and Democracy*. Edinburgh, Edinburgh University Press.

Barnhurst, K. (1998). 'Politics in the Fine Meshes: Young Citizens, Power and Media'. *Media Culture & Society* 20(2): 201–18.

Barnhurst, K (2000). 'Political Engagement and the Audience for News: Lessons from Spain'. *Journalism & Communication Monographs*, 2(1).

Bauman, Z. (1999). *In Search of Politics*. Cambridge, Polity.

Bauman, Z. (2001). *The Individualised Society*. Cambridge, Polity.

Beck, U. (1992). *Risk Society: Towards a New Modernity*. London, Sage.

Beck, U. (1997). *The Reinvention of Politics*. Cambridge, Polity.

Beck, U. (2000a). *What Is Globalisation?* Cambridge, Polity.

Beck, U. (2000b). 'The Cosmopolitan Perspective: Sociology of the Second Age of Modernity?' *British Journal of Sociology*, 51(1): 79–105.

Benhabib, S. (1996). 'Towards a Deliberative Model of Democratic Legitimacy'. In S. Benhabib (ed.), *Democracy and Difference*. Princeton, Princeton University Press, 67–94.

Bennett, L. (1998). 'The Uncivic Culture: Communication, Identity, and the Rise of Lifestyle Politics'. *PS: Political Science and Politics*, 31(4): 740–71.

Bennett, L. and R. Entman, (eds) (2001). *Mediated Politics*. Cambridge, Cambridge University Press.

Bennett, L. and Manheim, J. (2006). 'The One-Step Flow of Communication'. *The Annals of the American Academy of Political and Social Science*, 608: 213–32.

Bennett, W. (2004). 'Global Media and Politics: Transnational Communication Regimes and Civic Cultures'. *Annual Review of Political Science*, 7: 125–18.

Bentivegna, S. (2002). 'Politics and New Media'. In *The Handbook of New Media*. L. Lievrouw and Livingston (eds) S. London, Sage, 50–61.

Berg, L. and Wenner, L. (2004). 'Media Literacy and Television Criticism – Enabling an Informed and Engaged Citizenry'. *American Behavioral Scientist*, 48(2): 219–28.

Berlant, L. (1997). *The Queen of America Goes to Washington City*. Durham, NC, Duke University Press.

Bhavnani, K. (1991). *Talking Politics*. Cambridge, Cambridge University Press.

Bird, E. (2003). *The Audience in Everyday Life*. London, Routledge.

Blumler, J. and Gurevitch, M. (1995). *The Crisis of Public Communication*. London, Routledge.

Blumler, J. and Kavanagh, D. (1999). 'The Third Age of Political Communication'. *Political Communication*, 16: 209–30.

Boczkowski, P. J. (2004). *Digitising the News*. Cambridge, Mass.: The MIT Press.

Boggs, C. (1997) 'The Great Retreat: Decline of the Public Sphere in Late Twentieth-Century America'. *Theory and Society*, 26: 741–80.

Bohman, J. (1997). 'Deliberative and Democracy and Effective Social Freedom'. In J. Bohman J. and Rehg, W. (eds), *Deliberative Democracy*. Cambridge, Mass., MIT Press, 321–48.

Bohman, J. (2000). 'The Division of Labour in Democratic Discourse'. In S. Chambers and Costain, A. (eds), *Deliberation, Democracy and the Media*. Lanham, MD, Rowman and Littlefield, 47–64.

Bolter, R. and Grusin, D. (2001) *Remediation*. Cambridge, Mass., MIT Press.

Bonfadelli, H. (2002). 'The Internet and Knowledge Gaps: A Theoretical and Empirical Investigation'. *European Journal of Communication*, 17(1): 65–84.

Boorstin, D (1961). *The Image : or, What Happened to the American Dream*. London, Weidenfeld & Nicolson.

Bourdieu, P. (1984). *Distinction*. London: Routledge.

Bourdieu, P. (1990). *The Logic of Practice*. Cambridge, Polity.

Bromley, C., *et al.* (2004). *Is Britain Facing a Crisis of Democracy?* London, UCL Constitution Unit.

Buckingham, D. (2000). *Making Citizens*. London, Routledge.

Bucy, E. and Gregson, K. (2001). 'Media Participation: A Legitimising Mechanism of Mass Democracy'. *New Media & Society*, 3(3): 357–80.

Burbules, N (1998). 'Rhetorics on the Web: Hyperreading and Critical Literacy'. In I. Snyder (ed.), *Page to Screen: Taking Literacy into the Electronic Era*. New York, Routledge, 102–22.

Bryan, C. (1998). 'Manchester: Democratic Implications of an Economic Initiative'. In R. Tsagrousianou, D. Tambini and C. Bryan (eds), *Cyberdemocracy*. London, Routledge, 152–61.

Calhoun, C. (1992). 'Introduction'. In C. Calhoun (ed.), *Habermas and the Public Sphere*. Cambridge, Mass.; London, MIT Press, 1–48.

Cammaerts, B. and Van Audenhove, L. (2005). 'Online Political Debate, Unbounded Citizenship, and the Problematic Nature of a Transnational Public Sphere'. *Political Communication*, 22(2): 179–96.

Campbell, A. and Converse, P. (1972). *The Human Meaning of Social Change*. New York, Russell Sage Foundation.

Cappella, J. and Hall Jamieson, K. (1997). *The Spiral of Cynicism*. Chicago, Chicago University Press.

Castells, M. (2001). *The Internet Galaxy*. Oxford, Oxford University Press.

Cho, J. (2005). 'Media, Interpersonal Discussion, and Electoral Choice'. *Communication Research*, 32(3): 295–322.

Cohen, A., Adoni, H. and Bantz, C. (eds), (1990). *Social Conflict and Television News*. Newbury Park, CA: Sage.

Cohen, J. (1997). 'Deliberation and Democratic Legitimacy'. In J. Bohman and Rehg, W. (eds), *Deliberative Democracy*. Cambridge, Mass., MIT Press, 407–38.

Cohen, J. (1999). 'American Civil Society Talk'. In R. Fullinwider (ed.), *Civil Society, Democracy and Civic Renewal*. Lanham,MD, Rowman and Littlefield, 55–85.

Cohen, J. and Arato, A. (1992). *Civil Society and Political Theory*. Cambridge, Mass., MIT Press.

Coleman, S. (2001). 'The Transformation of Citizenship'? In B. Axford and Huggins, R. (eds), *New Media and Politics*. London, Sage, 109–26.

Coleman, S. (2003). 'A Tale of Two Houses: The House of Commons, the Big Brother House and the People at Home'. *Parliamentary Affairs*, 56(4): 733–58.

Coleman, S. (2005). 'The Lonely Citizen: Indirect Representation in an Age of Networks'. *Political Communication*, 22(2): 197–214.

Conover, P., Crewe, I. and Shearing, P. (1991). 'The Nature of Citizenship in the US and Great Britain'. *Journal of Politics* 53(3): 800–32.

Conover, P., *et al.* (2004). 'The Elusive Ideal of Equal Citizenship: Political Theory and Political Psychology in the United States and Great Britain'. *Journal of Politics*, 66(4): 1036–68.

Cook, R. (2005) 'The Abstention Party is the Biggest Threat, Not the Tories', *Guardian*, 18 Mar.

Corner, J. (1995). *Television Form and Public Address*. London, Edward Arnold.

Corner, J. and D. Pels, (eds) (2003). *Media and the Restyling of Politics*. London, Sage.

Cornfield, M. (2005). Buzz, Blogs and Beyond: the Internet and the National Discourse in the fall of 2004. Last available from http://www.pewinternet.org/ PPF/ p/1088/pipcomments.asp Accessed 26 Apr. 2006.

Costera Meijer, I. (1998). 'Advertising Citizenship'. *Media Culture & Society*, 20: 235–49.

Couldry, N. (2003a) *Media Rituals: A Critical Approach*. London: Routledge.

Couldry, N. (2003b). 'Passing Ethnographies: Rethinking the Sites of Agency and Reflexivity in a Mediated World'. In P. Murphy and M. Kraidy (eds), *Global Media Studies: Ethnographic Perspectives*. London, Routledge, 40–56.

Couldry, N. (2005a) 'The Individual Point of View: Learning from Bourdieu's *The Weight of the World*'. *Cultural Studies: Critical Methodologies*. 5(3): 354–72.

Couldry, N. (2005b) 'The Extended Audience: Scanning the Horizon'. In M. Gillespie (ed.), *Media Audiences*. Maidenhead: Open University Press, 182–222.

Couldry, N. (2006a). *Listening Beyond the Echoes: Media Ethics and Agency in an Uncertain World*. Boulder, CO: Paradigm Books.

Couldry, N. (2006b). 'Culture and Citizenship: the Missing Link?' *European Journal of Cultural Studies*, 9(3): 321–40.

Couldry, N. and Langer, A. (2003). 'The Future of Public Connection: Some Early Sightings'. *ESRC Cultures of Consumption Working Paper Series*. Available from www.consume.bbk.ac.uk

Couldry, N. and Langer, A. (2005). 'Media Consumption and Public Connection: Toward a Typology of the Dispersed Citizen'. *The Communication Review*, 8: 237–257.

Couldry, N., Livingstone, S. and T. Markham (forthcoming). 'Connection or Disconnection?: Tracking the Mediated Public Sphere in Everyday Life'. In R Butsch (ed.), *Media and the Public Sphere*. New York, Palgrave.

Crary, J. (1999). *Suspensions of Perception: Attention, Spectacle and Modern Culture*. Cambridge, Mass., MIT Press.

Croteau, D. (1995). *Politics and the Class Divide*. Philadelphia, Temple University Press.

Cruise, C., *et al.* (1996). 'Reactive Effects of Diary Self-assessment in Chronic Pain Patients'. *Pain* 67(2–3): 253–8.

Csikszentmihalyi, M. and Rochberg-Halton, C. (1990). *The Meaning of Things*. Chicago, Chicago University Press.

Dahl, R. (1989). *Democracy and Its Critics*. New Haven, Yale University Press.

Dahlgren, P. (2001). 'The Transformation of Democracy?' In B. Axford and Huggins, R. (eds), *New Media and Politics*. London, Sage, 64–88.

Dahlgren, P. (2003). 'Reconfiguring Civic Culture in the New Media Milieu'. In J. Corner and Pels, D. (eds), *Media and the Restyling of Politics*. London, Sage, 151–70.

Dahlgren, P. (2005). 'The Internet, Public Spheres, and Political Communication: Dispersion and Deliberation'. *Political Communication*, 22(2): 147–62.

Dahlgren, P. (2009). *Media and Political Engagement: Citizens, Communication and Democracy*. Cambridge: Cambridge University Press.

Dahlgren, P. and Olsson, T. (2008). 'Facilitating Political Participation: Young Citizens, Internet and Civic Cultures'. In K. Drotner and S. Livingstone (eds), *International Handbook of Children, Media and Culture*. London, Sage, 493–507.

Dahrendorf, R. (1974). 'Citizenship and Beyond'. *Social Research*, 41: 673–701.

Dalton, R. (1999). 'Political Support in Advanced Industrial Democracies'. In P. Norris (ed.), *Critical Citizens*. Oxford, Oxford University Press, 57–77.

Dalton, R. (2000). 'Value Change and Democracy'. In S. Pharr and Putnam, R. (eds), *Disaffected Democracies*. Cambridge, Mass., Harvard University Press, 252–69.

Dalton, R. J. and Wattenberg, M. P. (2000). *Parties Without Partisans*. Oxford, Oxford University Press.

Dayan, D. (2005). 'Mothers, Midwives and Abortionists: Genealogy, Obstetrics, Audiences and Publics'. In S. Livingstone (ed.), *Audiences and Publics*. Bristol, Intellect Press, 43–76.

Dayan, D. and Katz, E. (1992). *Media Events*. Cambridge, Harvard University Press.

De Grazia, S. (1962). *Of Time, Work and Leisure*. New York, Twentieth Century Fund.

Delli Carpini, M. and Keater, S. (1996). *What Americans Know About Politics and why It Matters*. New Haven, Yale University Press.

Delli Carpini, M. and Williams, B. (2001). 'Let Us Infotain You'., In L. Bennett, and Entman, R. (eds), *Mediated Politics*. Cambridge, Cambridge University Press, 160–81.

Delli Carpini, M., *et al.* (2004). 'Public Deliberation, Discursive Participation, and Citizen Engagement: A Review of the Empirical Literature'. *Annual Review of Political Science*, 7: 315–44.

Deutsch, K. (1966). *Nationalism and Social Communication*. Cambridge, Mass., MIT Press.

Dewey, J. (1946). *The Public and Its Problems*. Chicago, Gateway Books.

Dewey, J. (1993). *The Political Writings*. Indianopolis, Hackett.

van Dijk, T. (1988). *News as Discourse*. Hillsdale, NJ, Erlbaum.

Drezner, D. and Farrell, H. (2004a). *The Power and Politics of Blogs*. American Political Science Association Annual Conference, Chicago, Illinois.

Drezner, D. and Farrell, H. (2004b). 'Web of Influence'. *Foreign Policy*, (145): 32–40.

Drotner, K. (1992). 'Modernity and Media Panics'. In M. Skovmand and Schroeder, K. (eds), *Media Cultures: Reappraising Transnational Media*. London, Routledge, 42–62.

Drotner, K. (1994). 'Ethnographic Enigmas: "the Everyday" in Recent Media Studies'. *Cultural Studies*, 8(2): 341–57.

Drotner, K. (2005). 'Media on the Move: Personalised Media and the Transformation of Publicness'. In S. Livingstone (ed.), *Audiences and Publics*. Bristol, Intellect Press, 187–212.

Dutwin, D. (2003). 'The Character of Deliberation: Equality, Argument, and the Formation of Public Opinion'. *International Journal of Public Opinion Research*, 15(3): 239–64.

Easton, D. (1965). *A Systems Analysis of Political Life*. New York, John Wiley.

Eder, K. (2001). 'Social Movement Organisations and the Democratic Order'. In C. Crouch, Eder, K. and Tambini, D. (eds), *Citizenship, Markets, and the State*. Oxford, Oxford University Press, 213–37.

Eliasoph, N. (1998). *Avoiding Politics*. Cambridge, Cambridge University Press.

Eliasoph, N. (2004). 'Can We Theorise the Press Without Theorising the Public?' *Political Communication*, 21(3): 297–303.

Elliott, H. (1997). 'The Use of Diaries in Sociological Research on Health Experience'. *Sociological Research Online* 2(2).

Elshtain, J. (1997). 'The Displacement of Politics'. In J. Weintraub and K. Kumar (eds), *Public and Private in Thought and Practice*. Chicago, Chicago University Press, 103–32.

Elster, J. (1997). 'The Market and the Forum'. In J. Bohman and W. Rehg (eds), *Deliberative Democracy*. Cambridge, Mass., MIT Press, 3–34.

Eriksen, E. and Weigard, J. (2000). 'The End of Citizenship?' In C. Mackinnon and Hampshire-Monk, I. (eds), *The Demands of Citizenship*. London, Continuum, 13–34.

Ettema, J., *et al.* (1983). 'Knowledge gap effects in a health information campaign'. *Public Opinion Quarterly*, 47: 516–27.

Evans, G. and S. Butt (2005). 'Leaders or Followers? Parties and Public Opinion on the European Union'. *British Social Attitudes: The 22nd Report*. London, National Centre for Social Research.

Eveland, W. (2004). 'The Effect of Political Discussion in Producing Informed Citizens: The Roles of Information, Motivation, and Elaboration'. *Political Communication*, 21(2): 177–93.

Field, J. (2005). *Social Capital and Lifelong Learning*. Bristol, Policy.

Fine, B. (2001). *Social Capital Versus Social Theory: Political Economy and Social Science at the Turn of the Millennium*. London, Routledge.

Fine, G. and Harrington, B. (2004). 'Tiny Publics: Small Groups and Civil Society'. *Sociological Theory*, 22(3): 341–56.

Fleeson, W., *et al.* (2002). 'An Intraindividual Process Approach to the Relationship Between Extraversion and Positive Affect: Is Acting Extraverted as "good" as Being Extraverted?' *Journal of Personality and Social Psychology*, 83(6): 1409–22.

Flichy, P. (1995). *Dynamics of Modern Communication*. London, Sage.

Fraser, N. (1992). 'Rethinking the Public Sphere: a Contribution to the Critique of Actually Existing Democracy'. In C. Calhoun (ed.), *Habermas and the Public Sphere*. Cambridge, Mass., MIT Press, 109–43.

Frissen, Van, E. (2000). 'ICTs in the Rush Hour of Life'. *The Information Society*, 16: 65–75.

Gamson, J. (1998). *Freaks Talk Back: Tabloid Talk Shows and Sexual Nonconformity*. Chicago ; London, University of Chicago Press.

Gamson, W. (1992). *Talking Politics*. Cambridge, Cambridge University Press.

Gandy, O. (2002). 'The Real Digital Divide: Citizens Versus Consumers'. In L. Lievrouw and Livingstone, L. (ed.), *Handbook of New Media*. London, Sage, 448–60.

Garcia Canclini, N. (2001). *Consumers and Citizens*. Minneapolis, University of Minnesota Press.

Garnham, N. (2000). *Emancipation, The Media and Modernity*. Oxford, Oxford University Press.

Gauntlett, D. and Hill, A. (1999). *Television, Culture and Everyday Life*. London and New York, Routledge/BFI.

Gellner, E. (1983). *Nations and Nationalism*. Oxford, Blackwell.

Gerbner, G. *et al.* (1982). 'Charting the Mainstream: Television's Contributions to Political Orientations'. *Journal of Communication*, 32(2): 100–27.

Gerbner, G., *et al.* (1986). 'Living with Television: The Dynamics of the Cultivation Process. In J. Bryant and Zillman, D. (eds), *Perspectives on Media Effects*. Hillsdale, NJ, Erlbaum.

Gershuny, J. (2000). *Changing Times: Work and Leisure in Postindustrial Society*. Oxford, Oxford University Press.

Gershuny, J. (2004). 'Costs and Benefits of Time Sampling Methodologies'. *Social Indicators Research*, 67(1–2): 247–52.

Gershuny, J. and Sullivan, O. (1998). 'The Sociological Uses of Time-use Diary Analysis'. *European Sociological Review*, 14(1): 69–85.

Gerson, G. (2004). 'Deliberative Households: Republicans, Liberals, and the Public – private split'. *Political Research Quarterly*, 57(4): 653–63.

Geuss, R. (2001). *Public Goods, Private Goods*. Princeton, NJ, Princeton University Press.

Gibson, O. (2005) 'Young Blog Their Way to a Publishing Revolution'. *Guardian*, 7 Oct. 2005.

Gibson, O. (2006) 'News for the clickers and flickers'. *Guardian*, 1 May.

Gilligan, C. (1993) *In a Different Voice: Psychological Theory and Women's Development* (2nd edn). Cambridge, Mass.: Harvard University Press.

Giroux, H. (2001). *Public Spaces, Private Lives*. Lanham, MD, Rowman and Littlefield.

Gitlin, T. (1998). 'Public Sphere or Public Sphericules?' In T. Liebes and Curran, J. (eds), *Media Ritual and Identity*. London, Routledge, 74–89.

Goffman, E. (1974). *Frame Analysis*. Harmondsworth, Penguin.

Golding, P. (2000). 'Forthcoming Features: Information and Communications Technologies and the Sociology of the Future'. *Sociology*, 34(1): 165–84.

Graber, D. (2001). *Processing Politics*. Chicago, Chicago University Press.

Graber, D. (2004). 'Mediated Politics and Citizenship in the Twenty-first Century'. *Annual Review of Psychology*, 55: 545–71.

Grade, M. (2004). 'Building Public Value' Speech by Michael Grade, Chairman of the BBC, 29 June 2004 http://www.bbc.co.uk/pressoffice /speeches/stories/bpv_grade.shtml. Last accessed 5 May 2006.

Graham, S. and Marvin, S. (2001). *Splintering Urbanism*. London, Routledge.

Grant, M. (1994) *Propaganda and the Role of the State in Inter-War Britain*. Oxford: Oxford University Press.

Grant, L., *et al.* (2002). 'Women's Adaptation to Chronic Back Pain: Daily Appraisals and Coping Strategies, Personal Characteristics and Perceived Spousal Responses'. *Journal of Health Psychology*, 7(5): 545–63.

Griffiths, H. and Jordan, S. (1998). 'Thinking of the Future and Walking Back to Normal: an Exploratory Study of Patients' Experiences During Recovery from Lower Limb Fracture'. *Journal of Advanced Nursing*, 28(6): 1276–88.

Gronow, J. and A. Warde, (eds) (2001). *Ordinary Consumption*. London, Routledge.

Gunsteren, van H. (1998). *A Theory of Citizenship*. Boulder, CO; Westview.

Gunter, B. (1987). *Poor Reception*. Hillsdale, NJ, L. Erlbaum Associates.

Gunter, B. (2003). *News and the Net*. Mahwah NJ, Lawrence Erlbaum Associates.

Habermas, J. (1988) *Legitimation Crisis*. Cambridge: Polity.

Habermas, J. (1989). *The Structural Transformation of the Public Sphere*. Cambridge, Polity.

Habermas, J. (1996). 'Three Normative Models of Democracy'. In S. Benhabib (ed.), *Democracy and Difference*. Princeton, Princeton University Press, 21–30.

Habermas, J. (1996). *Between Facts and Norms*. Cambridge, Polity.

Hagen, I. (1994). 'The Ambivalences of Television News Viewing'. *European Journal of Communication*, 9(2): 193–220.

Hall, P. (2002). 'Great Britain: The Role of Government and the Distribution of Social Capital'. In R. Putnam (ed.), *Democracies in Flux*. Oxford, Oxford University Press, 21–58.

Hamilton, J., and Jenner, E. (2003). 'The New Foreign Correspondence. *Foreign Affairs*, 82(5), 131–8.

Hannerz, U. (2002). 'Among the Foreign Correspondents: Reflections on Anthropological Styles and Audiences'. *Ethnos*, 67(1): 57–74.

Hansard Society, The (2001). *None of the Above: Non-Voters and the 2001 Election*. London, Hansard Society.

Hargreaves, I. and Thomas, J. (2002). New News, Old News. London, ITC/BSC.

Hartley, J. (1999). *Uses of Television*. London, Routledge.

Haste, H. (2005) *My Voice, My Vote, My Community*. London: Nestle Social Research Programme.

Havens, J and Schervish, P. (2001), 'The Methods and Metrics of the Boston Area Diary Study'. *Nonprofit and Voluntary Sector Quarterly*, 30(3): 527–50.

Hays, W. (1988). *Statistics*. New York, Holt, Rinehart and Winston.

Haythornthwaite, C. and Wellman, B. (2002). 'The Internet in Everyday Life'. In B. Wellman and Haythornthwaite, C. (eds), *The Internet in Everday Life*. Oxford, Blackwell, 3–41.

Held, D. (1995). *Democracy and the Global Order*. Cambridge, Polity.

Held, D. (2004). *Global Covenant*. Cambridge: Polity.

Hermes, J. (1998). 'Cultural Citizenship and Popular Fiction'. In K. Brants, Hermes, J. and van Zoonen, L. (eds), *The Media in Question*. London, Sage, 157–67.

Hermes, J. and Stello, C. (2000). 'Cultural Citizenship and Crime Fiction: Politics and the Interpretive Community'. *Cultural Studies*, 3(2), 215–32.

Hill, K. and Matsubayashi, T. (2005). 'Civic Engagement and Mass – elite Policy Agenda Agreement in American Communities'. *American Political Science Review*, 99(2): 215–24.

Hilton, M. and Daunton, M. (2001). 'Material Politics: an Introduction'. In M. Daunton and Hilton, M. (eds) *The Politics of Consumption*. Oxford, Berg, 1–32.

Hirschauer, S. (2001). 'Ethnographic Writing and the Silence of the social – Towards a Methodology of Description'. *Zeitschrift Für Soziologie*, 30(6): 429–51.

Hirschman, A. (1969). *Exit Voice and Loyalty*. Cambridge, Mass., Harvard University Press.

Hirschman, A. (1982). *Shifting Involvements*. Oxford, Blackwell.

Hoijer, B. (2004). 'The Discourse of Global Compassion: the Audience and Media Reporting of Human Suffering'. *Media, Culture & Society*, 26(4), 513–31.

Hooghe, M. and Stolle, D. (2003). *Generating Social Capital*. New York and Basingstoke, Palgrave Macmillan.

Hoover, S. (2006). *Religion in the Media Age*. London, Routledge.

Hoover, S., Schofield Clarke, L. and Alters, D. (2004). *Media Home and Family*. London: Routledge.

Huckfeldt, R. and Sprague, J. (1995). *Citizens, Politics, and Social Communication*. Cambridge, Cambridge University Press.

Huggins, R. (2001). 'The Transformation of the Political Audience'. In B. Axford and Huggins, R. (eds), *New Media and Politics*. London, Sage, 128–47.

Huntington, S. (1975). 'The United States'. In M. Crozier, S. Huntington and J. Watarmiki (eds), *The Crisis of Democracy*. New York, New York University Press.

Inglehart, R. (1977). *The Silent Revolution*. Princeton: Princeton University Press.

Inglehart, R. (1997). *Modernisation and Postmodernisation: Cultural Economic and Political Change in 43 Countries*. Princeton, Princeton University Press.

Isin, E. (2002). *Being Political*. Minneapolis, University of Minnesota Press.

Jensen, K. (ed.) (2005). *Interface://Culture: The World Wide Web as Political Resources and Aesthetic Form*. Frederiksberg, Denmark, Samfundslitteratur Press/Nordicom.

Johnson, B. (2003). 'Backbench Bloggers', *Guardian*, Media section, 21 July.

Johnson, B. (2006). 'Britain Turns Off – and Logs On'. *Guardian*, 8 Mar.

Jones, D. (2002). 'The Polarising Effect of New Media messages'. *International Journal of Public Opinion Research*, 14(2).

Jones, R. (2000). 'The Unsolicited Diary as a Qualitative Research Tool for Advanced Research Capacity in the Field of Health and Illness'. *Qualitative Health Research*, 10(4): 555–67.

Jones, S. (1997). 'The Internet and Its Social Landscape'. In S. Jones (ed.), *Virtual Culture*. London, Sage, 7–35.

Katz, E., *et al.* (1973). 'On the Use of the Mass Media for Important things'. *American Sociological Review*, 38(2): 164–81.

Katz, E. and Lazarsfeld, P. (1955). *Personal Influence*. Glencoe, Ill, Free Press.

Katz, J. and Rice, R. (2002). *Social Consequences of the Internet: Access, Involvement and Interaction*. Cambridge, Mass., MIT Press.

Kavanagh, D. (1989). 'Political Culture in Great Britain: the Decline of the Civic Culture'. In G. Almond and Verba, S. (ed.), *The Civic Culture Revisited*. Newbury Park, Sage, 124–76.

Keane, J. (1998). *Civil Society: Old Images, New Visions*. Cambridge, Polity.

Keefe, F. J. *et al.* (2001). 'Giving with Rheumatoid Arthritis: The Role of Daily Spirituality and Daily Religious and Spiritual Coping'. *Journal of Pain*, 2(2): 101–10.

Keeter, S., Zukin, C. Andolina, M. and Jenkins, K. (2002). *The Civic and Political Health of the Nation: A Generational Portrait*. Available from www.pewtrusts.com/pdf/public_policy_youth_civic_poltiical_health.pdf Last accessed 3 Apr. 2006.

Keum, H., *et al.* (2004). 'The Citizen – Consumer: Media Effects at the Intersection of Consumer and Civic Culture'. *Political Communication*, 21(3): 369–31.

Khan, H. and Muir, R. (eds) (2006). *Sticking Together: Social Capital and Local Government*. London, IPPR and London Borough of Camden.

Kierkegaard, S. (1962). *The Present Age*. London, Fontana.

Kimberlee, R. (2002). 'Why Don't British Young People Vote at General Elections?' *Journal of Youth Studies*, 5(1), 85–98.

Kress, G. (2003). *Literacy in the New Media Age*. London, Routledge.

Kwak, N., *et al.* (2004). 'Connecting, Trusting, and Participating: The Direct and Interactive Effects of Social Associations'. *Political Research Quarterly*, 57(4): 643–52.

Kwak, N., *et al.* (2005). 'Talking Politics and Engaging Politics: An Examination of the Interactive Relationships Between Structural Features of Political Talk and Discussion Engagement'. *Communication Research*, 32(1): 87–111.

Lacey, K. (1996). *Feminine Frequencies : Gender, German Radio, and the Public sphere, 1923–1945*. Ann Arbor, University of Michigan Press.

LeBlanc, R. (1999). *Bicycle Citizens: The Political World of the Japanese Housewife*. Berkeley, University of California Press.

Lembo, R. (2000). *Thinking Through Television*. Cambridge, Cambridge University Press.

Levine, P., and Lopez, M. (2004). *Young People and Political Campaigning on the Internet – Fact Sheet:* CIRCLE – The Center for Information & Research on Civic Learning & Engagement, University of Maryland.

Lewis, J., Inthorn, S. and Wahl-Jorgensen, K. (2005). *Citizens or Consumers?* Maidenhead, Open University Press.

Lieberg, M. (1995). 'Public Space: Lifestyles and Collective Identity'. *Young*, 3(1): 19–38.

Liebes, T. (1992). 'Decoding Television News: The Political Discourse of Israeli Hawks and Doves'. *Theory and Society*, 21(3): 357–81.

Lievrouw, L. (2001). 'New Media and the 'Pluralisation of Lifeworlds': a Role for Information in Social Differentiation'. *New Media & Society*, 3(1): 7–28.

Lievrouw, L. and Livingstone, S. (2006). Introduction. In L. Lievrouw and Livingstone, S. (eds), *Handbook of New Media: Social Shaping and Social Consequences*. London, Sage, 1–14.

Liff, S. and Stewart, F. (2001). 'Community E-gateways: Locating Networks and Learning for Social Inclusion'. *Information, Communication and Society*, 4(3), 317–40.

Lindlof, T. and D. Grodin (1990). 'When Media Use Can't Be Observed: Some Problems and Tactics of Collaborative Audience Research'. *Journal of Communication*, 40(4): 8–28.

Lippman, W. (1922). *Public Opinion*. New York, Harcourt Brace and Company.

Lippman, W. (1925). *The Phantom Public*. New York, Harcourt Brace.

Lipset, S. M. (1963). *Political Man*. Garden City, NY, Doubleday Anchor Books.

Lister, R., Smith, N. Middleton, S. and Cox, L. (2003). 'Young People Talk About Citizenship: Empirical Perspectives on Theoretical and Political Debates'. *Citizenship Studies*, 7(2), 235–53.

Livingstone, S. (1998). *Making Sense of Television: The Psychology of Audience Interpretation*. London, Routledge.

Livingstone, S. (2002). *Young People New Media*. London, Sage.

Livingstone, S. (2004). 'Media Literacy and the Challenge of New Information and Communication Technologies'. *Communication Review*, 7: 3–14.

Livingstone, S. (2005a). 'On the Relation Between Audiences and Publics.' In S. Livingstone (ed.), *Audiences and Publics*. Bristol, Intellect Press, 17–42.

Livingstone, S. (2005b). 'Critical Debates in Internet Studies: Reflections on an Emerging Field'. In J. Curran and Gurevitch, M. (eds), *Mass Media and Society*. London, Sage, 9–28.

Livingstone, S. (2009). *Children and the Internet: Great Expectations and Challenging Realities*. Cambridge, Polity.

Livingstone, S. and Lunt, P. (1994). *Talk on Television*. London, Routledge.

Livingstone, S. and Bovill, M. (2001). *Children and Their Changing Media Environment*. Mahwah, NJ, Lawrence Erlbaum.

Livingstone, S. and Bober, M. (2004). *UK Children Go Online: Surveying the Experiences of Young People and Their Parents*. London, London School of Economics and Political Science.

Livingstone, S., Bober, M., and Helsper, E. (2005). 'Active Participation or Just More information?: Young people's take up of opportunities to act and interact on the internet'. *Information, Communication and Society*, 8(3): 287–314.

Livingstone, S., van Couvering, E. J. and Thumim, N. (2008). 'Converging Traditions of Research on Media and Information Literacies: Disciplinary and Methodological Issues'. In D. J. Leu, Coiro, J. Knobel, M. and Lankshear, C. *Handbook of Research on New Literacies*. Hillsdale, NJ, Lawrence Erlbaum Associates, 103–32.

Livingstone, S. and Markham, T. (2008). 'Mediating Public Participation: On the Political Significance of Everyday Media Consumption'. *British Journal of Sociology*, 59(2): 351–71.

Longhurst, B., Bagnall, G. and Savage, M. (2001). 'Ordinary Consumption and Personal Identity: Radio and the Middle Classes in the North West of England'. In J. Gronow and Warde, A. (eds), *Ordinary Consumption*. London; New York, Routledge, 125–42.

Loughborough, University of (2005) 'UK 2005 Election Study'. *Guardian* 2 May.

Luke, T. (2006). 'Power and Political Culture'. In L. Lievrouw and Livingstone, S. (eds) *The Handbook of New Media, (2nd edn.)*. London, Sage.

Lumby, C. (1997). *Gotcha: Living in a Tabloid World*. Sydney, Allen and Unwin.

Lunt, P. and Stenner, P. (2005). 'The Jerry Springer Show as an Emotional Public Sphere'. *Media Culture & Society*, 27(1): 59–81.

Lupia, A. and McCubbins, M. (1998). *The Democratic Dilemma*. Cambridge, Cambridge University Press.

Mackay, H. (ed.) (1997). *Consumption and Everyday Life*. London, Sage.

Madianou, M. (2005). 'The Elusive Public of Television News'. In S. Livingstone (ed.), *Audiences and Publics*. Bristol, Intellect Press, 99–114.

Mann, M. (1970). 'The Social Cohesion of Liberal Democracy'. *American Sociological Review*, 35(3): 423–39.

Marco, C. and Suls, J. (1993). 'Daily Stress and the Trajectory of Mood – Spillover, Response Assimilation, Contrast, and Chronic Negative Affectivity'. *Journal of Personality and Social Psychology*, 64(6): 1053–63.

Marcus, G. (1999). 'The Use of Complicity in the Changing Mise-en-scene of Ethnography'. In S. Ortner (ed.), *The Fate of "Culture" : Geertz and beyond*. Berkeley: University of California Press, 86–109.

Marshall, T. (1992). 'Citizenship and Social Class'. In T. Marshall and T. Bottomore (eds), *Citizenship and Social Class*. London, Pluto, 31–51.

Martin-Barbero, J. (1993). *Communication, Culture and Hegemony*. London, Sage Publications.

Marvin, C. (1988). *When Old Technologies Were New*. Oxford, Oxford University Press.

Mayhew, L. (1997). *The New Public*. Cambridge, Cambridge University Press.

McChesney, R. (2000). *Rich Media, Poor Democracy* New York, The New Press.

McCombs, M. and Shaw, D. (1972). 'The Agenda-setting Function of the Mass Media'. *Public Opinion Quarterly*, 36: 176–87.

Meth, P. (2003). 'Entries and Omissions: Using Solicited Diaries in Geographical Research'. *Area*, 35(2): 195–205.

Meyer, D. and Tarrow, S. (1998). 'A Movement Society: Contentious Politics for a New Century'. In D. Meyer and Tarrow, S. (eds), *The Social Movement Society*. Lanham, MD, Rowman and Littlefield, 1–28.

Michalski, M., Preston, A. Gillespie, M. and Cheesman, T. (2002). *After September 11: TV News and Transnational Audiences*. Milton Keynes: Open University/BFI.

Miller, D. (2000). *Citizenship and National Identity*. Cambridge, Polity.

Miller, T. (2002). 'Cultural Citizenship'. In E. Isin and Turner, B. (eds), *Handbook of Citizenship Studies*. London, Sage, 231–43.

Milner, H. (2002). *Civic Literacy*. Hanover, NH, Tufts University Press.

Misztal, B. A. (1996). *Trust in Modern Societies*. Cambridge, Polity.

Moore, C. (2005) 'Kingdom of Boredom', *Daily Telegraph*, 9 Apr.

Morley, D. (1986). *Family Television: Cultural Power and Domestic Leisure*. London, Comedia.

Morley, D. (1980) *The Nationwide Audience*. London, BFI.

Morley, D. (1992). Electronic Communities and Domestic Rituals: Cultural Consumption and the Production of European Cultural Identities'. In M. Skovmand and Schroder, K. C. (eds), *Media Cultures: Reappraising Transnational Media*. London, Routledge.

Morley, D. (1999). 'Finding About the World from Television News: Some Difficulties'. In J. Gripsrud (ed.), *Television and Common Knowledge*. London, Routledge, 136–58.

Morris, Z., John, P. and Halpern, D. (2003) 'Compulsory Citizenship for the Disenfranchised', *The Curriculum Journal*, 14(2): 1–19.

Morrisett, L. (2003). 'Technologies of Freedom?' In H. Jenkins and Thorburn, D. (eds), *Democracy and New Media*. Cambridge, MA: MIT Press, 21–32.

Mouffe, C. (1992). 'Democratic Citizenship and the Political Community'. In Mouffe, C. (ed.), *Dimensions of Radical Democracy*. London, Verso, 225–239.

Mouffe, C. (2000). *The Democratic Paradox*. London, Verso.

Mulgan, G. (2006). Central Reservations. *Guardian*. Society section, 1 Mar.

Murdock, G. (1999). 'Right and Representations: Public Discourse and Cultural Citizenship'. In J. Gripsrud (ed.), *Television and Common Knowledge*. London, Routledge, 7–17.

Murdock, G., P. Hartmann, and Gray, N. (1995). 'Contextualising Home Computing: Resources and Practices'. In N. Heep (ed.), *Information Technology and Society*. London, Sage, 269–283.

Narayan, U. (1997). 'Towards a Feminist Vision of Citizenship'. In M. Shenley and Narayan, U. (eds), *Reconstructing Political Theory*. Cambridge, Polity, 48–67.

Neuman, W., Just, M. and Crigler, A. (1992). *Common Knowledge*. Chicago, Chicago University Press.

Newton, K. and Norris, P. (2000). 'Confidence in Public Institutions'. In S. Pharr and Putnam, R. (eds), *Disaffected Democracies*. Cambridge, Mass., Harvard University Press, 52–73.

Nie, N., Junn, J. and Stehlik-Barry, K. (1996). *Education and Democratic Citizenship in America*. Chicago, Chicago University Press.

Nisbet, M. and Scheufele, D. (2004). 'Political Talk as a Catalyst for Online Citizenship'. *Journalism & Mass Communication Quarterly*, 81(4): 877–96.

Noelle-Neumann, E. (1984). *The Spiral of Silence: Public Opinion, Our Social Skin*. Chicago, University of Chicago Press.

Norris, P. (ed.) (1999). *Critical Citizens*. Oxford, Oxford University Press.

Norris, P. (2000). *A Virtuous Circle*. Cambridge, Cambridge University Press.

Norris, P. (2001). *Digital Divide*. Cambridge, Cambridge University Press.

Ouellette, L. (2002). *Viewers Like You*. New York, Columbia University Press.

Page, B. and Shapiro, R. (1992). *The Rational Public*. 1992.

Park, R. (1984). 'The Natural History of the Newspaper'. In R. Park and Burgess, E. (eds), *The City*. Chicago, Chicago University Press, 80–98.

Pateman, C. (1970). *Participation and Democratic Theory*. Cambridge, Cambridge University Press.

Pateman, C. (1989). 'The Civic Culture: A Philosophical Critique'. In G. Almond and Verba, S. (eds), *The Civic Culture Revisited*. Newbury Park, Sage, 57–102.

Pattie, C., Seyd, P. and Whiteley, P. (2004). *Citizenship in Britain: Values, Participation and Democracy*. Cambridge, Cambridge University Press.

Pels, D. (2003). 'Aesthetic Representation and Political Style: Re-Balancing Identity and Difference in Media Democracy'. In J. Corner and Pels, D. (eds), *Media and the Restyling of Politics*. London, Sage, 41–66.

Pharr, S. and Putnam, R. (eds), (2000). *Disaffected Democracies*. Cambridge, Mass., Harvard University Press.

Pharr, S., Putnam, R. and Dalton, R. (2000). 'Introduction: What's Troubling the Trilateral Democracies'. In S. Pharr and Putnam, R. (eds), *Disaffected Democracies*. Cambridge, Mass., Harvard University Press, 3–30.

Phillips, A. (1996). 'Dealing with Difference: A Politics of Ideas or a Politics of Presence?' In S. Benhabib (ed.), *Democracy and Difference*. Princeton, Princeton University Press, 139–52.

Philo, G., and Berry, M. (2004). *Bad News From Israel*. London: Pluto Press.

Phipps, L. (2000). 'New Communications Technologies: A Conduit for Social Inclusion'. *Information, Communication and Society*, 3(1), 39–68.

Plummer, K. (2003). *Intimate Citizenship*. Montréal, McGill-Queen's University Press.

Pollock, G. (1997). 'Individualisation and the Transition of Youth to Adulthood'. *Young* 5(1): 55–68.

Press, A. (1991). *Women Watching Television*. Philadelphia, University of Pennsylvania Press.

Preuss, U. (1995). 'Problems of a Concept of European Citizenship'. *European Law Journal*, 1(3): 267–81.

Prior, M. (2003). 'Any Good News in Soft News? The Impact of Soft News Preference on Political Knowledge'. *Political Communication*, 20: 149–71.

Prout, A. (2000). 'Children's Participation: Control and Self-realisation in British Late Modernity.' *Children & Society*, 14(4): 304–15.

Putnam, R. (2000). *Bowling Alone*. New York, Simon & Schuster.

Putnam, R.(2002). *Democracies in Flux*. Oxford, Oxford University Press.

Raboy, M. (1992). 'Media and the Invisible Crisis of Everyday Life'. In B. Dagenais and Raboy, M. (eds), *Media, Crisis and Democracy*. London, Sage, 133–43.

Radway, J. (1988). 'Reception study: Ethnography and the prblems of Dispersed Audiences and Nomadic Subjects'. *Cultural Studies*, 2(3): 359–76.

Rasmussen, C. and Brown, M. (2002). 'Radical Democratic Citizenship'. In E. Isin and Turner, B. (eds), *Handbook of Citizenship Studies*. London, Sage, 175–88.

Reckwitz, A. (2002). 'Toward a Theory of Social Practices'. *European Journal of Social Theory*, 5(2): 243–63.

Regan, T. (2004). 'Weblogs Threaten and Inform Traditional Journalism'. *Nieman Reports*, 57(3): 68–70.

Reilly, J. (1999). 'Just Another Food Scare?: Public Understanding and the BSE crisis'. In G. Philo (ed.), *Message Received: Glasgow Media Group Research 1993–1998*. London: Longman.

Reimer, B. (1995). 'Youth and Modern Lifestyles'. In *Youth Culture in Late Modernity*. In J. Fornas and Bolin, G. London, Sage.

Reith, J. (1924). *Broadcast Over Britain*. London, Hodder & Staughton.

Rheingold, H. (1995). *The Virtual Community: Finding Connection in a Computerised World*. London, Minerva.

Rice, R. and Haythornthwaite, C. (2006). 'Perspectives on Internet Use: Access, Involvement and Interaction'. In L. Lievrouw and Livingstone, S. (eds), *Handbook of New Media 2nd edn*. London, Sage, 92–113.

Robinson, J. P. and Converse, P. E. (1972). 'Social Change Reflected in the Use of Time'. In A. Campbell and Converse, P. E. (eds), *The Human Meaning of Social Change*. New York, Russell Sage Foundation.

Robinson, J. P. and Levy, M. R. (1986). *The Main Source: Learning from Television News*. Beverly Hills, Sage.

Robinson, J. and Godbey, G. (1997). *Time for Life: The Surprising Ways Americans Use Their Time (2nd edn)*. Philadelphia, Penn State University Press.

Roche, M. (2002). 'Citizenship Popular Culture and Europe'. In N. Stevenson (ed.), *Culture and Citizenship*. London, Sage, 75–98.

Rojek, C. (2001). *Celebrity*. London, Reaktion.

Rose, N. (1999). *Powers of Freedom*. Cambridge, Cambridge University Press.

Rousseau, J.-J., (1973). *The Social Contract and Discourses*. London, Dent.

Sancho, J. (2003). *Conflict Around the Clock*. London, Independent Television Commission.

Sandel, M. (1982). *Liberalism and the Limits of Justice*. Cambridge, Cambridge University Press.

Sassen, S. (2002). 'Towards Post-National and Denationalised Citizenship'. In E. Isin and B. Turner (eds), *Handbook of Citizenship Studies*. London, Sage, 277–81.

Scannell, P. (1989). 'Public Service Broadcasting and Modern Public Life'. *Media Culture & Society* 11: 135–66.

Schatzki, T. (1996). *Social Practices: A Wittgenstinian Approach to Human Activity and the Social*. Cambridge, Cambridge University Press.

Scheufele, D. and Nisbet, M. (2002). 'Being a Citizen Online: New Opportunities and Dead Ends'. *Press/Politics*, 7(3): 55–75.

Scheufele, D., et al. (2004). 'Social Structure and Citizenship: Examining the Impacts of Social Setting, Network Heterogeneity, and Informational Variables on Political Participation'. *Political Communication*, 21(3): 315–38.

Schlesinger, P. (1978) *Putting 'Reality' Together*. London, Methuen.

Schlesinger, P. (2000). 'The Nation and Communicative Space'. In H. Tumber (ed.), *Media Power, Professionals and Policies*. London, Routledge, 99–115.

Schlesinger, P. (2003) *The Babel of Europe?: An Essay on Networks and Communicative Spaces*. Arena Working Paper no 22, Nov.

Schlesinger, P. and Kevin, D. (2000). 'Can the European Union Become a Sphere of Publics?' In E. Eriksen and Fossum, J. (eds), *Democracy in the European Union*. London, Routledge, 206–29.

Schlesinger, P. and Tumber, H. (1994). *Reporting Crime*. Oxford, Clarendon Press.

Schroder, K. and Phillips, L. (2005). 'The Everyday Consumption of Mediated Citizenship'. In G. Lowe and P. Jauert (eds), *Cultural Dilemmas in Public Service Brodcasting*. Goteborg, Nordicom, 179–97.

Schudson, M. (1997). 'Why Conversation Is Not the Soul of democracy'. *Critical Studies in Mass Communication* 14(4): 297–309.

Schudson, M. (1998). *The Good Citizen*. Cambridge, Mass., Harvard University Press.

Schumpeter, J. (1950). *Capitalism, Socialism and Democracy*. (3rd ed). New York: Harper.

Schwebel, D., *et al*. (2002). 'Using an Injury Diary to Describe the Ecology of Children's Daily Injuries'. *Journal of Safety Research*, 33(3): 301–19.

Sennett, R. (2003). *Respect*. London, Allen Lane.

Shattuc, J. (1997). *The Talking Cure*. New York, Routledge.

Shields, C. (2002) *Unless*. London, Fourth Estate.

Silverstone, R. (1994). *Television and Everyday Life*. London, Routledge.

Silverstone, R. (2005). 'Mediation'. In C. Calhoun, Rojek, C. and Turner, B. (eds), *The Sage Handbook of Sociology*. London, Sage.

Silverstone, R (ed.) (2005). *Media, Technology and Everyday Life in Europe: from Information to Communication*. Aldershot, Ashgate.

Skocpol, T. and M. Fiorina, (eds) (1999). *Civic Engagement in American Democracy*. Washington, Brookings Institution Press.

Smith, A. (2008). *From BarackObama.com to Change.gov: Those Active in the Obama Campaign Expect to be Involved in Promoting the Administration*. Washington, D.C., Pew Internet & American Life Project.

Snyder, I., (ed.) (1998). *Page to Screen*. London, Routledge.

Southerton, D. and Tomlinson, M. (2005). ' "Pressed for time" – the Differential Impacts of a "Time Squeeze" '. *Sociological Review*, 53(2): 215–39.

Soysal, Y. (1994). *Limits of Citizenship*. Chicago, University of Chicago Press.

Statistiek, C. B. v. (2003). 'Meer belangstelling voor politiek in 2002'. *Webmagazine*.

Stensland, P. and Malterud, K. (1999). 'Approaching the Locked Dialogues of the Body – Communicating Symptoms Through Illness Diaries'. *Scandinavian Journal of Primary Health Care*, 17(2): 75–80.

Stevenson, N. (1997). 'Globalisation, National Cultures and Cultural Citizenship'. *Sociological Quarterly*, 38(1): 41–66.

Stevenson, N. (ed.) (2002). *Culture and Citizenship*. London, Sage.

Street, J. (1994). 'Political Culture: from Civic Culture to Mass Culture'. *British Journal of Political Science*, 24: 95–114.

Sunstein, C. R. (2001). *Republic.com*. Princeton, NJ ; Oxford, Princeton University Press.

Sussman, G. (2005). *Global Electioneering*. Lanham, MD, Rowman and Littlefield.

Szalai, A. (1972). *The Use of Time*. The Hague, Mouton.

Tarrow, S. (2000). 'Mad Cows and Social Activists'. In S. Pharr and Putnam, R. (eds), *Disaffected Democracies*. Cambridge, Mass., Harvard University Press, 270–90.

Taylor, C. (1989). 'Cross-Purposes: the Liberal – Communitarian Debate. In N. Rosenblum (ed.), *Liberalism and the Moral Life*. Cambridge, Mass., Harvard University Press.

Taylor, C. (2004) *Modern Social Imaginaries*. Durham, NC, Duke University Press.

Tewksbury, D. (2003). 'What Do Americans Really Want To Know?: Tracking the Behaviour of News Readers on the Internet'. *Journal of Communication*, 53(4): 694–710.

Theiss-Morse, E. and Hibbing, J. (2005). 'Citizenship and Civic Engagement'. *Annual Review of Political Science*, 8: 227–49.

Thiele, C., *et al*. (2002). 'Diaries in Clinical Psychology and Psychotherapy: A Selective Review'. *Clinical Psychology & Psychotherapy*, 9(1): 1–37.

Thompson, M. (2006). 'Creative Future: The BBC Programmes and Content in an On-demand World'. Royal Television Society Fleming Memorial Lecture, 25 Apr. http://www.bbc.co.uk/print/pressoffice/speeches/stories/thompson_fleming.shtml Last accessed 8 May 2006

Tilly, C. (1997). 'A Primer on Citizenship'. *Theory and Society*, 26: 599–602.

Topf, R. (1989). 'Political Change and Political Culture in Britain, 1959–1987'. In J. Gibbins (ed.), *Contemporary Political Culture*. London, Sage, 52–80.

Touraine, A. (2000). *Can We Live Together?* Cambridge, Polity.

Touraine, A. (2001) *Beyond Neoliberalism*. Cambridge: Polity.

Toynbee, P. (2005) 'It Is New Labour as Much as the Public That Lacks Trust', *Guardian*, 22 Nov.

Towler, R. (2001). *The Public's View 2001*. London: ITC/BSC research publication.

Tsagarousianou, R., Tambini, D. and Bryan, C. (1998). *Cyberdemocracy: Technology, Cities, and Civic Networks*. London, Routledge.

Tsfati, Y. (2003). 'Media Skepticism and Climate of Opinion Perception'. *International Journal of Public Opinion Research*, 15(1), 65–82.

Tumber, H. and Palmer, J. (2004). *Media at War: the Iraq Crisis*. London, Sage.

Turner, B. (2001). 'The Erosion of Citizenship'. *British Journal of Sociology*, 52(2): 189–209.

Turner, G. (2004). *Celebrity Culture*. London, Reaktion Books.

Turnock, R. (2000). *Interpreting Diana*. London, British Film Institute.

UCLA (2003). *The UCLA Internet Report: Surveying the Digital Future Year Three*. Los Angeles: UCLA Center for Communication Policy.

Ujimoto, K. V. (1990). 'Time – Budget Methodology for Research on Aging'. *Social Indicators Research*, 23(4): 381–93.

Unger, R. (1998) *Democracy Realised*. London: Verso.

USC (2004). *The Digital Future Report: Surveying the Digital Future Year Four – Ten Years, Ten Trends*. Available from www.digitalcenter.org

Vanek, J. (1974). 'Time Spent in Housework'. *Scientific American*, 231: 116–20.

Verba, S., Schlozman, K. and Nie, N. (1995). *Voice and Equality*. Cambridge, Mass., Harvard University Press.

Wahl-Jorgensen, K. (2002) 'The Construction of the Public in Letters to the Editor: Deliberative Democracy and the Idiom of Insanity'. *Journalism*, 3(2): 183–204.

Wajcman, J. (2002). *The Social World in the 21st Century: Ambivalent Legacies*. London, Sage.

Walzer, M. (1974). 'Civility and Civic Virtue in Contemporary America'. *Social Research*, 41: 593–611.

Walzer, M. (1983). *Spheres of Justice: a Defence of Pluralism and Equality*. New York, Basic Books.

Walzer, M. (1998). 'The Civil Society Argument'. In G. Shafir (ed.), *The Citizenship Debates*. Minneapolis, University of Minnesota Press, 291–308.

Ward, S., Gibson, R. and Lusoli, W. (2005). 'The Promise and Perils of "Virtual Representation" – The Public View. NOP opinion survey of online political transactions in the UK'. Feb. 2005. Available from www.ipop.org.uk.

Warde, A. (2005). 'Consumption and Theories of Practice'. *Journal of Consumer Culture*, 5(2): 131–53.

Warner, M. (2002). *Publics and Counter-Publics*. New York, Zone Books.

Webster, J. (2005). 'Beneath the Veneer of Fragmentation: Television Audience Polarisation in a Multichannel World'. *Journal of Communication*, 55(2): 366–82.

Weintraub, J. (1997). 'The Theory and Politics of the Public/Private Distinction'. In J. Weintraub and Kumar, K. (eds), *Public and Private in Thought and Practice*. Chicago, Chicago University Press, 1–42.

Wellman, B. and Hampton, K. (1999). 'Living Networked On and Offline'. *Contemporary Sociology*, 28(6): 648–54.

Wenger, E. (1998). *Communities of Practice*. Cambridge, Cambridge University Press.

Wilhelm, A. (2000). *Democracy in the Digital Age*. New York, Routledge.

Williams, B., Press, A. Moon, E. and Johnson-Yale, C. (2006) 'Comparative Issues in the Study of Media and Public Connection', paper presented to the annual International Communication Conference, Dresden, June.

Williams, R. (1961). *The Long Revolution*. Harmondsworth, Penguin.

Williams, R. (1976). *Drama in a Dramatised Society*. Cambridge, Cambridge University Press.

Williams, Z. (2006) 'No Respect in the House'. *Guardian* 10 Jan.

Wilson, W. (1996). 'The Poorest of the Urban Poor'. In M. Bulmer and A. Rees (ed.), *Citizenship Today*. London, UCL Press, 223–48.

Wuthnow, R. (1994) *Sharing the Journey: Support Groups and America's New Quest for Community*. New York: Free Press.

Wuthnow, R. (1999). 'The Role of Trust in Civic Renewal'. In R. Fullinwider (ed.), *Civil Society, Democracy and Civic Renewal*. Lanham, MD, Rowman and Littlefield, 209–20.

Wuthnow, R. (2002). 'The US: Bridging the Privileged and the Marginalised?' In R. Putnam (ed.), *Democracies in Flux*. Oxford, New York, Oxford University Press.

Wyatt, R. *et al.* (2000). 'Bridging the Spheres: Political and Personal Conversation in Public and Private Spaces'. *Journal of Communication*, 51(1): 71–92.

Young, I. (2000). *Inclusion and Democracy*. Oxford, Oxford University Press.

Young, J. (1999). *The Exclusive Society*. London, Sage.

Zaretsky, E. (1976). *Capitalism, the Family and Personal Life*. London, Pluto.

Ziehe, T. (1994). 'From Living Standard to Life Style'. *Young: Nordic Journal of Youth Research*, 2(2): 2–16.

Zolo, D. (1992). *Democracy and Complexity*. Cambridge, Polity.

Zoonen, van, L. (1994). *Feminist Media Studies*. London, Sage.

Zoonen, van, L. (2004). 'Imagining the Fan Democracy'. *European Journal of Communication*, 19(1): 39–52.

Index